The Essential
Guide to Ratzinger

The Essential Guide to Ratzinger
The Man and His Message

Matthew J. Ramage, Ph.D.

Our Sunday Visitor
Huntington, Indiana

Excerpts from the *Revised Standard Version of the Bible*—Second Catholic Edition (Ignatius Edition) Copyright © 2006 National Council of the Churches of Christ in the United States of America. Used by permission. All rights reserved worldwide.

Excerpts from the English translation of the *Catechism of the Catholic Church* for use in the United States of America Copyright © 1994, United States Catholic Conference, Inc.—Libreria Editrice Vaticana. Used with Permission. English translation of *the Catechism of the Catholic Church*: Modifications from the Editio Typica copyright © 1997, United States Conference of Catholic Bishops—Libreria Editrice Vaticana.

Every reasonable effort has been made to determine copyright holders of excerpted materials and to secure permissions as needed. If any copyrighted materials have been inadvertently used in this work without proper credit being given in one form or another, please notify Our Sunday Visitor in writing so that future printings of this work may be corrected accordingly.

Our Sunday Visitor Publishing Division
Our Sunday Visitor, Inc.
200 Noll Plaza
Huntington, IN 46750
www.osv.com
1-800-348-2440

ISBN: 978-1-63966-217-3   (Inventory No. T2906)
1. RELIGION—Christianity—Catholic.
2. RELIGION—Christian Theology—General.
3. RELIGION—Christian Education—Adult.
eISBN: 978-1-63966-218-0
LCCN: 2024947383

Cover and interior design: Chelsea Alt
Cover art: Alamy
Interior art: Adobe Stock

PRINTED IN THE UNITED STATES OF AMERICA

*In gratitude to the greatest theologian of our age and,
if the Holy Spirit wills, a future doctor of the Church*

My basic impulse ... was always to free up the authentic kernel of the faith from encrustations and to give this kernel strength and dynamism. This impulse is the constant of my life.

— Joseph Ratzinger

His specialty was the ability to unravel complicated issues, to see straight through mere superficialities in order to arrive at the genuine core of an issue.

— Peter Seewald, *Last Testament: In His Own Words*

In essentials, unity; in doubtful matters, liberty; in all things, charity.

— Saint Augustine

CONTENTS

The Importance of Benedict XVI's Thought for the World of Today

What does it mean to be a Catholic? Who, really, is Jesus Christ? Given all the turmoil in our world, can we trust his Church? Can we trust Scripture? If so, how do we interpret it? Hasn't science disproven Christianity? If I experience doubt, does it mean I have lost my faith? What are we to hope for? What defines love? How do I draw nearer to God in the face of suffering and death? What actions should I take to make the world a better place? Or is it more prudent to retreat into a Christian enclave until the storm subsides?

Amid chaos and confusion, many are looking for a trustworthy model that might help us find some sanity. As we live in a culture that constantly inundates us with conflicting opinions and heated debates, the need for a wise and charitable approach to navigating controversies has never been

more critical. As providence would have it, the Catholic Church has blessed us with just such a guide in the towering figure of Pope Benedict XVI
(Joseph Ratzinger).

Those who only knew Benedict as pope may be surprised to discover
the profound depth and sheer breadth of his thought. Some may also be
unaware of the many pivotal roles he played for over five decades in an
untiring quest to safeguard the Church in the truth and to promote the
gospel of Jesus Christ. Not only that, but it would also be easy to miss out
on the remarkable ways in which Benedict's lifelong ministry exemplified
humble, Christlike service. Crucially, this unassuming pope reminded us
that our primary concern as Christians should not be to win arguments or
to defend our cherished ideas. As he understood so well, our true objective
is to become ever more one with Jesus Christ. In his view, it is above all
through the witness of this friendship that souls are drawn to the Catholic
Church.

The constant goal of Benedict's life was to seek out that which is truly
essential and to adhere to this truth once it is discovered. He also considered it vital to strive to live in communion with all those he encountered,
regardless of whether they agreed with him or not. In this way, we can say
Benedict's ambition was to live by a timeless dictum typically attributed
to one his great inspirations, Saint Augustine: Believers should be *unified
in essential matters, enjoy liberty in those areas that are not so essential*, and
comport ourselves with charity in all things. The Church has never been a
stranger to strife, and she has always had access to this kernel of wisdom.
However, the sad reality is that we are having a hard time living it out today.

Herein lies the impetus for this book, and a key reason why Benedict
stands out as a shining example of how to navigate controversy and effectively propose the Gospel in our society. As pontiff, he urged the faithful to
strive for two complementary virtues: charity in truth, and truth in charity.
As this pontiff saw it, our desire to find and share the truth will be effective
only when carried out in a spirit of charity. He knew charity can achieve its
end only when it is practiced in the light of truth. But how, concretely, are
we to carry out this task when it comes to the myriad issues that require us
to cultivate a dynamic balance of truth and charity?

This volume takes Pope Benedict XVI as our guide for some cues to how this question can be answered. It is intended to serve as a primer on Joseph Ratzinger's thought, including what he taught as pope as well as the vast body of work that preceded his election as the Roman pontiff. The word *essential* in the title of this text does double duty.

First, it captures the book's primary aim. As a guide to Benedict, its goal is to equip you with the basics you need to delve deeply into the thought world of this illustrious theologian. Second, it points to something distinctive that lies at the core of Benedict's theological approach: his constant effort to get to the essence of things and present them to the faithful with clarity and love. Looking back on his life, Ratzinger himself said it well:

> Although the constellations in which I have found myself — and naturally also the periods of life and their different influences — have led to changes and development in the accents of my thought, *my basic impulse, precisely during the council, was always to free up the authentic kernel of the faith from encrustations and to give this kernel strength and dynamism. This impulse is the constant of my life.* ... Naturally the office gives an accentuation that isn't present as such when you are a professor. But nonetheless what's important to me is that I have never deviated from this constant, which from my childhood has molded my life, and that I have remained true to it as the basic direction of my life. (*Salt of the Earth,* 79)

In a time when competing voices make it increasingly difficult to attain clarity in matters of faith, this pontiff stands out more than ever for his unparalleled ability to illumine unwaveringly, yet in a language accessible to modern man, the traditional teachings of Catholicism. This, when combined with his especially keen pastoral sensitivity to the most pressing concerns of our day, accounts for why Benedict has long been — and continues to be — a singularly dependable guide for believers trying to find their way through the turbulent waters of the present age.

In this book, we will tease out the fundamental strands of Benedict's thought, offer a brief overview of his primary works, explore the profound impact he had on theology, and highlight the continued relevance of his work. Over the course of this journey, we will examine how his key insights developed over more than fifty years. Covering some of Professor Ratzinger's most salient early thoughts, we will examine his important role during the Second Vatican Council, his work as the Prefect of the Congregation for the Doctrine of the Faith and President of the Pontifical Biblical Commission, and, finally, how his vibrant theological insights continued during his tenure as Pope Benedict XVI and even afterward throughout his retirement. In the end, we will discover that Benedict's wisdom offers a reliable compass by which to navigate complexities in the life of the Church and world today. And he shows us how to go about this with charity, poise, and an unwavering commitment to the truth.

One final note: At the end of each chapter, you will find a targeted list of recommendations for further reading on the specific themes under discussion. Some sources are repeated across various chapters — this is inevitable given the integrated nature of Ratzinger's theology, in which he always manages to weave together ideas across disciplines into a coherent whole rather than treating them as isolated topics.

CHAPTER 1

The Life and Legacy of
Joseph Ratzinger

When Joseph Alois Ratzinger was born on Holy Saturday of 1927, no one thought this Bavarian son of a police officer and a baker's daughter would one day become the worldwide leader of the Catholic Church and the most distinguished theologian of the past century.

The story of Joseph Ratzinger's childhood and early adulthood merits an entire book in its own right, and thankfully such texts have been written. (See especially Ratzinger's 1977 autobiography *Milestones*; *Benedict XVI: A Life*, Vol 1, 1–162; *Benedict XVI: His Life and Thought*, 1–99.) But, for our purpose of getting acquainted with the highlights of Ratzinger's thought, it is important to note that young Joseph's later theological vision was profoundly shaped by the traumatic times he endured as part of a devout Catholic family living under a brutal Nazi regime during World War II. Like his father, Joseph was a staunch opponent of Nazism and could clearly see that the tenets of this totalitarian system went against everything Jesus Christ and his Church stood for. Already as a teenager, Ratzinger concluded that the Catholic Faith was the sole sure defense of truth and justice against the atheistic reign of terror unleashed in his fatherland. This resolute belief, coupled with an upbringing steeped in the simple piety of his Bavarian household, proved to be the pivotal catalyst that led this remarkable adolescent to enter the diocesan seminary in 1939. Despite his opposition to the regime, at the age of sixteen, Ratzinger was conscripted into the German army along with countless other youths. Not two years afterward, he deserted the *Wehrmacht* — fully aware that those caught doing so would be subject to the death penalty.

Joseph was able to resume his formation after the war at Freising and then Munich, armed with firsthand experience of the horrific effects of political ideologies. He had the zeal to understand the misguided philosophies undergirding them, and had the goal to prevent recent history from ever transpiring again. Ratzinger's intellectual influences were many and diverse during this time, including the likes of Hans Urs von Balthasar, Romano Guardini, Luigi Giussani, Josef Pieper, Max Scheler, and the Jewish philosopher Martin Buber. Ordained in 1951, Father Ratzinger learned under the tutelage of luminaries such as the New Testament scholar Friedrich Wilhelm Maier, who helped Ratzinger to see the value in the modern historical-critical approach to biblical interpretation. Even as the student perceived the method's limitations more than his professor, Ratzinger would long hold a deep sympathy for Maier, who was censured by Rome for advancing interpretations of Scripture that are now widely recognized as legitimate ("Exegesis and the Magisterium of the Church," 127).

Two men stood out as key mentors in Ratzinger's theological formation. One was Alfred Läpple, who instilled in the young scholar a passion for the theology of St. John Henry Newman. Läpple also introduced the budding theologian to Henri de Lubac, whose book *Catholicism* Ratzinger later described as the single most important text he read in all his years of study. Then there was Gottlieb Söhngen, a deep believer and relentless inquirer who would wind up directing both of Ratzinger's major academic projects on great saints, and whose thought exerted a powerful impact on Ratzinger for the rest of his life. A man who called himself a "decided Augustinian," Ratzinger completed his doctorate in theology in 1953 with the thesis "The People and the House of God in St. Augustine's Doctrine of the Church." After this came his habilitation thesis, a postdoctoral manuscript required to attain full professorship at a German university. The intrigue surrounding the drafting of this work makes for its own dramatic chapter in the saga of Ratzinger's life (see *Benedict XVI: A Life*, Vol. 1, 345–63). After initially failing due to the obstructions of one especially ill-tempered professor, Ratzinger eventually passed in 1957, and the work was then published under the title *The Theology of History in St. Bonaventure.*

Beginning with teaching stints in Freising and Munich, Professor Ratzinger traveled widely across his native land, during which time he quickly distinguished himself as the most renowned theologian in Germany. Students eagerly packed his lecture halls, and his lessons were diligently transcribed and distributed across the country. The fruits of Ratzinger's teaching also contributed to his increasingly prolific body of writing, which aimed to reach a broad range of audiences. His 1968 *Introduction to Christianity* became a worldwide bestseller, and its message remains as timely today as ever. The text's intention was to present a credible and moving account of the faith in the face of the "oppressive power of unbelief" that Ratzinger saw beginning to overtake Western society. In so doing, he sought to showcase the "real content and meaning of the Christian faith" in an age where Christianity finds itself "enveloped in a greater fog of uncertainty than at almost any earlier period in history" (*Introduction to Christianity*, 31).

While still in his thirties, the achievements of this rare intellect earned Father Ratzinger the invitation to serve as an official theologian (*peritus*) at the Second Vatican Council from 1962 to 1965. Alongside his teaching duties at Bonn and then Münster, for the council's duration he acted as an adviser and speechwriter for one of the council's most important bishops: Cardinal Joseph Frings of Cologne. From this moment forward, Ratzinger would be present as a crucial force for good at all the pivotal moments in Church history for half a century to come.

Father Ratzinger's impact began even before the council started, with a 1961 speech that he was tasked to write for Cardinal Frings. The purpose of this talk, delivered in Genoa as part of a series of briefings to help prepare the bishops for Vatican II, was to compare the circumstances at the

time of Vatican I (1869–1870) with those of the upcoming gathering nearly a century later. One of the lecture's most incisive themes was a strong
insistence that the next council should strike a more inviting tone than
had been typical of the ecclesial discourse in prior decades, taking care not
to become a counterwitness to the truth of the Faith it sought to proclaim.

A couple of months later, Pope John XXIII unexpectedly summoned
Frings to a meeting, at which point the cardinal honestly feared he was
about to be rebuked for having been too bold in Genoa. Instead, what
happened was the opposite: The pope elatedly rushed up to Frings and
embraced him, saying, "Eminence, I must say thank you. Last night I read
your speech. *Che bella coincidenza del pensiero*! What beautiful harmony of
thought! You have said everything that I've thought and wanted to say, but
was unable to say myself." The pope was surprised to learn that Frings's
assistant had been the one who actually wrote the speech, but that did not
change his appraisal (*Benedict XVI: A Life*, Vol. 1, 444).

In this lecture, Ratzinger successfully set the tone for the upcoming
council, accurately analyzed the signs of the times, and laid out the specific
kind of renewal and reform the Church needed at this pivotal moment
in history. Indeed, so much did Pope John esteem Ratzinger's wisdom
that his own opening speech for Vatican II drew lines from it word-for-
word. Other key lines in this talk similarly carry an unmistakably vintage
Ratzinger tone, such as the pope's memorable formula that "substance of
the ancient doctrine of the deposit of faith is one thing, and the way in
which it is presented is another."

As history would have it, Ratzinger's impact would continue to increase as the council began in earnest. Over the course of its proceedings,
the young prelate regularly provided incisive and persuasive analyses of
the initial working documents (*schemata*). These he criticized for a lack of
pastoral and ecumenical sensitivity — a concern that was especially dear to
the young priest as the citizen of a nation that was largely Protestant. Perhaps most significantly, Ratzinger was the leading force behind a meeting
he later described as the "turning point" of the council.

At this gathering, Ratzinger led the charge calling for the council fathers to reject the council's initial draft document on divine revelation,
originally titled *De fontibus revelationis* (On the Sources of Revelation). In

Ratzinger's judgment, this document, put together by a small preparatory commission in Rome, was entirely one-sided and imbued with an overly defensive "antispirit of negation" that was more interested in condemning errors than proclaiming Christianity's truth, goodness, and beauty. Along with many others, he predicted that the aggressive tone of this text would certainly lead to "a cold, even shocking" reception by the faithful. With input from this meeting, Ratzinger wrote a counterproposal. With this in hand, Frings then wrecked the Curia's plans to push through declarations that were crafted in advance by a small cadre of prelates, effectively asking the more than two thousand bishops who had been invited to Rome to rubber stamp them.

At the same time, Ratzinger drafted the opening chapter of what he considered a more suitable statement of the Church's teaching on divine revelation. In contrast with the earlier neoscholastic draft he had critiqued so harshly, this revised version underscored that the Bible is not an ahistorical repository of abstract propositions (*Benedict XVI: A Life*, Vol. 1, 495). Sacred Scripture indeed reveals the truth, Ratzinger maintained, yet it communicates this precisely through the history of God's chosen people. As such, he insisted it can only be understood as part of the gradual journey that culminated in the person of Jesus Christ. The history books now record the Constitution on Divine Revelation *Dei Verbum* as one of the council's greatest fruits, a tour de force that showcases the truly human and truly divine dimensions of Scripture. Building on this early foundational work at the council, over the next few years Ratzinger assisted the Doctrinal Commission in its work on *Dei Verbum*'s sixth chapter ("Sacred Scripture in the Life of the Church"). He also made contributions to Vatican II's Dogmatic Constitution on the Church (*Lumen Gentium*) and its Decree on Missionary Activity (*Ad Gentes*).

Ratzinger proved himself to be of incalculable importance at Vatican II in another way as well. Cardinal Frings was a senior member of the International Pontifical Theological Commission in Rome, and he was habitually among the first to address a given issue when it came up for debate. As *peritus* for Frings, Ratzinger, the council's youngest theological adviser, wrote the bulk of this cardinal's eleven electrifying speeches. The nearly blind prelate memorized these verbatim from Ratzinger's pen and then delivered their pivotal message before the council fathers.

Given this and everything else we have touched on only briefly here, the annals of history make it hard to argue that any single entity was more influential for the passage of Vatican II's corpus than the duo of Ratzinger and Frings. Indeed, Ratzinger had helped to prepare and define the council, he significantly shaped many of its key events through his timely contributions, and he supplied it with a positive orientation grounded in God's revelation with a focus on proclaiming Christ's message of reconciliation and salvation. As his biographer Peter Seewald has observed, when we take all this into account, Ratzinger's later branding by progressives as having betrayed the spirit of Vatican II is "surely one of the most bizarre aftermaths of the Vatican Council" (*Benedict XVI: A Life*, Vol. 1, 563–68).

With the close of Vatican II in 1965, a new task lay before Ratzinger that would be a momentous struggle and arguably remain his top priority for the next fifty years. The heart of this work was quite simple: to make the council's authentic intentions and teachings known. As the pontiff recollected in the autumn of his life, "To make clear what we really want and what we don't want. That is the task I have undertaken since 1965" (*Benedict XVI: A Life*, Vol. 1, 568). Over the course of this expansive period of time, Ratzinger's name has been etched into history as the council's foremost interpreter, the man who was second to none in his ability to express the purpose of Vatican II accurately and compellingly. Moreover — and this is a key reason why he is such a sure guide in today's turbulent times — given the many decades he spent as either the number one or two man in the Church, no one in the past century has been more qualified than Benedict to say what exactly the Church's teaching on any given subject truly is.

Ratzinger's vision of the council's goals coincides with what he took to be his personal vocation as a theologian: "to rescue the faith from the rigidity of the system and reawaken its original vital power, without giving up what is really valid in it." As he said in a speech written for Cardinal Frings, the council's goal was "to renew Christian life and to adapt church discipline to the demands of the time, so that witness to the faith can shine with a new brightness in the darkness of this world" (*Benedict XVI: A Life*, Vol. 2, 20).

As reading the documents themselves enables one to attest, Ratzinger insisted that the council texts were in complete continuity with the vast Catholic tradition they sought to re-propose to modern man. Yet, as a progressivist interpretation of Vatican II's "spirit" was gaining a foothold in popular culture, Ratzinger and other council fathers found themselves increasingly on the defense. In the face of a formidable "underground council" whose iconoclastic designs went either beyond or even directly contrary to the conciliar texts themselves, the need for a *Reconquista* of the Church's teaching became apparent. To counter these radical misrepresentations of the truth, Ratzinger collaborated with Henri de Lubac and Hans Urs von Balthasar to found the international theological journal *Communio* in 1972.

During this period, he took up further teaching positions at Tübingen and later at Regensburg. However, his meteoric rise as an exceptional theologian took an unexpected turn in 1977, when Ratzinger sacrificed his academic career to assume a role he had never sought out: Pope Paul VI appointed him to the position of cardinal archbishop of Munich and Freising.

Even as Cardinal Ratzinger was busy at work shepherding his archdiocese, within a few years a new pope was bent on snatching him away from his homeland and bringing him to Rome. After a failed first attempt to persuade the archbishop to join him, in 1981 Pope John Paul II finally succeeded in convincing Ratzinger to accept the appointment as Prefect of the Congregation for the Doctrine of the Faith (CDF). Confident that he "was able to say something to humanity," Ratzinger's one condition for taking on this role is that he would still be allowed to publish his private research — a request the pope was happy to grant (*Benedict XVI: A Life*, Vol. 2, 778). In addition to this position, generally considered the most significant in the Church after the papacy itself, Ratzinger would also serve as president of the Vatican's International Theological Commission (ITC) and Pontifical Biblical Commission (PBC).

Ratzinger's feats during his twenty-four-year tenure as Karol Wojtyła's right-hand man are legendary. Walking step-in-step with the pope amid struggle after struggle, the cardinal presided over the publication of numerous touchstone theological works. Among others, these include the PBC's *Interpretation of the Bible in the Church* (1993) and *The Jewish People and Their Sacred Scriptures in the Christian Bible* (2002), as well as the CDF's historic *Joint Declaration on the Doctrine of Justification* (1999) and its pivotal declaration *Dominus Iesus* (2000). In terms of the cardinal's most significant achievements with lasting impact, it is hard not to think of his work as head of the pontifical commission that published the 1992 *Catechism of the Catholic Church*. Sometimes informally referred to as the "Catechism of the Second Vatican Council," it is the vision enshrined in this monumental work that Ratzinger and Wojtyła spent so many years defending. The achievement is all the more remarkable considering it was shepherded by a man of poor health who had suffered a brain hemorrhage the previous year and had unsuccessfully begged his boss on multiple occasions to let him retire to a life of study and prayer.

Upon the passing of John Paul II in 2005, at the age of seventy-eight the precocious boy from a small village in Bavaria, with not the least desire for power, became the first German in half a millennium to become the Vicar of Christ. Alongside all his other liturgical and pastoral activities, Pope Benedict XVI beatified three people and canonized forty, including Cardinal John Henry Newman and Pope John Paul II. Despite his increasingly frail health, he also traveled to nearly every continent over the course of twenty-three apostolic visits and three World Youth Days. But this is not the part of Benedict's life for which he is most recognized. That, rather, would be his towering intellect and masterful command of the written word.

Although his pontificate lasted just shy of eight years, during that time Benedict penned a stunning number of seminal texts, which have had, and will almost certainly continue to have, a profound impact on theology and the life of the Church for a very long time. His opus included seventy-four major speeches and lectures, eleven *motu proprios*, a momentous apostolic constitution *Anglicanorum coetibus*, four apostolic exhortations, and four landmark encyclicals including a tour de force on Catholic social teaching and a trio on the theological virtues (the last of which was finished and published by his successor, Pope Francis, four months after Benedict's retirement in 2013). Amidst all this, Benedict's scholarly corpus reached its pinnacle with his *Jesus of Nazareth* books. Instant worldwide bestsellers, these continue to be widely regarded as the preeminent illustration of how to interpret Sacred Scripture within the heart of the Catholic Church. Considering all this, it has not taken long for scholars to arrive at the conclusion that Benedict was possibly the greatest theologian ever to occupy the chair of Saint Peter, or at least the most exceptional since St. Gregory the Great at the end of the sixth century (*Benedict XVI: A Life*, Vol. 2, 20; Emery de Gaál, *The Theology of Pope Benedict XVI*, 13).

An easily missed feature of Benedict's output is that a significant portion of it was communicated orally rather than in writing. For instance, on the Vatican website you can read the pontiff's countless audiences and homilies, where his ability to captivatingly present the truth and beauty of the Faith set a standard that will be a stretch for any of his successors to approximate. Benedict's numerous book-length interviews are especially worth reading. In fact, picking up one of these can be the easiest entry point into this pope's thought world. In his conversations, you not only get to see how he deals with a wide range of topics, but his short and off-the-cuff answers are especially revealing of this man's unassuming and charming character. Vittorio Messori's 1985 exchange with Cardinal Ratzinger called *The Ratzinger Report* is an earlier interview that made headlines and remains an informative read today. Peter Seewald's 1996 *Salt of the Earth* is the most extensive and far-reaching work of this genre.

His body emaciated and riddled with arthritis, his left eye having gone completely blind, and his hearing and memory failing, Benedict made the surprise announcement of his retirement on February 11, 2013. This made him the first pope in a thousand years to resign, and the first ever to do so because of old age. Under the impression that he did not have long left on this earth, the first-ever "pope emeritus" astonishingly lived nine more years until at long last he returned to the Lord on December 31, 2022.

At the time of his resignation, Benedict would have been the last person to think that he had long to live, but as time went on many people began to wonder if he would ever speak or write again. While exercising humble deference toward his legitimate successor and largely leading a life of prayerful solitude, the emeritus pontiff who now simply went by "Father Benedict" did manage to continue some of the intellectual activities he had longed to pursue. His final expansive interview, 2016's *Last Testament*, is a must-read for anyone who wants to hear some of Benedict's final thoughts on this side of eternity. Near the end of his earthly life, we were also blessed with access to previously unpublished words of the emeritus pontiff thanks to Seewald's magisterial two-volume *Benedict XVI: A Life*. Last but not least, there is the collection of texts that the emeritus pontiff wrote after his resignation entitled *What Is Christianity?* Edited by Elio Guerriero and Benedict's longtime assistant Msgr. Georg Gänswein, these essays were published after Benedict's death. Gänswein also published a book *Who Believes Is Not Alone*, which includes selections from the homilies that Benedict delivered to the small community of vowed religious who cared for him in his final days.

The Richness and Distinctive Marks of Ratzinger's Mind

There's a library in Spain that warns the pilgrim: "He who says he has read all of Saint Augustine's works is a liar." The same might very well be said of anyone who says he has read all of the works of Joseph Ratzinger, who is arguably that saint's greatest intellectual and pastoral heir in the modern world. It is virtually impossible to mine the depths of Benedict's thought, and it would require volumes to detail all his major contributions. As an initiation into the world of this extraordinary figure, there is nevertheless something important we can do: Seek to follow the pontiff's example and get down to the core of his message, gaining some pointers for how to find the golden threads that run throughout his written corpus. As the following chapters unfold, we will walk alongside Ratzinger in his quest to teach the faith in the present age, engaging with a wide assortment of his works: from his unpublished lecture notes from the 1950s, to his homilies as bishop, to documents he wrote as a Vatican official, to his papal encyclicals, and to his final works penned shortly before his definitive encounter with Our Lord. The following are some of the notable characteristics of Ratzinger's theology that we will encounter throughout his oeuvre.

Breadth of Thought

Ratzinger wrote on seemingly every topic imaginable, and his ability to speak competently and insightfully across all these domains is nothing short of staggering. Among his boundless interests, prominent subjects included Sacred Scripture, Patristics, the Church, liturgy, the sacraments, prayer, Christ and the Trinity, the saints, anthropology, creation, ethics and the virtues, beauty and the arts, the environment, social justice, ecumenism, interreligious dialogue, salvation, eschatology, and the dialogue between faith and science.

Touching the Hearts of Men

A large part of what makes Ratzinger's forays into these subjects so fascinating is that he was always conscientious to ensure his reflections were not merely cerebral. It is hard to conceive of someone more widely cultured than Ratzinger, who was conversant in many ancient and modern languages, a lover of the arts, and an aficionado of Mozart and Beethoven. This dimension of his character permeates his prose, which has a unique depth that is often meditative and even lyrical. Although he was comfortable speaking extemporaneously, Benedict remained committed to writing out his speeches ahead of time in an effort to present his message in the most beautiful and relatable way possible. The goal of his ministry was not merely to win arguments but to draw souls to Christ, and he went to great lengths to develop stimulating images, symbols, and cultural references that would aid him in that endeavor. At a time when a highly scholastic presentation of faith was the norm, Ratzinger's added emphasis upon friendship with Christ and a personal relationship with the Holy Trinity stood out. He was second to none in the ability to integrate the truths of the faith with a central emphasis on living out these realities in our daily lives (Emery de Gaál, *The Theology of Pope Benedict XVI*, 16).

Both-and

Another feature of Ratzinger's thought that makes it so compelling is his unrivaled synthetic capability. Reading Ratzinger gives you an experience similar to what you find when reading Thomas Aquinas, albeit in a more modern idiom. In reading Ratzinger, you are not just reading one author. With all the background and references he provides, you encounter the entire Catholic tradition so straightforwardly that it's easy to miss what is happening. In this regard, one cannot overstate how important it is that Ratzinger always sought to bring together domains that are often separated: He embraced both faith *and* reason and drank deeply from both ancient *and* modern sources of wisdom. Ratzinger's entire life and ministry enshrined the Catholic "both-and" principle.

Rising to Meet Modern Challenges

For those who knew Ratzinger well, one characteristic that stood out was his constant ability to keep current amid changing times while at the same time remaining a foremost expert on the Catholic Tradition. Part of this was surely thanks to his natural giftedness, but another motivating force was his willingness to be challenged. Far from being afraid of what is new, Ratzinger found strength in the knowledge that all truth, no matter what its source, is of the Holy Spirit. This gave him the confidence that the Church is strong enough to stand up to any challenge the modern world might throw her way. It also emboldened him to achieve a feat that eludes so many: to serenely meet contemporary challenges head-on and learn from those with whom he disagreed. By doing this, he honed the skill to rectify others' mistakes as well as to remedy deficiencies in our own tradition.

As his biographers have noted, throughout his life Benedict was fearless about asking uncomfortable questions and exploring thorny topics others preferred to dodge. As one of his early students reflected, Ratzinger was a fascinating teacher "because you always felt he was giving answers to particular questions" (*Benedict XVI: A Life*, Vol. 1, 342). Quite likely, these were often questions the teacher himself was wrestling with. Whether it was a sin of the past from which the Church needed to repent or biblical interpretation that required reconsideration in light of newfound scientific knowledge, he wanted to leave an example of how to confront our own deficiencies and to learn from our past mistakes in a spirit of inquiry and faithfulness to the Church. In this regard, his approach resembles that of St. Thomas Aquinas, who was also keenly aware of the need to abandon a particular position if it is proven to be false, lest Scripture be exposed to the ridicule of unbelievers and obstacles posed to their believing (Aquinas, *Summa Theologiae*, I, q. 68, a. 1).

Getting to the Heart of the Matter

The heart of Ratzinger's theology is on display when he sets out to provide compelling answers to the day's most pressing questions. One of his biographers put it well when he observed, "His specialty was the ability to unravel complicated issues, to see straight through mere superficialities ... in order to arrive at the genuine core of an issue" (Seewald, *Last Testament*, xx). No matter the topic, Ratzinger always found a way to peer through the externals and get to the heart of the matter. He would seek to contextualize a problem, acknowledge past mistakes, take the best of whatever anyone had to say about it, and then articulate a path forward in a fresh way that anyone could understand. Far from trying to say anything brand new, Ratzinger's creative genius lay in his unsurpassed ability to make core Christian teachings accessible, presenting them in an intelligent and captivating way that kindled in the faithful the desire to live by the gospel of Jesus Christ.

As I noted in the preface to this book, no one has better summed this up than Cardinal Ratzinger himself in response to an interview question about his vocation as a theologian: "[M]y basic impulse ... was always to free up the authentic kernel of the faith from encrustations and to give this kernel strength and dynamism. This impulse is the constant of my life" (*Salt of the Earth*, 79). Later in this same conversation, Ratzinger was asked to address the claim circulated by those who thought there were in fact "two Ratzingers" — one a progressive teenager and the other a resigned conservative ecclesial official. To this charge, he responded that the fundamental thread of his work always remained continuous: "I want to be true to what I have recognized as essential and also to remain open to seeing what should change." While not denying that his thought developed over time, he added, "I hold firmly that it is a *development and change within a fundamental identity*" and said, "Here I agree with Cardinal Newman, who says that to live is to change and that the one who was capable of changing has lived much" (*Salt of the Earth*, 115–16).

———————————— ◆ ————————————

In this introductory chapter, we have sought to highlight the key features of Joseph Ratzinger's life and thought that are essential to understanding the man and his message. When we consider all his achievements and account for the multitude of souls whose faith has been profoundly strengthened by his teachings over the years, a very strong case can be made that Benedict has been the modern era's most formidable teacher of the Christian faith. Indeed, contemplating the vast array of subjects he illumined has led some to suggest that Benedict may one day be reckoned as a Doctor of the Church.

While it is impossible at present to say whether this prospect will ever come to fruition, this book aspires to show why it is that Benedict is regarded as the greatest synthesizer of the faith in our age. A modern-day Thomas Aquinas, his unparalleled skill in extracting wisdom from everywhere led to the matchless ability to capture the core of Christian teachings and render them understandable to modern believers. Yet, even as he ranked among the most eminent minds in Christian history, for this thinker the faith was always and above all a matter of the heart. Above all, Joseph Ratzinger was a dedicated disciple of Jesus Christ and a man of the Church. At the same time, the Bavarian pope's great emphasis on the centrality of love was the very reason he endeavored to offer a rigorous presentation of what it is we believe and why we do so. Without further delay, then, let us delve into some of the subjects that were closest to Benedict's heart and see what makes him such a compelling teacher of the Catholic Faith in a world that needs its message more than ever.

READING LIST

♦ Benedict XVI. *Last Testament: In His Own Words*. New York: Bloomsbury, 2016.

♦ Benedict XVI. *Light of the World*. San Francisco: Ignatius Press, 2010.

♦ Gaál, Emery de. *O Lord, I Seek Your Countenance: Explorations and Discoveries in Pope Benedict XVI's Theology*. Steubenville, OH: Emmaus Academic, 2018.

♦ Gaál, Emery de. *The Theology of Pope Benedict XVI: The Christocentric Shift*. New York: Palgrave Macmillan, 2010.

♦ Gänswein, Georg. *Who Believes Is Not Alone: My Life Beside Benedict XVI*. Notre Dame, IN: St. Augustine's Press, 2023.

♦ Guerriero, Elio. *Benedict XVI: His Life and Thought*. San Francisco: Ignatius Press, 2018.

♦ Nichols, Aidan. *The Thought of Pope Benedict XVI*. New York: Burns & Oates, 2007.

◆ Ratzinger, Georg. *My Brother, the Pope*. San Francisco: Ignatius Press, 2012.

◆ Ratzinger, Joseph. *God and the World*. San Francisco: Ignatius Press, 2002.

◆ Ratzinger, Joseph. *Milestones: Memoirs: 1927–1977*. San Francisco: Ignatius Press, 1988.

◆ Ratzinger, Joseph. *Salt of the Earth*. San Francisco: Ignatius Press, 1997.

◆ Rowland, Tracey. *Beyond Kant and Nietzsche: The Munich Defence of Christian Humanism*. Edinburgh: T&T Clark, 2021.

◆ Rowland, Tracey. *Ratzinger's Faith: The Theology of Pope Benedict XVI*. Oxford: Oxford University Press, 2008.

◆ Seewald, Peter. *Benedict XVI: A Life: Volume 1*. New York: Bloomsbury, 2020.

◆ Seewald, Peter. *Benedict XVI: A Life: Volume 2*. New York: Bloomsbury, 2021.

CHAPTER 2
Divine Revelation
Old and New from the Storehouse

For many readers of this book, it will come as no surprise that internal discord among the Catholic faithful has dramatically proliferated in recent years. Browse the internet or ask a fellow Catholic in the flesh, and it will not take you long to find yourself in a fierce debate over any number of practical and theological matters. These arguments often center around the question of whether or not the issue at hand represents an authentic development within the Catholic tradition.

Our goal in this chapter is to unfold Benedict's approach to interpreting Catholic doctrine when it is difficult to distinguish what is essential to the faith from what is changeable over time. An especially crucial topic that comes into focus here is the relationship between the teachings of the Second Vatican Council and the tradition that preceded it. Enter Benedict's call for a "hermeneutic of renewal and reform," where the pontiff emphasizes the preservation of essential matters of faith while allowing legitimate development in its less central elements. We will also discuss how it is that one can go wrong by failing to properly make this distinction.

Put differently, following Benedict will allow us to discover how to remain steadfast in our adherence to the definitive teachings of the Catholic Church, avoiding the pitfalls of a relativistic progressivism on the one hand and a reactionary traditionalism on the other. Especially in the jungle of the World Wide Web, it has been common for sensationalistic popularizations of online Catholicism to overshadow official doctrine, becoming a rival Magisterium ultimately undermining the reliability of the institutional Church founded by Jesus Christ. Yet, to be able to grasp what Benedict is up to when making his key distinctions, we must first address something even more fundamental: the pontiff's comprehensive understanding of revelation and the dynamic interplay between Scripture and Tradition that provides the basis or "deposit" of Christian faith.

Ratzinger at the Second Vatican Council

An ideal entry point into Ratzinger's perspective on the relationship between Scripture and Tradition can be found in his reflections on the Second Vatican Council's 1965 Dogmatic Constitution on Divine Revelation. While the document we now know as *Dei Verbum* is often considered one of Vatican II's great achievements, Divine Revelation was a subject of fierce debate during the document's long preparatory phase. Importantly for our purposes, this issue held special significance for the young Father Ratzinger in his capacity as a theological expert for Cardinal Joseph Frings.

As we discussed in the last chapter, Ratzinger found two faults in the first draft of this document, which was initially titled *On the Sources of Revelation*. First, he perceived that its rigid, one-sided, and combative tone was not going to lead to a fruitful reception. This is the critique we hear from the mouth of Cardinal Frings, who delivered these words verbatim from Ratzinger's pen: "In the schema put before us today, I think the voice that can be heard is not that of a mother or guide, not that of the Good Shepherd who calls his sheep by name, so that they hear his voice. Rather, it is the language of a schoolmaster or professor, which does not nourish or stimulate."

More substantially, the bold up-and-coming Bavarian theologian critiqued the council's initial draft on revelation for having a flawed theology of revelation. The text had planned to treat Scripture and Tradition as separate and independent vessels, declaring that revelation is partially derived from each. As Ratzinger saw it, however, this distribution of revelation was unnatural, mechanical, and not in fact traditional. Moreover, it failed to grasp that revelation is not merely a collection of statements or propositions dropped down from on high. Ironically, had this view prevailed, it would have contradicted the original vision of the Church Fathers, who never thought of Tradition as a set of affirmations alongside Scripture. Recalling Pope John's desire that the teachings of the Second Vatican Council be made in accessible language that takes its cue from Christ rather than any single school of philosophy, Frings's speech thus explained:

> That pastoral voice is so important that Pope John wishes dearly that it should be used for all the utterances of the Second Vatican Council. But the language we have here does not go to the depths. It operates on the level of our human knowledge. But on the level of being, there is only one single source, which is revelation itself, the Word of God. And it is very regrettable that there is nothing, almost nothing, said about it in this schema. (*Benedict XVI: A Life*, Vol. 1, 493)

In sum, Ratzinger rejected the council's initial "two sources" schema for being bereft of nuance and ignoring Jesus Christ as the one source of Divine Revelation.

After reflecting on Frings's incisive analysis, Pope John made a stunning decision. Against all expectations, the speech led the pope to withdraw the prepared text of *De fontibus revelationis* and assemble a new committee to revise it. As commentators including Ratzinger himself have noted, this marked a "turning point" for the future of the council, and therefore for the future direction by which the Church would go about her work of proclaiming the Gospel. The council fathers had taken an unambiguous stand "against the one-sided continued promotion of anti-modernist spirituality" and in its place "decided in favor of a new way of positive thinking and speaking" to people living in the world today (*Benedict XVI: A Life*, Vol. 1, 497).

As Providence would have it, Cardinal Frings was on the committee that would go on to make the revisions called for by Ratzinger. This is how the young Father Ratzinger came to write the initial chapter to the landmark constitution we now know as *Dei Verbum*. A text many regard as the most important and beautiful among the sixteen documents of Vatican II, it is a tour de force of Catholic teaching on the nature of revelation and principles for its proper interpretation. For those who read enough Ratzinger, it is easy to see the parallel between *Dei Verbum*'s articulation of the dynamic interplay between Scripture and Tradition, and Pope Benedict's characterization of that interplay as a "polyphonic hymn" and "symphony of the word" (*Verbum Domini*, 7).

One of Benedict's most significant contributions to understanding divine revelation is his contention that Scripture and Tradition are not the sources of revelation but rather its *witnesses*. In a 1962 address to the German-speaking bishops in which he critiqued *De fontibus revelationis*, Ratzinger emphasized a point he had discovered over the course of preparing his postdoctoral thesis on Saint Bonaventure's theology of history. Revelation is God's communication with mankind and his action in history, but Ratzinger found it crucial to remember that the Lord's manifestation always outstrips man's attempts to capture it. As he would later write as pope, the revelation of God's word "precedes and exceeds sacred Scripture." Ratzinger described Scripture and Tradition, which together constitute the Church's supreme rule of faith, as revelation's inspired *testimony* (*Verbum Domini*, 18). For Benedict, as for the Catechism whose production he oversaw as cardinal, the revealed word of God ultimately does not reside on paper (CCC 108). Transcending its witness in Scripture and Tradition, revelation is none other than the person of Jesus Christ — in whom we see the Father and whose self-manifestation would not be exhaustively captured even with a library that measured the breadth of the world itself (Jn 14:9; 21:25).

Scripture's Origin in the Heart of the Church

Benedict's concept of Sacred Tradition is all-encompassing. He thought of it as a multilayered yet unified presence of the mystery of Christ in the world. In a shift from the language used at the Council of Trent where the word was deployed in the plural form ("traditions"), Benedict preferred to speak of it in the singular, Tradition. Unsurprisingly, this usage aligned with the theology of Vatican II's *Constitution on Divine Revelation* he helped to write.

According to Benedict, Tradition is transmitted in three ways: teaching, life, and worship. Doctrinal statements are certainly a part of Tradition, but the pontiff understood that it also includes other vital aspects of our faith that are harder to pin down in formulas. This perspective mirrors the view of Yves Congar, who described Tradition as encompassing not just dogma but indeed all facets of Christianity, including its customs, ecclesiastical structures, powers of ministry, liturgical practices, and sacraments. Speaking in his capacity as pope, Benedict eloquently captured this thought when he explained that tradition connects us to its source in Christ and makes us participants in God's activity in the world: "Tradition is not the transmission of things or words, a collection of dead things. Tradition is the living river that links us to the origins, the living river in which the origins are ever present, the great river that leads us to the gates of eternity" (General Audience, April 26, 2006).

To further reinforce his conviction that Christianity is not primarily a religion of the book, Cardinal Ratzinger contrasted Catholicism's understanding with Martin Luther's doctrine of *sola scriptura* (Bible alone). In place of this truncated motto, Ratzinger suggested that the better motto to describe the Catholic approach would actually be *sola traditio* (Tradition alone). The reason for Ratzinger's support of this sharp alternative is his recognition that the entirety of Scripture is in fact nothing other than Tradition, which is simply the early Christian memory solidified in written form. As Ratzinger asserted in his classic text *Principles of Catholic Theology*, the "seat of all faith" is not Scripture or Tradition but "the memory of the Church" (23–24).

As pope, Benedict consistently stressed the historical truth that the Christian deposit of faith was a reality even before the Bible was formed. Contrary to a commonly held but insufficiently reflective Christian view, Benedict knew the early Church could not wait for an authoritative written code to live out her faith in Christ. When it comes to the origin of the Bible within this matrix, the pontiff described its formation using the imagery of generation and birth: "As the word of God became flesh by the power of the Holy Spirit in the womb of the Virgin Mary, so sacred Scripture is born from the womb of the Church by the power of the same Spirit" (*Verbum Domini*, 19). As Benedict wrote in his commanding foreword to the first installment of his *Jesus of Nazareth* series, Scripture emerged from the living heart of the Church, and it is precisely within the life of the Church that the words of the Bible remain present still today.

To say that the deposit of faith lies primarily in the heart of the Church is by no means to say that the interpretation of God's word is conducted through a democratic process. Ratzinger consistently emphasized that Scripture and Tradition are so connected with the Magisterium of the Church that they comprise a single living organism and therefore stand or fall together. The Church's teaching office is essential, yet Benedict insisted it should not be considered superior to God's word as if it were its master. As the Second Vatican Council teaches in a text Ratzinger helped to draft and which he would cite at his papal installation: "This teaching office is not above the word of God, but serves it, teaching only what has been handed on" (Homily, May 7, 2005; *Dei Verbum*, 8).

For over fifty years, Benedict would continue to reflect on the role of the Magisterium as the custodian of Christ's teachings. In fact, so dear was this point to his heart that the emeritus pontiff chose it as a theme for one of his last essays penned during retirement:

> Sacred Scripture speaks only in the living community of the Church. There is a twofold exchange here, a relation of subordination and superiority. On the one hand, the Church is clearly subordinate to the Word of God, since she must always allow herself to be guided and judged by it; on the other hand, though, Scripture, in terms of its totality, can be interpreted adequately only in the living Church. ("The Christian-Islamic Dialogue," in *What Is Christianity?*, 45)

What is more, the emeritus pontiff demonstrated this lifelong conviction with the example of his life up to his dying days. As John Paul II was purified with physical suffering in his final years, so Our Lord provided Benedict with a prolonged opportunity for a martyrdom appropriate to his persona. For nearly a decade after retiring, he would humbly remain out of the limelight, united in prayer for the universal Church. Even as it became undeniable that his heir had sought to part ways with many aspects of Benedict's theological and pastoral approach, the emeritus pope continued to show the same humility and self-restraint that had always been essential features of his character. As a faithful son of Holy Mother Church, Benedict's entire habit of being remained one of deference to the authority of the legitimately elected Roman pontiff, even when he personally judged his successor's decisions to be mistaken (Georg Gänswein, *Who Believes Is Not Alone*, 230–31).

Identifying Genuine Tradition

When discussing the subject of Divine Revelation, Ratzinger invariably grounded his remarks in the Second Vatican Council's teaching that tradition "develops in the Church with the help of the Holy Spirit," and over time "there is a growth in the understanding of the realities and the words which have been handed down" (*Dei Verbum*, 8). Benedict's insights into this conciliar text are particularly enlightening, and he deemed it so important that he would return to it throughout his papacy.

One critical and delicate point that Ratzinger underscores is an issue that he wished the Second Vatican Council had addressed: the fact that not everything in the history of the Church is unequivocally good. In Ratzinger's words, "legitimate" tradition can coexist alongside "distorting" tradition (*Dogmatic Constitution on Divine Revelation*, 184–85). This crucial observation often goes unacknowledged, but to grasp it is to understand what precisely it was that preoccupied Ratzinger over the next fifty years: elucidating criteria by which to faithfully receive, soberly evaluate, and fruitfully renew Tradition within the Church.

Even as a young priest, Ratzinger made capturing and presenting the essence of Catholicism one of his top priorities. Importantly, this endeavor was informed by his profound awareness that the trend of atheistic secularism cannot be effectively countered merely by grasping onto "the precious metal of the fixed formulas of days gone by" (*Introduction to Christianity*,

32). To effectively evangelize, he believed that knowledge of the Church's traditional doctrines will always remain necessary, yet he also stressed *aggiornamento*, or "updating" — the vital importance of presenting the substance of the Church's ancient Faith in fresh new ways.

The necessity of Ratzinger's distinction between authentic and inauthentic traditions became evident immediately after the closing of the council in 1965. As we have noted, the conciliar texts did not provide guidance for how to adapt longstanding traditions to modern contexts. Consequently, some Catholics at the time rushed to interpret the council as a call to completely discard the Church's ancient traditions in the name of *aggiornamento*. As pope, Benedict described this as a time when "two councils" emerged: the real council that embraced the Church's ancient wisdom, and the "council of the media" that was hostile toward tradition and actively sought to overthrow it (Christmas Address to the Roman Curia, 2005).

Benedict lamented that the latter "council" unfortunately had a more significant influence on society, with the result that the official documents of Vatican II often went unread and thus unheeded. Ratzinger's dismay at this state of affairs is plain to see in his describing the zeitgeist as having a "euphoria of reform" and a "naïve progressivist utopianism" that "can only be called neurotic" (*Principles of Catholic Theology*, 227, 373). At the same time, however, Ratzinger was also keenly aware of another disturbing trend. In response to this one extreme, another reaction materialized just as forcefully but in the opposite direction. This was the launch of a movement in which Tradition would be accepted only up to a certain historical point, leading to the rejection of all developments in the Church at and after the council. Like the original "council of the media," the Church has also witnessed a meteoric rise of this "council of reaction" in present-day society.

Benedict's characteristic poise was always evident in how he distanced himself from both trends. On the one hand, he repudiated radical traditionalism, which refuses to accept legitimate postconciliar developments and the continuing authority of the Church's Magisterium. At the same time, he decisively rejected radical progressivism, which wishes to remake the Church in the image of elitist postmodern culture. Cardinal Ratzinger's pointed response to an interviewer on this subject is revealing:

It is impossible ("for a Catholic") to take a position for or against Trent or Vatican I. Whoever accepts Vatican II, as it has clearly expressed and understood itself, at the same time accepts the whole binding tradition of the Catholic Church, particularly also the two previous councils. And that also applies to the so-called "progressivism," at least in its extreme forms … It is likewise impossible to decide in favor of Trent and Vatican I, but against Vatican II. Whoever denies Vatican II denies the authority that upholds the other two councils and thereby detaches them from their foundation. And this applies to the so-called "traditionalism," also in its extreme forms … Every partisan choice destroys the whole (the very history of the Church) which can exist only as an indivisible unity." (*The Ratzinger Report*, 28–29)

Later, in an important speech to the Roman Curia in the first year of his pontificate, Benedict would say that the aforementioned extremes ironically have in common the same unstable foundation he labeled a "hermeneutic of discontinuity and rupture" (Christmas Address to the Roman Curia, 2005).

Bringing Tradition into the Modern World

Benedict rejects the idea that we must choose between strict continuity and acute rupture when it comes to Tradition. In place of these, in the above-mentioned speech he proposed a "hermeneutic of reform, of renewal in the continuity of the one subject-Church which the Lord has given to us." Far from seeing the *aggiornamento* called for by Vatican II as either a rejection of all that came before or a refusal to acknowledge change, the pontiff declared concisely: "It is precisely in this combination of continuity and discontinuity at different levels that the very nature of true reform consists" (Christmas Address to the Roman Curia, 2005).

Benedict's approach does not buy into the myth that Catholicism prior to the council had remained entirely unchanged over the centuries. He acknowledges that novel elements have emerged in the Church over time while maintaining that the Faith's fundamental identity remains ever the same. To name just a few examples, we might think of developments in

Trinitarian theology, the papacy, and the canon of Scripture. Neither the word "Trinity" nor the word "pope" are used in the Bible, and for that matter even the word "Bible" is not used in Scripture in reference to itself (the word in Greek simply means "book"). The same goes for the two natures of Jesus Christ, purgatory, transubstantiation, and so many other teachings — both those that are distinctively Catholic and those which all Christians hold in common.

Benedict's understanding of doctrinal development echoes the language of *Dei Verbum* and draws inspiration from the thought of St. John Henry Newman. In fact, Ratzinger's affirmation that the Church's "continuity of principles" has never been abandoned is a verbatim citation from Newman's second "note" for distinguishing genuine development from corruption of doctrine. Moreover, Benedict's teaching that the Church has preserved the past, while enjoying the capacity to assimilate what is new, mirrors Newman's ideas on how a healthy tradition has a robust "power of assimilation" and exerts "conservative action" upon the past. Last but not least, Benedict's frequent efforts to locate the "essential" or "core" dimension of Tradition coincide remarkably well with Newman's belief that Catholic doctrine has been one in substance from the beginning.[1]

Discerning the Essential: Embracing the Old and the New

As we have been discussing, Benedict's quest to identify the core, unchanging aspect of Tradition throughout history is his way of addressing that crucial issue that the Second Vatican Council left unresolved: how to differentiate the Church's unchanged fundamental realities from those aspects of Catholicism that can and sometimes must change in light of new discoveries and varying cultural circumstances. The existence of this distinction is the linchpin that allows Benedict to grant the presence of both continuity and discontinuity in the Church throughout the ages. This is how the Bavarian theologian could see himself to be both a conservative and a reformer (Seewald, *Benedict XVI: A Life*, 407). At bottom, Benedict wanted the same thing his friend Henri de Lubac so earnestly sought: to revive the memory of the church's great tradition (*ressourcement*), identify

---

1. For further reading on this element of Newman's thought, see *An Essay on the Development of Christian Doctrine*. University of Notre Dame Press, 1989. See also *John Henry Newman and Joseph Ratzinger: A Theological Encounter*. The Catholic University of America Press, 2024.

what lies at its heart, and propose it in a fresh way to the modern world. In this, the pontiff aspired to Our Lord's image of the householder who brings forth things both new and old from his storehouse (Mt 13:52).

As we discussed in the opening chapter of this book, at the heart of Ratzinger's life-long project was the endeavor to implement the *aggiornamento* ("updating") called for by Pope St. John XXIII in his opening speech for Vatican II. In this pivotal lecture, the pope seconded the themes of Cardinal Frings's pivotal speech that Ratzinger had composed on the eve of the council. Stressing the importance of holding fast to the core or substance of our Faith while also learning to present it afresh, he recognized that it was even necessary to let go of certain incidentals when they hold us back from effectively proclaiming the Gospel. In the words of Ratzinger, we accomplish this by distinguishing the Church's "actual belief" from its "time-conditioned clothing" (*"Das Konzil und die moderne Gedankenwelt,"* 174).

Ever a lover of the arts, Ratzinger would later develop an analogy from Michelangelo to illustrate this point. Like the Renaissance master who beheld his subject residing within the block of marble even before setting out to sculpt it, the task of the theologian is not to create something entirely new but rather to unveil what is essential. Extending this analogy, Ratzinger explained that some things in the Church can be compared to temporary scaffolding, which is useful for a specific time but may become obsolete — and even hinder us from seeing what is truly essential if we refuse to let it go when it is no longer needed. Alluding to his beloved mentor Saint Bonaventure, Ratzinger summarizes his point by saying that the Church's reforming task is fundamentally the same as that of our journey of personal conversion. It is largely a work of *ablatio*: the "removal" of what is inauthentic to make way for faith's true form to emerge (*Called to Communion*, 141–142).

Ratzinger returned to this subject many times and even made it the topic of the 1990 CDF *Instruction on the Ecclesial Vocation of the Theologian*. As this document candidly acknowledges, "It could happen that some Magisterial documents might not be free from all deficiencies." However, the text immediately proceeds to stress that this recognition does not undermine the core tenets of faith. Some past judgments of the Church were justified given the information available at the time, but the document observes that with deeper learning it became clear that these decisions "contained true assertions and others which were not sure" (*Donum Veritatis*, 24). Ratzinger's personal commentary on this magisterial text is especially noteworthy given his position as then-prefect of the CDF:

> The text also presents the various forms of binding authority which correspond to the grades of the Magisterium. It states — perhaps for the first time with such candor — that there are magisterial decisions which cannot be the final word on a given matter as such but, despite the permanent value of their principles, are chiefly also a signal for pastoral prudence, a sort of provisional policy. Their kernel remains valid, but the particulars determined by circumstances can stand in need of correction. (*The Nature and Mission of Theology*, 106)

Illustrations of Developments from Recent Memory

One might wonder what kind of cases Ratzinger has in mind with talk of nonessential details or "scaffolding" that might fade away over time. Never content to remain at the level of mere generalizations, he naturally provides concrete examples to illustrate his point. In the above document, he discusses two such instances. One of these revolves around "the pontifical statements of the last century regarding freedom of religion" (*The Nature and Mission of Theology*, 106). Magisterial documents such as Pius IX's 1864 *Syllabus of Errors* once anathemized the proposition that every person enjoys the freedom of religion that his reason judges to be true. A century later, the Second Vatican Council would reverse this policy, declaring that "the human person has a right to religious freedom" (*Dignitatis Humanae*, 2). As pope, Benedict himself would underscore that religious freedom "is not the exclusive patrimony of believers, but of the whole family of the earth's peoples" and "an essential element" in societal governance (January 1, 2011, Message for the World Day of Peace).

Commenting on this declaration, which he considered long overdue, Ratzinger frankly deemed it "scandalous" that it took so long and required so much prodding from the non-Christian world for the Church to make the clarification that finally came in 1965 (*Theological Highlights of Vatican II*, 210). Importantly, Ratzinger would affirm that Vatican II's authoritative and strongly worded reversal of prior policy was by no means tantamount to a total rejection of previous Church teaching. On the contrary, he saw the Church's willingness to move away from "outmoded political-religious positions" as an endeavor to unfold the essence of Christian doctrine and to help the Church recover from a misstep that had gravely damaged its credibility for a century and a half.

Making this frank admission is precisely what allows Ratzinger to turn his attention to identifying the heart of Church teaching on the issue of religious freedom. It turns out, he concludes, that the teaching of the prior century was the same that we find in the Second Vatican Council and in the teachings of recent popes: *a truly religious act requires that it not be compelled by force*. Having said that, Ratzinger was fully aware of how easy it is to fall into the error of conceiving freedom as the ability to follow whatever strikes one's fancy irrespective of whether it is good and true. In reality, religious freedom is a right that is accompanied by a crucial duty: the requirement to seek the truth and, once it is found, to order our entire lives in accord with it (*Dignitatis Humanae*, 2).

Another magisterial decision of the past that Ratzinger more than once identified as provisional centered on "the anti-modernist decisions of the then Biblical Commission" (*The Nature and Mission of Theology*, 106). In a series of decrees in the opening years of the twentieth century, the Pontifical Biblical Commission weighed in on a number a highly technical scholarly disputes. The concern of these dictates was to defend the reliability and proper interpretation of Scripture. It sought to do so primarily by affirming that its books were authored by the writers to whom they were traditionally attributed: for example, the Pentateuch to Moses, the Psalms to David, the second part of Isaiah to the prophet bearing the book's name, and the Gospels to the four evangelists as opposed to their disciples.

Unfortunately, as Ratzinger remarked more than once, these ordinances of the PBC wound up forbidding Catholics to entertain certain positions that later became so widely accepted than Benedict XVI and John Paul II themselves later considered them noncontroversial. For instance, it is clear in the writings of these pontiffs that they viewed the

Pentateuch, Isaiah, and John as composed by multiple authors. They also took no issue with the scholarly consensus that Mark wrote the first Gospel and that Matthew made use of preexistent sources to craft his account of Christ's life. For Benedict, it was evident that the Pentateuch took shape gradually over many centuries and is a much more complex work than the PBC of a century prior was willing to grant. More fundamentally still, he was not in favor of the Vatican weighing in on questions of authorship in the first place. As then-Cardinal Ratzinger explained with regard to the Pentateuch, the biblical text is inspired regardless of who wrote it, and so "the question of whether or not Moses may have been a writer is one we can happily leave to one side" (*God and the World*, 151–52).

At this point, one may wonder why the PBC dedicated such effort to weigh in on academic disputes in the first place, especially when leading churchmen like Benedict would later deem their conclusions wanting. Here, as ever, Ratzinger had a firm grasp of the issue and offered an explanation that was at once critical and charitable:

> The process of intellectual struggle over these issues that had become a necessary task can in a certain sense be compared with the similar process triggered by the Galileo affair. Until Galileo, it had seemed that the geocentric world picture was inextricably bound up with the revealed message of the Bible, and that champions of the heliocentric world picture were destroying the core of Revelation. It became necessary fully to reconceive the relationship between the outward form of presentation and the real message of the whole, and it required a gradual process before the criteria could be elaborated. … Something analogous can be said with respect to history. At first it seemed as if the ascription of the Pentateuch to Moses or of the Gospels to the four individuals whom tradition names as their authors were indispensable conditions of the trustworthiness of Scripture and, therefore, of the faith founded upon it. Here, too, it was necessary for the territories to be re-surveyed, as it were; the basic relationship between faith and history needed to be re-thought. This sort of

clarification could not be achieved overnight. ("Exegesis and Magisterium of the Church," 134)

Ratzinger's incisive analysis in this passage goes a long way toward illuminating why it is that certain features of the PBC's early decrees stood "in need of correction." Those who crafted the statements had assumed that the trustworthiness of Scripture would be undermined if the Church were to accept the findings of modern scholarship. The fear was straightforward: to acknowledge discrepancies between modern discoveries and certain ancient traditions concerning Scripture was to threaten the foundations of the Faith itself. Fully cognizant of this apprehension, Ratzinger's entire life was nevertheless dedicated to demonstrating that precisely the opposite is the case. As he saw it, the credibility of the Christian Tradition requires an ongoing conversation between the old and the new, a synthesis that draws from the best of both while acknowledging their respective limitations.

Ratzinger's assessment of the Church's anti-modernist decrees is especially blunt in the notebook he kept during the Second Vatican Council. In brief, the eminent theologian saw these as saturated with "cramped thinking" that was symptomatic of an "anti-modernistic neurosis which had again and again crippled the Church since the turn of the century" (*Theological Highlights of Vatican II*, 23, 42–43). These are not merely the words of what some have construed as a younger, more progressive Ratzinger, for this is the same evaluation that he would give in his official capacity as president of the Pontifical Biblical Commission. In an address delivered on the one hundredth anniversary of this office, Cardinal Ratzinger acknowledged that with these judgments "the Magisterium overextended the range of what faith can guarantee with certainty and that, as a result, the Magisterium's credibility was injured and the freedom needed for exegetical research and interrogation was unduly narrowed" ("Exegesis and the Magisterium of the Church," 133).

With regard to the authorship of the Gospels, the then-president of the PBC departed from the commission's earlier rulings on the subject of the Two-Source Theory (the idea that the many similarities between Matthew and Luke can be accounted for by their reliance on Mark and another shared source). While not repeating the past mistake of characterizing this conclusion as a matter of faith, Ratzinger described this approach as being "almost universally accepted" ("Exegesis and the Magisterium of the Church," 127). Ratzinger exemplifies this same conviction elsewhere when he remarks that Mark is the oldest among the Gospels and that "Matthew and Luke have, so to speak, taken Mark as their basic framework and have enriched it with other traditional materials that were available to them." While aware of the venerable tradition that considers Matthew the first of the Gospels, Ratzinger clearly accepts — with appropriate nuances and modifications — the standard suggestions of modern scholarship regarding the origin and relationship of the Synoptic Gospels.

And yet, his willingness to part with this or that assumption of a bygone era is not where Ratzinger's greatest genius lies. Indeed, one of Benedict's greatest traits is that his allegiance was never to a particular scholarly hypothesis or a particular theological figure but rather *to Christ and his Church*. Because of this, he had the remarkable ability to turn on its head the somewhat arcane debate over who wrote which Gospel and when. In place of this never-ending academic quarrel, Ratzinger focused on the *ecclesial* nature of the Bible and the interdependence of the Gospels. Indeed, he provided a breath of fresh air by underscoring a new and more holistic way to think about the matter — namely, that "the first three Gospels were not just written by one writer in each case but were based on the transmission of material by the whole believing Church" (*God and the World*, 228–30).

As Ratzinger details, the formation of the gospels was a gradual and complex process that involved bringing together a wealth of source material. In this connection, he makes it a point to confirm modern scholarship's findings on the presence of significant redactions to the biblical text from the second century. For instance, on the subject of the Gospel of Mark's longer ending (see 16:9–20), he states, "In the second century, a concluding summary was added, bringing together the most important Resurrection traditions and the mission of the disciples to proclaim the Gospel to the whole world" (*Jesus of Nazareth: Holy Week*, 262). Whether this epilogue was written by Mark himself or another early disciple, Benedict stresses that the fundamental reality to bear in mind is that the Scriptures are inspired by the Holy Spirit, and that in the end "the question about particular people is secondary."

In light of the above, it is clear that Benedict was not shy to admit some of the Church's past anti-modernist claims on technical matters have since been revealed to be highly questionable. Nonetheless, he insisted that their core concerns remain legitimate today. True man of the Church that he was, Benedict was able to look past the shortcomings of this bygone era and see the perennial validity of the Church's call for prudence against a hasty embrace of all things new simply because they are new. Looking back a century later, Ratzinger could see that the essential purpose and central message of these decrees did not lie in their debatable claims regarding when and by whom particular biblical books were composed. Instead, Ratzinger believed that the core of what the Magisterium intended to convey at that time — and which remains valid today — is the importance of safeguarding the authority of the Scriptures, the historicity of Jesus, and the divine foundation of the Church. Indeed, he went so far as to express that these decisions served well to defend the Church against deconstructive intellectual trends that sought to undermine the foundations of faith. All the same, Cardinal Ratzinger never tired of reiterating, "Nevertheless, with respect to particular aspects of their content, they were superseded after having fulfilled their pastoral function in the situation of the time" (*The Nature and Mission of Theology*, 106).

Benedict would take up this subject again as pope, underscoring the need to distinguish permanent from changeable features of the Faith. Addressing the Church's past statements on particular issues involving politics and biblical interpretation, the pontiff explained:

> In this process of innovation in continuity we must learn to understand more practically than before that the Church's decisions on contingent matters — for example, certain practical forms of liberalism or a free interpretation of the Bible — should necessarily be contingent themselves, precisely because they refer to a specific reality that is changeable in itself. It was necessary to learn to recognize that in these decisions it is only the principles that express the permanent aspect, since they remain as an undercurrent, motivating decisions from within. On the other hand, not

so permanent are the practical forms that depend on the historical situation and are therefore subject to change. Basic decisions,
therefore, continue to be well-grounded, whereas the way they are
applied to new contexts can change. (Christmas Address to the
Roman Curia, 2005)

Once again, Benedict demonstrated the need to embrace the best that both
the ancient *and* modern world have to offer. To be sure, there is always
the lurking danger of progressivism, with its eagerness to cast off what it
perceives to be the shackles of Tradition. Yet, Benedict was also concerned
that we not cling rigidly to the past and throw out the proverbial baby with
the bathwater of modernity. As Maurice Blondel memorably put it, the
appropriate response to Modernism is not Veterism.

Doctrine versus Discipline

The cases we have just discussed revolve around questions of theory, but
the fruitfulness of Benedict's distinction between essentials and non-es-
sentials is equally applicable in the practical realm. A major application
of the pontiff's principles in this domain can be found in the distinction
between doctrines that cannot change and disciplines that can. For example, the Church's faith in the Lord's real presence in the Eucharist will never
pass away, but many details regarding how we go about the liturgy might
vary over time and place. For instance, Catholics in America kneel during
the entire Eucharistic prayer. Go somewhere else in the world, such as Europe, and you will likely find that the faithful stand up for the remainder
of the prayer after singing the Memorial Acclamation ("We proclaim your
Death, O Lord").

Similarly, priests in the Roman rite are celibate, but celibacy is not a
requirement in other rites. In fact, even here exceptions can be made, as in
the case of a married Protestant pastor who converts to Catholicism. As we
see in the Church's practice, this matter is a discipline that is in principle
subject to change and exceptions, yet the Church's fundamental theology
of the sacramental priesthood cannot. Significantly, Cardinal Ratzinger
himself addressed this point in his capacity as the CDF's doctrinal chief. In
the face of public dissent from the pope's definitive teaching on this sub-

ject, the cardinal-prefect forcefully defended John Paul II's declaration that "the Church has no authority whatsoever to confer priestly ordination on women and that this judgment is to be definitively held by all the Church's faithful" (John Paul II, *Ordinatio Sacerdotalis*, 4). In other words, while the question of marriage for priests is a disciplinary matter, the reservation of the priesthood to males is a matter of doctrine.

Examples of Irreformable Doctrines

We have seen that Benedict was happy to provide examples of specific dimensions of Catholicism that are subject to change over time, but how are we to identify those doctrines that are not subject to change? Cardinal Ratzinger penned a document in which he provided concrete examples of Church teachings that cannot and therefore never will pass away. Published in his official capacity as prefect of the CDF under Pope John Paul II, the 1998 *Doctrinal Commentary on the Concluding Formula of the Professio Fidei* did not seek to offer an exhaustive list of such doctrines, yet it is noteworthy that among the "irreformable" teachings that it mentions we find a list that includes the following: the articles of the Creed; the Church's various Christological and Marian dogmas; the validity of the sacraments; the real and substantial presence of Christ in the Eucharist; the sacrificial nature of the Eucharistic celebration; the foundation of the Church by the will of Christ; the primacy and infallibility of the Roman pontiff; the existence of original sin; the immortality of the spiritual soul and its immediate judgment after death; the inerrancy of Scripture; the grave immorality of murder; the illicitness of fornication, prostitution, and euthanasia; and the reservation of the priesthood to men. With such a robust set of examples, Ratzinger makes it clear that recognizing the history of doctrinal development within the Church is a far cry from the supposition that everything in the Church is subject to change with the passing of time.

―――――――――― ◆ ――――――――――

In this chapter, we have seen that Ratzinger's approach to Scripture and Tradition emphasizes their unity and interconnectedness. Throughout his writings, he consistently endeavors to identify the central aspects of Tradition while recognizing that some elements can and indeed must change from time to time in order for the substance of the Faith to remain the same. In this connection, he more than once referenced Newman's saying that "to live is to change, and to be perfect is to have changed often." As we will have occasions to observe in various contexts throughout this book, Ratzinger's answer to the challenge of understanding the Deposit of Faith in the face of modern developments was rigorous and balanced. Among Benedict's greatest hallmarks was his willingness to assimilate contemporary insights while unwaveringly maintaining allegiance to the faith of our fathers.

But, as Ratzinger himself would characteristically say, a question still remains: What should believers do when confronted with the concern that a cherished tradition might change at some point in the future? Anticipating precisely this sort of eventuality, Benedict provided sage advice:

> Of course we always need to ask what are the things that may once have been considered essential to Christianity but in reality were only expressions of a certain period. What, then, is really essential? This means that we must constantly return to the gospel and the teachings of the faith in order to see: First, what is an essential component? Second, what legitimately changes with the changing times? And third, what is not an essential component? (*Light of the World*, 141)

Crucially, Joseph Ratzinger constantly stressed that the only competent authority in such matters is the Magisterium of the Catholic Church, governed by the pope and bishops. By humbly acknowledging this, this theological giant who became Supreme Pontiff revealed himself as a faithful disciple of Jesus Christ and a humble man of the Church. In so doing, he offers us all an example of joyful submission to divine revelation witnessed in Scripture and Tradition. While he valued the need for ongoing renewal within the Church, a hallmark of Benedict's work was his unwavering focus on the nonnegotiable revealed teachings of Catholicism. In his own words, these are "the things we have not made, but have received from the Lord" (*God and the World*, 453).

READING LIST

♦ Benedict XVI. Address to the Parish Priests and Clergy of Rome. February 14, 2013.

♦ Benedict XVI. Christmas Address to the Roman Curia. December 22, 2005.

♦ Benedict XVI. Christmas Address to the Roman Curia. December 21, 2012.

♦ Ratzinger, Joseph. "Exegesis and the Magisterium of the Church." In *Opening Up the Scriptures: Joseph Ratzinger and the Foundations of Biblical Interpretation*, edited by José Granados, Carlos Granados, and Luis Sánchez-Navarro, 126–36. Grand Rapids, MI: Eerdmans, 2008.

♦ Ratzinger, Joseph. *The Nature and Mission of Theology*. San Francisco: Ignatius Press, 1995.

♦ Ratzinger, Joseph. *Principles of Catholic Theology*. San Francisco: Ignatius Press, 1987.

♦ Ratzinger, Joseph. *The Ratzinger Report*. San Francisco: Ignatius Press, 1985.

♦ Ratzinger, Joseph. *Salt of the Earth*. San Francisco: Ignatius Press, 1997.

♦ Ratzinger, Joseph. *Theological Highlights of Vatican II*. New York: Paulist Press, 1966.

CHAPTER 3

Sacred Scripture and Its Interpretation

Now that we have explored Benedict's fundamental perspective on Divine Revelation and the dynamic interplay between Scripture and Tradition in the Church, in this chapter we turn our attention to Benedict's approach to biblical interpretation. Operating in concert with Vatican II's teaching that the study of the sacred page is the soul of theology, we will survey the key principles that Benedict provides to guide us in studying Scripture within the heart of the Church. As we are about to see, this renowned method at once seeks to uphold the ancient Catholic Tradition while at the same time updating it through a robust engagement with modern scholarship. In keeping with Benedict's perspective, this chapter also aims to be concrete by applying his methodology to particular biblical passages where its importance is especially evident. For example, we will address what to make of passages that appear to be mistaken in their understanding of who God is, how he expects us to live, and what happens after death.[2] In later chapters, we will follow up by addressing the question of how to explain confusing biblical passages that appear to indulge in mythological fancies, false understandings of the natural world, and even Christological heresies.

Benedict's "Method C" Interpretive Approach

Without question, one of Benedict's most enduring contributions to the Church's understanding of Scripture lies in his touchstone two-pronged strategy for biblical exegesis (interpretation).

The best way to grasp Benedict's vision is by examining how then-Cardinal Ratzinger summarized it following his 1988 Erasmus Lecture in New York City. Ratzinger argued that Christians interested in plumbing the depths of Scripture should be eager to draw on both the best of the ancient Christian Tradition and the discoveries of the various modern sciences. This endeavor he calls "Method C" exegesis: "You can call the patristic-medieval exegetical approach Method A. The historical-critical approach, the modern approach ... is Method B. What I am calling for is not a return to Method A, but a development of a Method C, taking advantage of the strengths of both Method A and Method B, but cognizant of the shortcomings of both" ("The Story of an Encounter," 107–08).

Ratzinger's shorthand term "Method A" stands in for a core set of principles that united Christian interpreters of the patristic and medieval eras, from the apostles to Saint Augustine to St. Thomas Aquinas and beyond. Setting them apart from many in our day, the major strength of this perspective is that it holds the inspiration, truth, and transformative power of Scripture as nonnegotiables. "Method B," meanwhile, refers to the common ground shared by more contemporary readers of the Bible. As we will discuss below, this modern method benefits from discoveries and tools that were not available even to the greatest minds in antiquity.

While Ratzinger deployed the shorthand expression "Method C" just this one time, he repeated over the years the call for this same twofold interpretive procedure in many places and from a variety of angles. For instance, sometimes he differentiates between a "historical hermeneu-

---

2. For a more detailed exploration of these themes and the principles outlined in this chapter, see my book *Dark Passages of the Bible: Engaging Scripture with Benedict XVI and Thomas Aquinas* (The Catholic University of America Press, 2013).

tic" from a "faith hermeneutic." Other times, he speaks of "scholarly" and "scientific" exegesis and distinguishes these from prayer with Scripture or *lectio divina*, insisting that "both [are] necessary and complementary in order to seek, through the literal meaning, the spiritual meaning that God wants to communicate to us today" (Angelus, October 26, 2008). By way of meditating on the birth of Christ, Benedict gave us his most direct explanation of how to put the "two stages" of his approach into practice: "Firstly, one has to ask what the respective authors intended to convey through their text in their own day — the historical component of exegesis. But it is not sufficient to leave the text in the past and thus relegate it to history. The second question posed by good exegesis must be: is what I read here true? Does it concern me? If so, how?" (*Jesus of Nazareth: The Infancy Narratives*, xi).

In passages like this, we witness Benedict powerfully reaffirming the Church's traditional doctrine of Scripture's fourfold sense. Alongside its emphasis on the need to interpret individual biblical passages in light of the whole of Sacred Scripture and Sacred Tradition, underscoring the Bible's multiple senses is a special strength of "Method A." As expressed by Hugh of Saint-Victor nearly a millennium ago and taught in the *Catechism of the Catholic Church*, these senses are the literal, the allegorical, the moral, and the anagogical (General Audience, November 25, 2009; *Catechism of the Catholic Church*, 115–19). The foundational sense of Scripture is the literal, which is to say the original intended meaning of the text. The other three comprise the spiritual sense, whose rich layers concern how the ancient biblical text finds perennial expression in the life of Christ (allegorical), how we are to live our life on earth (moral), and what we have to hope for in heaven (anagogical).

Since we are already blessed with the witness of so many Fathers and Doctors of the Church whom Benedict groups under the banner of "Method A," we might wonder why he considers the modern interpretative method so pivotal to understanding Scripture. As the pontiff routinely demonstrated, a unique contribution of the modern method lies in its remarkable toolbox of resources that deepen our understanding of the Bible's literary genre and meaning in its original context. While it is important for Christians to consult traditional sources like the Church Fathers when seeking to resolve difficulties in Scripture, Benedict was aware of a serious issue: the authors of these sources — giants on whose shoulders we all stand — lacked vital knowledge that is well established today.

As we have seen in the case of doctrine, the pontiff stressed that Christians who wish to study the Bible in our age must acknowledge the need to set aside some untenable features and assumptions of *particular traditions* without abandoning the enduring and authoritative tenets of *Sacred Tradition*. Benedict was never of the persuasion that having a vibrant faith requires the Christian to espouse all our forefathers' assumptions. On the contrary, he was convinced that our commitment to the faith may even receive a boost by entertaining positions that differ in some respects from those held by the faithful of ages past. On this score, Ratzinger cautioned against falling into the common temptation of rejecting modern critical scholarship as a whole. He likened this overly simplistic and exclusive reliance on ancient ecclesial sources among Catholics to biblical literalism in Protestantism, deeming it a "merely positivistic and rigid ecclesiasticism" ("The Story of an Encounter," 107–08). Ratzinger thus insisted that our adherence to the Christian Tradition and pronouncements of the Magisterium should not prevent us from imitating our forefathers in their openness to wedding their faith with mankind's ongoing discoveries. Instead, he encouraged the faithful to consider the possibility that Scripture's mysteries might be more deeply penetrated with the help of contemporary insights.

For Benedict, then, engaging the greatest challenges to Scripture of our day necessitates that we consult up-to-date sources of wisdom in conversation with the Christian Tradition. This is where modern exegesis, or "Method B," comes in. If a hallmark of the patristic-medieval or "Method A" approach is that it sees Scripture from a spiritual perspective and seeks to discern the voice of Christ speaking to us, then a strength of modern historical criticism or "Method B" stance is that it attends to Scripture's original meaning in its native historical context, language, mindset, and culture. This second method is distinct from the important enterprise of praying with Scripture and applying its message to our lives today. Nevertheless, it is especially crucial for engaging people who sense that traditional believers often skip a step in the process of biblical interpretation by failing to acknowledge that its present-day spiritual applications were probably not on the radar of the Bible's human authors. With this in mind, Benedict provides the parameters of historical-critical work in the foreword to the first volume of his *Jesus* trilogy: "It attempts to identify and to understand the past — as it was in itself — with the greatest possible precision, in order then to find out what the author could have said and intended to say in the context of the mentality and events of his time" (*Jesus of Nazareth: From the Baptism*, xvi).

In the quest to ascertain the original meaning of Scripture, modern scholarship employs all the scientific resources at our disposal today. These bodies of knowledge and tools include new and rediscovered competence in the ancient languages relevant to the Bible, archaeological discoveries that give us insight into the ancient Near Eastern cultural milieu in which the Bible was written, and the availability of a host of ancient religious texts that are pivotal to understanding the world of the Bible. On the side of the empirical sciences, it derives benefits from paleontological discoveries that have brought to light knowledge about the earth's long history and the common ancestry of all life.

If a Method C approach to biblical interpretation involves a mutual purification of both old and new methods of biblical interpretation, then what does the Church's ancient perspective offer as a corrective to the modern historical-critical method?

For starters, we should be aware that the "critical" attitude of historical criticism is not inherently a negative thing, and the method itself is by no means antithetical to faith. In contrast with the way we tend to use the word "critical" in our culture today, historical criticism involves the endeavor to judge (Greek *krinō*) what the intended meaning of a given biblical text was in its original context. In Benedict's view, grasping the meaning of thorny biblical texts requires that traditional Christians not bypass modernity but that we rather tackle contemporary challenges from within by engaging the modern method directly on its own terms and even learning from it. However, we should also be aware that doing so will require us to ask certain questions — and entertain some potentially uncomfortable corresponding answers — that the faithful of previous ages simply did not raise or countenance. As we will discuss in later chapters, some examples of such questions are whether all biblical authors are in agreement regarding the possibility of life after death, whether the Old Testament presents a unified account of who God is, and whether the Bible is entirely accurate in its understanding of evil.

Having said that, Benedict warned that not all is well among practitioners of the historical-critical method. Cognizant that the method has sometimes been deployed in the attempt to undermine the Christian Faith, then-Cardinal Ratzinger accused some in the field of being under the sway of unwarranted "academic dogmas" — such as the unproven and unprovable atheistic assumption that God does not exist and therefore cannot work in human history. In light of this, Ratzinger famously called for what he called a "criticism of the criticism" that can help us avoid antifaith presuppositions when using the valid tools of modern biblical scholarship.

Frustrated that the results of investigations into Scripture's meaning are sometimes sealed before one even opens the book, Ratzinger contended that the debate about how to engage in proper exegesis is at its core not a historical matter but rather a philosophical debate ("Biblical Interpretation in Conflict," 19). Importantly — and counter to the pretensions of many in the field — Ratzinger insisted that "there is no such thing as pure objectivity" (*Introduction to Christianity*, 175). The key quest is not to rid ourselves of underlying beliefs when reading the Bible. As Ratzinger saw it, the pivotal question is, What prior commitments best position us for an accurate understanding of the Bible?

It certainly would be nice if there were a definitive list of steps we could use to answer this question and interpret the Scriptures using Benedict's exegetical principles, but the reality is that Method C is not really a method in the way people usually think. In other words, it refers not to a collection of procedural rules that can be applied systematically to achieve a specific outcome, but rather to the holistic posture we should adopt in our encounter with God's word. This aligns with Benedict's understanding of Catholicism as a whole when he said, "Christianity is not an intellectual system, a collection of dogmas, or moralism. Christianity is instead an encounter, a love story; it is an event" ("Funeral Homily for Msgr. Luigi Giussani," *Communio* 31.4 (2004): 685–87). Like the Faith itself, Benedict sees Method C exegesis as a *proposal*: a summons to rejoice in the full breadth of reason and to harness every resource at our disposal in the effort to illumine the Deposit of Faith.

Divine Pedagogy: Scripture's Telos in Christ

Now that we have defined what Benedict's Method C vision is at its heart, it will be valuable to detail some of its main features. Above all, the pontiff held that a correct interpretation of Scripture requires us to grasp two key principles. We will delve into the first of these here and return to the second in the next section.

The first main feature consists in the necessity of reading Scripture in light of Jesus Christ, who is its unifying principle and goal (Greek *telos*), its Alpha and Omega. Throughout his long service in the Church, Benedict often spoke of the need to bear in mind how a given text fits into the overall canon of Scripture that was gradually composed over the span of more than a millennium. As emeritus pontiff, Benedict would describe the seventy-three biblical books as "diversified millennial literature":

> Their authority is different, and the individual parts can be understood correctly only in the totality of the journey that they represent ... For this reason, it is not possible to speak about a verbal inspiration of the Bible. The meaning and the authority of the individual parts are correctly gathered only from the Bible as a whole and in light of Christ's coming. All this means that the Christian faith is not a religion of the book. ("The Christian-Islamic Dialogue," in *What Is Christianity?*, 44, referencing CCC 108)

As Benedict saw it, this background is the key to understanding why God's holy word contains what from our human perspective look to be defects, such as scientific inaccuracies (such as creation happening over seven days approximately six thousand years ago) and seemingly immoral imperatives (such as God's command to wipe out entire peoples). It allows us to admit the obvious — that the Old Testament does not yet reveal the fullness of truth — while continuing to venerate it as God's word. As he said a number of times as cardinal, neither "the criterion of inspiration nor that of infallibility can be applied mechanically. It is quite impossible to pick out one single sentence and say, right, you find this sentence in God's great book, so it must simply be true in itself" (*God and the World*, 153; Address to Participants in the Plenary Meeting of the Pontifical Biblical Commission, May 2, 2011).

Benedict explored this point in depth in his 2010 apostolic exhortation on the word of God (*Verbum Domini*), where the pontiff noted that God's manifestation to his people was "suited to the cultural and moral level of distant times." This, he emphasizes, is why the Bible sometimes narrates scandalous behavior and echoes of questionable ideas that "can cause the modern reader to be taken aback." When we encounter bizarre texts that seem to stand in tension with the message of Christ, Benedict stresses that the key is for us to remember that God's plan was "manifested progressively and it is accomplished slowly, in successive stages and despite human resistance." In the end, the pontiff concluded that correct interpretation requires two things: "a training that interprets the texts in their historical-literary context" (i.e., Method B) along with the readiness to see Scripture "within the Christian perspective" (i.e., Method A) whose ultimate interpretative key is "the Gospel and the new commandment of Jesus Christ brought about in the paschal mystery" (*Verbum Domini*, 42).

Once you become aware of how central this theme is in Benedict's thought, you begin to see it everywhere. For example, he taught that the key to interpreting Genesis is to recall that the Bible narrates a twofold struggle:

> The Bible is thus the story of God's struggle with human beings to make himself understandable to them over the course of time; but it is also the story of their struggle to seize hold of God over the course of time. ... The whole Old Testament is a journeying with the Word of God. Only in the process of this journeying was the Bible's real way of declaring itself formed, step by step. ... For the Christian the Old Testament represents, in its totality, an advance toward Christ; only when it attains to him does its real meaning, which was gradually hinted at, become clear. (Ratzinger, *In the Beginning*, 10–11)

From this perspective — which he applies to make sense of all manner of passages — Divine Revelation is best understood not as a catalog of propositions dropped from on high, but rather as the ongoing dialogue between God and his people. The pages of Sacred Scripture are the authoritative witness to this conversation, but Ratzinger was also always on the lookout to underscore its continued relevance in the present day. Describing man as the "creature of dialogue" who necessarily learns the truth slowly and only over an extensive time period, he added, "The dialogue of God is always carried on in the present ... with the intention of forcing us to reply" (Ratzinger, "Chapter I: Revelation Itself," 171).

What Ratzinger is advocating with this approach is known across the wider Catholic tradition as a hermeneutic of *divine pedagogy*. This interpretive key was first articulated by early Church Fathers such as St. Irenaeus of Lyons. The same insight was captured well by Gregory the Great in the sixth century and by St. Thomas Aquinas in the thirteenth when they reflected on the way an individual human grows in knowledge over time. This piecemeal mode of learning, they observe, is mirrored in the history by which the Old Testament People of God progressively grew in divine knowledge over the course of salvation history. According to the Angelic Doctor, the reason for this slow development is not because God is a mediocre teacher, but rather because he knows that we frail humans learn only little by little. In consideration of this reality, he gives us precisely what we need at every moment in our journey toward Christ (*De veritate*, q. 14, a. 11; *Summa Theologiae*, I–II, q. 98, a. 2 ad 1; II–II, q. 2, a. 3). This hermeneutic even made its appearance in the *Catechism*, which spells it out in this way: "The divine plan of revelation ... involves a specific divine pedagogy: God communicates himself to man gradually. He prepares him to welcome by stages the supernatural revelation that is to culminate in the person and mission of the incarnate Word, Jesus Christ" (CCC 53).

To understand what theologians like Benedict and Aquinas are suggesting in these texts, we need only consider what it would be like to proclaim the Gospel for the first time. Think about someone who does not know even the most basic concepts that we Christians take for granted, such as the existence of God, hope for life after death, and a robust moral code. In these instances, a missionary must be patient and not overload the person with more than he can handle at any given time. He must also accept that at any given time a catechumen is going to have in his head a mix of correct and incorrect notions, which can be refined and purified only incrementally.

The Christology of Scripture

How can it be that the Bible contains so many apparent defects? One part of the answer that we have already given has to do with the reality that the recipients of God's revelation were imperfect human beings. The other lies in the astonishing reality that God wished to make his creatures true authors of his holy word, humbling himself to speak in a way that appears imperfect from our limited human point of view. This leads us to the second key principle of Benedict's Method C vision: the incarnational nature of God's word.

One of the most fundamental points of Catholic teaching with regard to Scripture is its inspiration, which informs us that God is the primary author of the sacred page. Yet, Catholic doctrine also emphasizes that the Lord "condescended" to man in such a way that he achieved his purpose by employing feeble humans as his secondary causes. In a document that Joseph Ratzinger himself helped to prepare, the Second Vatican Council tells us that these humble fleshly instruments wrote down everything God wanted them to write, and nothing more (*Dei Verbum*, 11). At the same time, the council is clear in its teaching that the Bible's human authors were not just God's puppets or scribes recording dictations from above. In fact, they are true authors, fully deploying all their talents in the effort to render God's own ineffable word into human words that his people could understand.

Describing this dynamic, the Church developed what might be called a *Christology of Scripture*. According to this teaching, which Benedict emphasized in his own exhortation on God's word, the nature of Scripture is best understood by way of an analogy with Jesus Christ himself: "The words of God, expressed in human language, are in every way like human speech, just as the word of the eternal Father, when he took on himself the weak flesh of human beings, became like them" (*Verbum Domini*, 13; *Dei Verbum*, 13).

Inerrancy and the Literal Sense

Grasping the incarnational character of Sacred Scripture opens up another important point of Catholic teaching about God's word: the doctrine of biblical inerrancy. How can a text without error contain defects and problems of various kinds? To address this point, Benedict grounds his thought in the Second Vatican Council's reaffirmation of the Church's traditional teaching that "everything asserted by the inspired authors or sacred writers must be held to be asserted by the Holy Spirit." As a result, the council adds that all the books of Scripture teach "without error that truth which God wanted put into sacred writings for the sake of salvation" (*Dei Verbum*, 11). This means that even the most apparently unscientific and outdated passages of Scripture must in some way teach truth. Yet, if everything asserted by Scripture's inspired authors is to be considered without error, how do we know what precisely is being asserted as true in the biblical text? This is where the literal sense of Scripture comes in.

For Benedict and the Catholic tradition, reading Scripture according to its literal sense is not the same thing as subscribing to literal*ism*, where one assumes that the Bible contains the sort of raw history that would be captured on a video camera. Contrary to a *literalistic* approach, the truly literal sense of Scripture is perhaps better described as its *literary* sense. It is a reading that considers not just the bare meaning of a passage's words but what its human authors meant to convey to the people of their time by means of their immense literary craft. Armed with this background, a literate reader of Scripture is capable of identifying its authors' communicative acts for what they are in each given instance — whether it be historical record, moral injunction, joke, parable, or some other mode of communication. Nowhere has this task been more aptly summarized than in this passage where the Second Vatican Council identifies the crucial importance of grasping Scripture's diverse literary genres:

> To search out the intention of the sacred writers, attention should be given, among other things, to "literary forms." For truth is set forth and expressed differently in texts which are variously historical, prophetic, poetic, or of other forms of discourse. The inter-

preter must investigate what meaning the sacred writer intended to express and actually expressed in particular circumstances by using contemporary literary forms in accordance with the situation of his own time and culture. For the correct understanding of what the sacred author wanted to assert, due attention must be paid to the customary and characteristic styles of feeling, speaking and narrating which prevailed at the time of the sacred writer, and to the patterns men normally employed at that period in their everyday dealings with one another. (*Dei Verbum*, 12)

With this guidance, we are enabled to understand that the literal sense of Scripture will look quite different in different books across the canon due to the simple fact that the Bible is not just one book, but a book of books. Each of these texts in the library of the Bible has its own unique literary style. In fact, it often happens that different styles are present in the same book. For example, Ratzinger dedicated considerable time to explaining how Genesis 1–11 stands in a league of its own, differing in genre not only from other biblical books but even from the rest of Genesis. These opening chapters of the Bible read quite differently from that of a psalm, whose style can differ significantly from another psalm, which in turn has quite a distinct character from what we encounter in wisdom books such as Job. Moreover, none of these is the same genre as the Gospels, which Benedict describes as "interpreted history" (*Jesus of Nazareth: The Infancy Narratives*, 17). Indeed, we find a plenitude of literary motifs even within the Gospels. Among these, there are *parables* (e.g., The Good Samaritan), *hyperbole* ("If your right eye causes you to sin, pluck it out"), and echoes of the Old Testament prophets' *apocalypticism* ("The sun shall be turned to darkness, and the moon to blood"). It may sound ironic given our culture's use of the term, but the literal (i.e., author-intended) sense of a biblical passage can be symbolic or figurative. For instance, consider the famous passage about the valley of dry bones: "Behold, I will open your graves, and raise you from your graves, O my people; and I will bring you home into the land of Israel" (Ez 37:12). In this sixth-century context, the Lord deployed a vivid metaphor — resurrection of the body — to foretell the historical restoration of the exiles in Babylon to their homeland in Israel. A similar point can be made concerning the Bible's opening chapters, where God "formed man of dust from the ground, and breathed into his nostrils the breath of life" (Gn 2:7). As we will discuss later in this book, what we have here is an intricate metaphor that is revelatory in its fullest sense. It may appear to stand in tension with modern scientific discoveries about human origins, but this is not an issue when we grasp that its fundamental purpose was not scientific in nature. With his relentless dedication to seeking out the truly literal meaning of Scripture, Benedict was therefore not at all bothered by passages that appear to contradict the findings of science or even other biblical texts. In fact, he maintains that this state of affairs is precisely what we should expect given the nature of Christianity: "It is because faith is not set before us as a complete and finished system that the Bible contains contradictory texts, or at least ones that stand in tension to each other" (*God and the World*, 152). Yet, the pontiff was thoroughly persuaded that these tensions admit of a powerful resolution when we cease reading biblical texts in isolation and learn to see Scripture and Tradition as a cohesive whole. All the while, he encouraged the faithful to embrace the challenges set before them — and not to fear when beset by doubts concerning the Bible's truthfulness. The following words of wisdom apply equally in the case of obscure texts from God's word and unclear teachings of the Magisterium:

> Doubt need not be immediately associated with a fall from faith. I can sincerely take up the questions that press upon me while holding fast to God, holding to the essential core of faith. On the one hand, I can try to find solutions for the seeming contradictions. On the other hand, I can also be confident that, though I can't find them all, there are solutions even when I can't find them. There are things that remain unsolved for the moment that should not be explained by forced interpretations. (*Salt of the Earth*, 31)

In all events, Ratzinger saw it as critical that Catholics not fall prey to "forced interpretations" in the effort to account for apparent contradictions that they encounter in the Bible or Church documents. Whatever point may be at issue, Benedict stressed that the task is to remain faithfully in Christ, keep inquiring with confidence, and always embrace the essential core of the Catholic Faith.

Scripture's Threefold Authorship and Discerning the Essential Point

Discovering these principles of biblical interpretation, the task of applying them personally may seem overwhelming. Fortunately, Benedict made a concerted effort to demonstrate this process repeatedly throughout his body of work.

According to Benedict and the Church's traditional wisdom that he sought to put into practice, the key to understanding biblical inerrancy is to be on the lookout to identify a given passage's intention, the message being taught. This is what he refers to as the text's "essential point" or "kernel." Benedict contrasts the heart of a passage with what is incidental to its message — the "shell" or literary vehicle by which the sacred author seeks to convey his meaning (*Jesus of Nazareth: Holy Week*, 43). One of the pontiff's enduring concerns was to defend the truth of Scripture against those who failed to make such a distinction. He was especially concerned with countering the deconstructive approach propagated by those whom Ratzinger described as "men who thought they could not save the faith without throwing away the inner core along with the expendable shell" (*Theological Highlights of Vatican II*, 41).

As you explore Benedict's oeuvre, you will find that he articulates his crucial kernel-shell distinction in a variety of complementary ways. For example, when encountering a biblical passage that seems to contain an error, he says that we must learn to distinguish the "content" or "doctrinal message" of the Bible from its "framing worldview" or the "temporary contingent vehicle for its real theme" ("Farewell to the Devil?," 198–99). To adapt Galileo's famous phrase that Benedict and John Paul II both valued, we should be trying to determine what it is in Scripture that helps us go to heaven, not what it thinks about how the heavens go. That is to say, Benedict encourages us to ask the following question when it comes to any challenging issue: Does this particular matter change who God is and what he is calling us to do, or does it not? Here is how Ratzinger answers this query when it comes to scientific matters: "The figure of Jesus, his spiritual physiognomy, does not change whether the sun revolves around the earth or the earth revolves around the sun, whether or not the world came to be through evolution" ("Farewell to the Devil?," 202).

The above distinction is crucial, for it is precisely this that allows Benedict to admit that not every biblical author personally has a perfect understanding of every last fact about our world. This in turn enables him to constructively revisit the traditional understanding of what it means to seek out the sacred author's intention. What Benedict ingeniously did was to shift the focus from Scripture's individual human authors and ancient redactors to *Scripture itself* as the subject of intentions or affirmations. He thus often uses "text" or "Scripture" as a stand-in for "author" when identifying the assertion of a challenging biblical passage.

Benedict's core contribution here is rooted in his insight that the Bible's authors and redactors were never working in isolation but rather as common participants in salvation history. This comes across especially well in the foreword to the first volume of his *Jesus* trilogy. In this context, Benedict departs from the traditional language of Scripture having two authors (divine and human) and instead introduces the concept of three "interlocking subjects" who composed the Scriptures. The first of these is a text's individual human writer (or, as Benedict notes, a "group of authors" such as the Pentateuch). The second subject is the People of God (the Church), whom Benedict identifies as "the deeper 'author' of the Scriptures." In other words, for Benedict the Church's rationale for including a particular text in the biblical canon holds the most importance, and that intention — not necessarily the interior thoughts of an individual author — is what is considered to be without error. Finally, the third subject is of course God himself, as the tradition has always held. In the words of Benedict, it is ultimately the Lord himself who is speaking "at the deepest level" in Sacred Scripture (*Jesus of Nazareth: From the Baptism*, xx–xxi).

Illustrations
This may be all well and good in the abstract, but the full value of Benedict's principles does not truly become clear until we see how he applies his methodology to concrete biblical passages. While there are many strong candidates on which to focus, here we will keep our gaze on just a few

thorny issues: times when Scripture's authors appear to reject the afterlife, make mistakes in their understanding of the divine nature, and advocate unbridled violence in the name of God.

Passages That Deny the Afterlife

When it comes to death, it may surprise some to learn that Ratzinger was not bothered by those moments when people in Scripture categorically deny the afterlife. Think, for example, of the outcry that "all is vanity," seeing as "the dead know nothing, and they have no more reward" (Eccl 9:5). Ratzinger was aware that affirming desperate outbursts like this were not the central point of the books in which they appear, nor the reason the Church included them in the canon. The official religion of Israel at the time had endorsed what scholars refer to as a "theology of retribution." The worldview we find in texts such as Proverbs 10 was based on the premise that a life of virtue leads to earthly success (e.g., long life, land, and descendants) while sin leads to misfortune (e.g., suffering, childlessness, and premature death).

Meanwhile, in early Israelite theology it was believed that everyone — just and unjust alike — spent eternity in Sheol, the underworld (see, for example, Sir 17:27–30). Israel was not unique in her view of death and Sheol, as it closely resembles what we find in Norse, Roman, and Greek mythology. In fact, the Greek translation of the Old Testament translates Sheol with the Greek word *Hades*. However, this recognition did not disturb Benedict in the least, for he recognized that it "simply illustrates a stage of awareness found in all cultures at a certain point in their development." In other words, it represents a stage in our family history, a moment when we were on our way toward Christ but not yet prepared to receive the fullness of truth (*Eschatology*, 83–84).

Beyond this, Ratzinger also explains what needed to happen in order for Israel to achieve a deeper understanding of death and the afterlife. Ecclesiastes is by no means alone in this bleak outlook on life, as this perspective is amply recorded in Job and Psalms, for example (especially Jb 7:9; Jb 14:11; and the entirety of Ps 88). While these texts may come across as inordinately bleak at points, Ratzinger says that this is because their purpose was to "canonize the collapse of the ancient assumptions." Their point, in other words, was to document the developments that happened at the time of the Babylonian exile of the sixth century when Israel's overly simplistic view of divine judgment was brought "to its knees" (*Eschatology*, 86).

Benedict returned to this point again as pope, explaining that the endless centuries of oppression and suffering were making it increasingly obvious that it is not truthfulness and virtue that pay dividends in this vale of tears, but rather cynicism and vice. Benedict sees the divine pedagogy on full display in texts that wrestle with this harsh reality, and in them he says that we catch a vivid glimpse of Israel's proverbial "struggle" with God (*Jesus of Nazareth: From the Baptism*, 212–13). When countless righteous Israelites died without any trace of evidence of having received an earthly reward for their trials, the patient endurance of this suffering is paradoxically what opened God's people to the possibility that the ultimate reward for righteousness — and punishment for it opposite — lies not here but on the other side of eternity (*Eschatology*, 91). For this reason, it is only in texts composed after the exile that we see unambiguous evidence of the afterlife in Sacred Scripture. In fact, belief in the resurrection of the dead did not coalesce until after yet another dire wave of persecutions in the second century BC, a development expressed with particular power and clarity in 2 Maccabees 6–7 and 12. And, even given that revelation, the definitive manifestation of man's hope for resurrection of the body would not arrive until the first Easter Sunday.

Passages That Assume Polytheism and Divine Mutability

An imperfect understanding of the afterlife was not the only area of Israel's early theology that deepened over time. Significantly, Ratzinger stressed that the official religion of Israel held not only to Sheol but for a long time also to the existence of other gods alongside Yahweh (*Eschatology*, 83–84). This polytheistic worldview is prevalent throughout the Old Testament, but it is especially evident in passages where Yahweh is depicted as the chief divinity in a "divine council," a pantheon of many gods that the ancients believed in even as a particular nation might privilege the worship of just one among them. This is the background to texts such as Psalm 82:1, where we hear: "God has taken his place in the divine council; / in the midst of the gods he holds judgment," as well as Psalm 86:8: "There is none like you among the gods, O Lord, / nor are there any works like yours." It also underlies echoes of a divine plurality in Genesis 3:22, where God punishes man for having "become like one of us." It is natural for the Christian to interpret passages like these in a Trinitarian key (i.e. the "us" = the three divine persons), and rightly so. However, Benedict would remind us that we can only do so if we neglect the fact that the Triune nature of God had not yet been revealed to the human authors of these texts.

However, it is not solely the presence of polytheistic tendencies that poses challenges for Scripture's portrayal of the divine nature. Beyond affirming that there is only one God, the Christian Tradition also insists that God's nature cannot suffer change (the doctrine of divine immutability). If the Lord were somehow to change by acquiring a new attribute, then it would mean he now possesses what he previously lacked, in which case he had not been God but only now is. On the other hand, if God changes by losing an attribute that he previously had, then he was God but now is not.

Relatedly, Catholic theology professes that God is also all-knowing (omniscient) and all-good (omnibenevolent). And, yet, Scripture speaks of instances where the Lord alters his will, changes his mind, learns novel things, or forgets something that he previously knew. For example, after Moses intercedes for the people, the Lord is said to have "repented of the evil which he thought to do to his people" (Ex 32:14). Similarly, Scripture seems to indicate that God acquired new knowledge after Abraham demonstrated the willingness to offer his son Isaac: "*Now* I know that you fear God, seeing you have not withheld your son, your only son, from me" (Gn 22:12).

As in the case of the afterlife, Benedict understood that a fuller grasp of the divine nature would have to wait until after God's people had gone through the experience of the Babylonian Exile. Paradoxically, the people's understanding of the divine made its greatest progress in the crucible of suffering, and it was only after that experience that a true understanding of God's oneness and its accompanying attributes began to take root. In his important address at the University of Regensburg where he had once taught, Pope Benedict described this process:

Within the Old Testament, the process which started at the burn-

ing bush came to new maturity at the time of the Exile, when the
God of Israel, an Israel now deprived of its land and worship, was
proclaimed as the God of heaven and earth and described in a
simple formula which echoes the words uttered at the burning
bush: "I am." This new understanding of God is accompanied
by a kind of enlightenment, which finds stark expression in the
mockery of gods who are merely the work of human hands. (Address "Faith, Reason and the University: Memories and Reflections," September 12, 2006)

It is significant that the pontiff spoke of Israel's knowledge of God in
terms of a *process* that exhibited development over the centuries. It was
only at the time of the Exile that Israel finally understood that Yahweh
was not merely *their* God — the divinity of a specific people who rules
their land in Canaan — but rather the *only* God whose dominion is the
entire cosmos. Meanwhile, all the other gods that were once acknowledged as "gods" but not worshiped in Israel were now revealed to be either merely human fabrications (Is 44–45), or in some cases demons (as
in the Greek version of Ps 96:5).

Providentially, then, Israel's national defeat ends up being their greatest
spiritual gain. Yet, this was by no means a foregone conclusion, as Ratzinger explains in his book on the relationship of Christianity and other religions. Under ordinary circumstances, he notes, a god who loses his land
and abandons his people is overthrown. No longer deemed deserving of
worship, he either gets demoted or vanishes from history. Against all odds,
however, the opposite happened when Israel went into exile. Ratzinger understood that, astonishingly, this was precisely the time when the faith of
God's people "at last took on its true form and stature." Yes, God had let
his chosen son Israel suffer tragic defeat, but this was allowed "so as to
awaken it thereby from its false religious dream" (*Truth and Tolerance*, 148).
This point held such significance for Benedict that it was among the final
subjects he revisited shortly before returning to the home of his heavenly
Father. "Only during the time of the Exile did monotheism develop completely in Israel," the pontiff emeritus wrote. "Israel had been robbed of
its land, and this normally put an end to the divinity of a country or of a

nation. A god who was not capable of defending his people and his land could not be a god. In Israel, on the contrary, the opposite train of thought was followed." ("Monotheism and Tolerance," in *What Is Christianity?*, 35).

Passages That Endorse Violence in God's Name

One of the most common obstacles to belief in our post-Christian era stems from the violence that the Old Testament portrays as being commanded or perpetrated by God. In his apostolic exhortation on the word of God, Benedict referred to these distributing texts as the "dark passages" of the Bible. Aware that their presence in Scripture has posed hurdles for many struggling or would-be Christians across the ages, the pope exhorted theologians to develop approaches by which to help the faithful interpret them in the full light of Jesus Christ (*Verbum Domini*, 42).

Benedict was familiar with many passages of this kind, from the global devastation wrought by the flood (see Gn 7:23), to the death of Egypt's firstborn (Ex 12:29), to the words of the psalmist who declares blessed those who would take his enemies' children and "dash them against the rock" (Ps 137:9). However, the Old Testament narrative describing Israel's conquest of the Promised Land typically draws the most critical attention in popular culture. Along their march toward Canaan, Scripture says that God commanded his people to "utterly destroy" the nations that lay before them and to "show no mercy to them" (Dt 2:34; 7:2; Jos 6:21). This ancient Near Eastern practice of totalizing *herem* warfare is reflected in other texts where the Israelites are said to have "utterly destroyed" entire cities — exterminating men, women, children, and animals alike (1 Sm 15:3–9). The difficulty posed by such passages is that they seem scarcely compatible with the existence of a God who is love itself. Indeed, Benedict took to heart the charge that these passages sound like they belong not in the Bible but in the Qur'an. How, then, is the Christian to respond to this charge?

Benedict addressed this question a number of times, always following his characteristic hermeneutic of divine pedagogy. The reason that Scripture narrates "acts of violence and massacre, without explicitly denouncing the immorality of such things" is that the Lord's revelation was adjusted "to the cultural and moral level of distant times" (*Verbum Domini*,

42). Like a parent or a missionary teaching the Faith, the Lord patiently helped the Israelites to understand his will as best as was possible for them at every moment on their path toward Jesus Christ. Accordingly, Benedict acknowledges that the Lord initially permitted the Israelites to think that he directly willed violence because that was their societal norm and thus the starting point of their education in divine matters. When he took up this subject a final time in retirement, the emeritus pontiff further noted that the "intolerance" of Israel's monotheism was motivated by the conviction that the people inhabiting the territories to be conquered posed an existential threat. Having defiled the land with their abominations, their idolatry reached such an extent that Israel considered their rights revoked. The land, it was believed, needed to be restored to its proper dignity — and cultures at the time had no reservations about waging wars of extermination to achieve this end ("Monotheism and Tolerance," in *What Is Christianity?*, 29).

Benedict's exploration of how to interpret Scripture's "dark passages" is a perfect example of his constant emphasis on the truth that God respects the fact that we only learn the truth slowly and within a specific cultural context. In the present case, it is pivotal to observe that the ancient Israelites were not yet privy to a distinction that we now know centuries later — namely, that God does not actively will evil but rather *permits* them as part of his salvific plan. With this distinction in place, after many centuries God's people would eventually be prepared to learn the full truth concerning how to treat our enemies.

And what is this truth? It is the "hard saying" that we are called not to destroy but rather *love* and *pray for* the conversion of our enemies to Christ, who is love itself (see Mt 5:39–4; 1 Jn 4:16). Emphasizing the necessity of interpreting the Old Testament in light of Jesus Christ, Benedict declared in his 2006 Regensburg Address that "violence is incompatible with the nature of God and the nature of the soul" ("Faith, Reason and the University: Memories and Reflections," September 12, 2006). Yet, before Israel could understand that the Lord is both all-powerful and all-good, they first had to learn the more fundamental lesson that there is only one God.

Last but not least, Benedict does not think that the problem of violence in the Old Testament admits of any resolution — and any clear differentiation from an Islamic approach — apart from this Christological perspective. While he duly acknowledged of Christianity and Islam that "there is some good and some bad in both," Benedict also knew that the Muslim cannot appeal to a definitive principle at the end of the Qur'an, which would reveal that all things are to be interpreted on the basis of love. In Christianity, however, Benedict tells us that there is a "relativization" of individual texts within the canon. This is not to deny the truth and perma-nent value of the Old Testament, but it is rather an acknowledgment that violence of God's people in times past was never meant to represent the Lord's final word. In one of Benedict's final essays, he explained:

> For Christians ... it is possible to grasp the Old Testament cor-rectly only in terms of the new interpretation that it had in the words and actions of Jesus Christ. The New Testament gives valid witness to this interpretation. The two collections of texts — the Old and the New Testaments — refer to each other in such a way that the New Testament is the interpretive key to the Old. From a Christian perspective, only in terms of the New Testament can we establish what the lasting theological significance of the Old Testament is. ... The meaning and the authority of the individual parts are correctly gathered only from the Bible as a whole and in light of Christ's coming. ("Monotheism and Tolerance," in *What Is Christianity?*, 43–44)

Aside from their being a step on Israel's journey to Christ, do these violent passages hold any enduring relevance for believers today? Inspired by the Fathers of the Church, Benedict found it significant that there is a profound *spiritual sense* to the Old Testament's dark passages. For example, while he grants that passages like Moses's slaughter of the idolaters in Exodus 32 do sound "terribly bloodthirsty," he finds they conceal a deeper meaning if we "look forward, toward Christ." The Israelites at the time had not yet fully grasped the full implications of the fifth commandment that would ultimately be revealed in Christ's command to love our enemies. Yet, even while saying that, Benedict confidently affirms that the death of heathens at the hands of Israel's faithful "expresses the truth that anyone who turns from God not only departs from the Covenant but from the sphere of life; they ruin their own life and, in doing so, enter into the realm of death" (*God and the World*, 168). A similar hermeneutic is applicable to passages where the Israelites are reported to have wiped out entire populations. From the perspective of past greats such as St. Benedict of Nursia and St. Gregory of Nyssa, the command to "destroy" or "drown" our enemies and their "firstborn" should be seen as an exhortation to put to death everything in our lives that is not of God, no matter how small it might seem.

Furthermore, if we take seriously the Second Vatican Council's emphasis on the need to grasp the literary form of thorny biblical passages, then another fascinating possibility emerges for the interpretation of Scripture's dark passages. In 2014, the Pontifical Biblical Commission published a document whose work had been initiated during the tenure of Pope Benedict. In this text, the Pontifical Biblical Commission crucially notes that many instances of violence in the Old Testament "do not have the characteristics of a historical account" (*The Inspiration and Truth of Sacred Scripture*, 147). As we see in works from other cultures of that time, the extent of violence depicted in these passages was quite likely overstated in order to foster a sense of national identity and inspire total devotion to God's laws. With this knowledge in hand, the PBC notes that the purpose of Israel's ancient vindictiveness was exhortative, and "the apparently violent action is to be interpreted as concern to remove evil" (*The Inspiration and Truth of Sacred Scripture*, 147). In other words, it was designed as a summons for the Israel of its day to imitate the zeal of the ancients portrayed in these texts.

Remarkably, this more recent interpretive trend represents a return to the old. On this score, the PBC concurs with what we discovered above, that "the best interpreters of the patristic tradition" already read the conquest narrative symbolically. To this, it adds that a given passage where we encounter divinely sanctioned violence "requires a nonliteral interpretation" and that "we must understand the entire event of the conquest as a sort of symbol" (*The Inspiration and Truth of Sacred Scripture*, 146–47). Reading these texts in light of the revelation of God's abundant mercy in Christ, we learn that what should be "devoted to destruction" in our lives is not other sinners but rather *our sinful ways*. Ultimately, it is these, and not other people, that prevent us from being true disciples of Jesus.

————— ◆ —————

As we have seen in this chapter, Benedict's approach to Scripture strikes a unique balance with his capacity to acknowledge periodic tensions between the biblical text all while embracing the full revelation of God in Jesus Christ. Rather than rejecting Scripture or burying our heads in the sand, the biblical-scholar-pope maintained that the truth shines forth on every page of Sacred Scripture. To see this truth, he insisted that believers must have the courage to embrace the full breadth of reason, drawing on wisdom from traditional sources while also welcoming the challenge of putting the Church's ancient faith into conversation with new discoveries. Furthermore, he stressed that the Bible is not just one book, but a book of books, each of which has its own literary genius and a specific message that its authors wanted to convey by means of their craft. In other words, Scripture is both an ancient text to be studied and as a living word to be prayed and lived. As the pontiff wrote in his "Spiritual Testament" bequeathed to the Church upon his death, the question before us is this: "How, indeed, can we properly understand a biblical text — not coming up with ideas of our own, but remaining honest with ourselves as interpreters of history — and yet, without doing violence to the text, inquire into its relevance for the present?"

Perhaps above all, for Benedict the key to understanding the Bible is to recognize that it is both truly divine and truly human, aware that this reality carries with it important ramifications. On the eve of Vatican II, the young Joseph Ratzinger summarized this point well:

> According to a practically irrefutable consensus of historians there definitely are mistakes and errors in the Bible in profane matters of no relevance for what Scripture properly intends to affirm. ... The true humanity of Scripture, behind which the mystery of God's mercy arises all the more, is now finally dawning on our awareness; namely that Scripture is and remains inerrant and beyond doubt in everything that it properly intends to

affirm, but this is not necessarily so in that which accompanies the affirmation and is not part of it. (Wicks, "Six Texts by Prof. Joseph Ratzinger," 280)

This small passage ties together a number of key themes we have discussed in this chapter, in particular the true humanity of Scripture and the necessity of distinguishing its core affirmations from the vehicle by which they are conveyed. All the while, Ratzinger's conviction undergirding texts like this is that a reluctance to concede the Bible's imperfections represents more than a failure of reason. To overlook this is to miss the opportunity to marvel at the remarkable journey by which the Lord painstakingly prepared his people to reach the ultimate goal of divine revelation: welcoming the incarnation of our Lord and Savior, Jesus Christ.

READING LIST

♦ Benedict XVI. *Verbum Domini*. Apostolic Exhortation. September 30, 2010.
♦ Pidel, Aaron. *The Inspiration and Truth of Scripture: Testing the Ratzinger Paradigm*. Washington, DC: The Catholic University of America Press, 2023.
♦ Ramage, Matthew. *Dark Passages of the Bible: Engaging Scripture with Benedict XVI and Thomas Aquinas*. Washington, DC: The Catholic University of America Press, 2013.
♦ Ramage, Matthew. *Jesus, Interpreted: Benedict XVI, Bart Ehrman, and the Historical Truth of the Gospels*. Washington, DC: The Catholic University of America Press, 2017.
♦ Ratzinger, Joseph. "Biblical Interpretation in Conflict: On the Foundations and the Itinerary for Exegesis Today." In *Opening Up the Scriptures: Joseph Ratzinger and the Foundations of Biblical Interpretation*, edited by José Granados, Carlos Granados, and Luis Sánchez-Navarro, 1–29. Grand Rapids, MI: Eerdmans, 2008.
♦ Ratzinger, Joseph. *Called to Communion: Understanding the Church Today*. San Francisco: Ignatius Press, 1996.

◆ Ratzinger, Joseph. "Dogmatic Constitution on Divine Revelation: Chapter II: The Transmission of Divine Revelation." In *Commentary on the Documents of Vatican II*, ed. edited by Herbert Vorgrimler, vol. III, 181–98. New York: Herder and Herder, 1967–1969.

◆ Ratzinger, Joseph. "Exegesis and the Magisterium of the Church." In *Opening Up the Scriptures: Joseph Ratzinger and the Foundations of Biblical Interpretation*, edited by José Granados, Carlos Granados, and Luis Sánchez-Navarro, 126–36. Grand Rapids, MI: Eerdmans, 2008.

◆ Ratzinger, Joseph. "Observations on the Schema *De fontibus revelationis*." English translation in Jared Wicks, "Six Texts by Prof. Joseph Ratzinger as *Peritus* before and during Vatican Council II," in *Gregorianum* 89 (2008): 233–311, at 271.

◆ Ratzinger, Joseph. *Principles of Catholic Theology*. San Francisco: Ignatius Press, 1987.

◆ Stallsworth, Paul. "The Story of an Encounter." In *Biblical Interpretation in Crisis: The Ratzinger Conference on Bible and Church*, 102–90. Grand Rapids, MI: Eerdmans, 1989.

CHAPTER 4

The Harmony of
Faith and Reason

With a good sense of Benedict's approach to interpreting the Bible, we are now well positioned to consider his hallmark insights for how to navigate issues at the intersection of faith and reason — especially when the discoveries of modern science appear to contradict the testimony of Sacred Scripture. As we will explore, one of Ratzinger's most enduring concerns was the question of how to affirm the Church's ancient faith in light of modern scientific discoveries, like the shared ancestry of all life that has come clearly into view only over the past two centuries.

In what follows, I aim to showcase Benedict's thought as a priceless wellspring of wisdom that can resolve apparent contradictions between faith and reason. In particular, the pontiff's constant endeavor to pinpoint the essence of Christian teaching amid so much confusion over these subjects has been an indispensable model for countless Catholics. As we will see, Benedict's balanced approach refuses to privilege the findings of science against the Church's ancient faith, or pit a literal interpretation of Scripture against legitimate scientific developments. This great lover of the truth was convinced that modern scientific advances are not merely to be begrudgingly tolerated, but rather to be welcomed as gifts that enable the Church to penetrate the Deposit of Faith ever more deeply.[3]

At the Intersection of Faith and Reason

There is a prevailing notion among many today that we are compelled to choose between faith and reason, or between religion and science. On the one hand, it is commonplace in popular culture to encounter the allegation that modern empirical discoveries have made the "God hypothesis" no longer necessary. Not a few Christians have lost their faith over the years as a result of assaults along these lines. On the other hand, Christians are sometimes encouraged to be skeptical of all things new, insinuating that a commitment to faith precludes their acceptance of modern advancements in the sciences. This can lead believers to perceive novel theories as threats to be rejected out of hand alongside other positions that rightly deserve our condemnation. For instance, the question arises: Why would we trust the conclusions of scholars about the nature of the universe when they are so clearly mistaken on such fundamental questions as when a human life begins and the complementarity of man and woman? In this respect, it is hard to blame believers who are skeptical of science when hearing a claim made "in the name of science."

Yet, regrettably, the sense of apprehension about new ideas and reflexive dismissal of science are also significant contributors to our society's loss of faith, especially among the young. When sincere Christians take a spurious approach toward the enterprise of science, for example, it tends to lead to a scenario in which people feel backed into a corner. They have encountered compelling evidence for a specific rational assertion, and their impression that it runs counter to the faith is not allayed by a well-intentioned citation from Scripture, a Church Father, or magisterial document. In the words of Joseph Ratzinger's dear friend and theological mentor Henri de Lubac: "To one who has seen a problem, the most beautiful and

---

3. An in-depth treatment of the themes explored in this and the following chapter can be found in my book *From the Dust of the Earth: Benedict XVI, the Bible, and the Theory of Evolution* (The Catholic University of America Press, 2022).

true things, uttered by someone who has not seen it, are but words and yet more words" (*Paradoxes of Faith*, 54).

As a loving pastor and relentless inquirer, Benedict deeply appreciated the wariness of traditional believers when it comes to modern empirical breakthroughs. After all, all experts — whether they be scientists, philosophers, or biblical scholars — are fallible mortals who can have their own prejudices and agendas. This is a phenomenon the pontiff described when he observed, "Science has opened up major dimensions of reason that previously had not been accessible. ... But in its joy over the greatness of its discoveries, it tends to confiscate dimensions of our reason that we still need" (*Creation and Evolution*, 145). Combine this with the realization that some things once widely assumed by Christians are today generally acknowledged to be otherwise, and what you get, says Ratzinger, is the following:

> There is an almost ineluctable fear that we will gradually end up in emptiness and that the time will come when there will be nothing left to defend and hide behind, that the whole landscape of Scripture and of the faith will be overrun by a kind of "reason" that will no longer be able to take any of this seriously.
>
> Along with this there is another disquieting consideration. For one can ask: If theologians or even the church can shift the boundaries here between image and intention, between what lies buried in the past and what is of enduring value, why can they not do so elsewhere — as, for instance, with respect to Jesus' miracles? And if there, why not also with respect to what is absolutely central — the cross and the resurrection of the Lord? (*In the Beginning*, 6–7)

Put another way, one can easily imagine a slippery slope in which the Church's gradual acceptance of groundbreaking scientific theories results in "the impression that the faith of the Church is like some kind of jellyfish, where there is nothing solid to grab onto, nothing firm at the center of it all that can be built upon" (*The Divine Project*, 22).

In the same way that the Church had to grapple with the emerging theory of heliocentrism at the time of Copernicus and Galileo, a similar challenge confronts us today in the case of Mendel and Darwin with their insights into the laws of genetics and life's evolutionary past. How are today's Christians to navigate the dramatic tension between the realms of faith and reason in a way that is "both intellectually honest and genuinely faithful" (*The Divine Project*, 17)? At the core of Benedict's concern was not so much the question of how to defend the faithful against the advances of modernity, rather it was how we can actively engage in conversation with it. In the end, this dialogue aims to penetrate the mysteries of the Christian faith with the aid of human reason and, in turn, to illumine the findings of reason with the light of faith.

Benedict captures the heart of this task with a scientific metaphor. Just as no experiment guarantees a given outcome in advance, so Benedict writes that Catholicism requires making an "experiment of faith." In Benedict's own words, this involves existential "risk" — the possibility that we may have to revise certain preconceptions in response to the outcomes of our venture (*Introduction to Christianity*, 51–52). On this point, Benedict agreed with his friend Henri de Lubac's wise saying that authentic love of truth never goes without daring and that the fear of falling into error should never prevent us from daring to attain the truth (Henri de Lubac, *Paradoxes of Faith*, 101). In conformity with this, Cardinal Joseph Frings delivered the following words prepared by Father Ratzinger on the eve of the Second Vatican Council: "Today's man must be able to recognize again that the Church is neither afraid of nor need be afraid of science, because she is sheltered in the truth of God" ("Das Konzil und die moderne Gedankenwelt," 174).

Benedict would return to this theme five decades later in a landmark lecture at one of his former teaching posts, the University of Regensburg. In this 2006 address, the pontiff stressed that a compelling reproposal of the faith in today's world requires of the disciple a willingness to "enter into the debates of our time," armed with "the courage to engage the whole breadth of reason." Rather than fighting modern advances and dwelling on the dangers that they might pose for traditional Christian doctrine, Benedict affirmed that "the positive aspects of modernity are to be acknowledged unreservedly" (Address "Faith, Reason and the University,"

September 12, 2006). The pontiff's overarching concern was to encourage everyone to devote themselves to attaining the truth of things, even when that truth is difficult to bear or complicates our lives.

For Benedict, there was never any doubt that the Church can withstand any challenge presented by reason. However, even this core conviction was simply an echo of his predecessor John Paul II's teaching that "truth cannot contradict truth" and St. Thomas Aquinas's centuries-old dictum that "all truth, no matter what its source, is of the Holy Spirit" (Aquinas, *De Veritate*, q. 1, a. 8; John Paul II, October 22, 1996, Message to the Pontifical Academy of Sciences). Simply put, whether the wisdom was being propounded by a believer or a non-Christian made no difference to any of these theological greats. In reference to this, Church Fathers such as Origen of Alexandria even went so far as to encourage believers to "plunder the Egyptians."

On more than one occasion, Benedict raised the stakes with the suggestion that believers incur great "risk" by *not* daring to pursue the truth wherever it may be found. The reluctance to accept recent discoveries, he maintains, prevents many from fully grasping the truth of the Christian faith:

> It seems to me that we quite often run a particular risk: that of not wanting to see these things. We live with shades down over our windows, so to speak, because we are afraid that our faith could not stand the full, glaring light of the facts. So we shield ourselves against this and push these facts out of our consciousness, so as to avoid falling on our face. But a faith that will not account for half of the facts or even more is actually, in essence, a kind of refusal of faith, or, at least, a very profound form of skepticism that fears faith will not be big enough to cope with reality. … In contrast to that, true believing means looking the whole of reality in the face, unafraid and with an open heart, even if it goes against the picture of faith that, for whatever reason, we make for ourselves. (*What It Means to Be a Christian*, 19–20)

Regrettably, the reality is that many Christians find it too daunting to take up this challenge. As we have already seen him point out, the temptation is to retreat into perceived safe havens such as strict biblical literalism (a wooden reading of the Bible, treating it as if it were a textbook on history and science) or what Cardinal Ratzinger called "a positivistic and rigid ecclesiasticism" (an overly simplistic and exclusive reliance on documents of the Church).

The Church and Evolutionary Theory

We will be focusing on the subject of creation more in the next chapter, but at this point it is helpful to pause and consider Benedict's approach to evolutionary theory as a shining example of his wisdom in navigating issues at the intersection of faith and reason. While many Christians find the theory of evolution to be noncontroversial, Benedict was sensitive to the experience of those who have difficulty accepting the proposition that every living species on our planet descends from a shared ancestor that lived roughly four billion years ago. As a good shepherd, Benedict's approach to this subject was therefore gentle. Rather than mandating that the faithful embrace the science of evolution, the pontiff's strategy for addressing the topic was more of an invitation to contemplate how to understand the science of evolution in light of the Catholic Faith. In turn, he urged us to consider how our understanding of divine revelation might be enriched through dialogue with modern science.

For Benedict, like those well versed in the field, the science of evolution is not "just a theory" in the popular sense of the term. This would unduly reduce the mountain of scientific evidence supporting the theory to the status of mere conjecture (while effectively doing the same for other well-established theories such as heliocentrism, gravity, the Big Bang, and plate tectonics). As distinguished Catholic voices such as St. John Henry Newman and Pope St. John Paul II have understood, evolution is "more than a hypothesis," and its conclusions are based on the confluence of findings across many independent fields (Message to the Pontifical Academy of Sciences, October 22, 1996, 4). Speaking on this topic during his own tenure as pontiff, Benedict even spoke of the "many scientific proofs in favor of evolution" (Meeting with Clergy of the Dioceses of Belluno-Feltre and Treviso on July 24, 2007).

The theme of how to engage evolution in the light of faith occupied Benedict's mind throughout his life. Already as a young professor, Father Ratzinger had described the basic truths described by evolutionary theory as "self-evident" (*Introduction to Christianity*, 66). In his 1964 course on the doctrine of creation, he fittingly spoke of God's providential governance of the universe across time as "evolutionary creation." The word "evolutionary" is the modifying term in this expression, as it clarifies that the Lord's creation of the world out of nothing is the more fundamental reality and that evolution is simply the *means* by which God guides and sustains the universe.

Ratzinger took up this subject a number of times during his tenure as cardinal-prefect of the Congregation for the Doctrine of the Faith and president of the Church's International Theological Commission. In a document penned under his leadership, the commission explained in detail: "There is general agreement among them that the first organism dwelt on this planet between three-and-a-half and four billion years ago. Since it has been demonstrated that all living organisms on earth are genetically related, it is virtually certain that all living organisms have descended from this first organism" (*Communion and Stewardship*, 63). Appealing to "converging evidence from many studies in the physical and biological sciences," this study proceeds to emphasize that there is little doubt among experts as to whether all life shares a common genetic ancestry. The document then wraps up its summary of man's evolutionary history by noting that while the precise narrative "is complex and subject to revision, physical anthropology and molecular biology combine to make a convincing case for the origin of the human species in Africa about 150,000 years ago in a humanoid population of common genetic lineage."

Cardinal Ratzinger made some exceptionally insightful remarks on this subject in a 1981 homily and a 1985 meditation on Genesis's creation account with its depiction of Adam's origin from the "dust of the ground" (Gn 2:7). Reflecting on the depth and power of this text, Ratzinger could not help but confront the issue head-on: "All well and good, we might say, but is not all this ultimately refuted by our scientific knowledge of man's descent from the animals?" The ancient words of Genesis are beautiful indeed, but are they also true? Ratzinger acknowledged that "everything seems to speak against" the truth of the Bible's creation narrative. Phrased somewhat differently, it would appear that "science has long since disposed of the concepts" that are bound up with it.

Ratzinger immediately anticipates the skeptic's next thought. The stories in Genesis, so the indictment reads, arose out of "the reveries of the infant age of human history, for which we occasionally experience homesickness but to which we can nevertheless not return." In other words, given what science has revealed over the past millennium, it is difficult — if not impossible — to honestly accept such naïve stories at face value.

Ratzinger's answer to this challenge echoes that of St. Thomas Aquinas with his twin principles for interpreting Genesis's creation narratives: First, we must hold the *truth* of Scripture unwaveringly. Second, we should be ready to abandon any particular *explanation* of Scripture if our interpretation is proven to be false — lest Scripture be exposed to the ridicule of unbelievers and obstacles posed to the believers (*Summa Theologiae*, I, q. 68, a. 1). Like Augustine and Aquinas, Ratzinger was deeply concerned about avoiding making the faith look absurd to would-be and struggling believers. Indeed, his entire interpretive approach served as a caution against adhering to rigidly literal interpretations of Genesis, especially when engaging with individuals outside the Christian fold who know well that such an approach is intellectually untenable.

Cardinal Ratzinger's response to the formidable challenge presented by evolution was especially noteworthy. Stressing "the inner unity of creation and evolution, of faith and reason," he remarked that this is not an "either-or" situation. In reality, Ratzinger observed that we should not say "creation *or* evolution" but should actually be saying "creation *and* evolution," seeing these as answers to two different questions (*The Divine Project*, 77–78; *In the Beginning*, 3–4, 50).

If the relationship between these two domains is a both-and matter, then what comes next? In other words, what is the task that lays before us? As the Ratzinger-helmed ITC put it, the real issue for scientists has to do with mapping out the details of precisely how life evolved, while for theologians the question has to do with *its theological implications*. With this in mind, the Vatican charged theologians with "the responsibility to locate modern scientific understandings within a Christian vision of the created universe" (*Communion and Stewardship*, 66). In the words of John Paul II, our newfound knowledge of mankind's long biological backstory puts us in a position to ask the following: "Does an evolutionary perspective bring any light to bear upon theological anthropology, the meaning of the human person as the *imago Dei*, the problem of Christology — and even upon the development of doctrine itself?" This line of reasoning fits well with the overall approach of Benedict's predecessor, who memorably explained, "Science can purify religion from error and superstition; religion can purify science from idolatry and false absolutes" (John Paul II, June 1, 1988, Letter to George Coyne, SJ, Director of the Vatican Observatory).

While John Paul II is known as the pope who wrote an entire encyclical devoted to the subject of faith and reason, Ratzinger was always right there at his side, not only helping him craft *Fides et Ratio* but also engaged in his own efforts to showcase the harmony of these two domains. As Benedict put it both as cardinal and then later as pope, engaging in sincere dialogue between faith and reason can be a crucial countermeasure against two opposite errors. On the one hand, reason's openness to faith can be an antidote against "a pathology of reason" that would reduce Jesus to a mere man and man to mere material. At the same time, religion's willingness to engage reason's discoveries can serve as an antidote against "a pathology of religion" that would have us close our eyes to the truths unveiled in creation, the other "book" authored by God.

Benedict disavowed this latter disease on many occasions, notably his critiques of fundamentalist ideologies that irrationally advocate violence in the name of God. This critique also extends to his frequent repudiations of biblical literalism and the related error of fideism, which refers to the "desire to believe against reason" which the Catholic Church has rejected from her very beginning (*Values in a Time of Upheaval*, 160; 2006 Address at the University of Regensburg, September 12, 2001; General Audience of November 21, 2012). In his final words bequeathed to the Church, the emeritus pontiff wrote that the openness to being challenged by the discoveries of the natural sciences enables faith to "understand the limits of the scope of its affirmations and thus its own specificity" (Spiritual Testament, December 31, 2022).

Lessons Learned from the Galileo Affair

As we discussed in Chapter 2, the essential dogmas of Catholicism are irreformable, meaning that they can never change. However, Benedict also knew that positions long associated with these dogmas at times stand in need of emendation as mankind's treasury of knowledge increases. Just to take one prominent example from the turbulent yet rich history of the encounter between science and theology, we can consider the sixteenth-century Galileo affair. At that moment in history, many in the Church rejected the new science of heliocentrism propounded by Copernicus and Galileo. While they also had valid scientific reasons for doing so, the reticence toward this new theory stemmed from the assumption that acknowledging the idea of the Earth orbiting the Sun contradicted the teachings of Scripture and thereby the core of Christian faith. And yet, most of us today would find ourselves hard pressed to find a Catholic who disputes the theory, continuing to insist that the sun revolves around the earth ("Farewell to the Devil?," 198).

In his role as head of the Pontifical Biblical Commission, Cardinal Ratzinger noted that the underlying problem at the time of Galileo was the widespread assumption that "the geocentric world picture was inextricably bound up with the revealed message of the Bible, and that champions of the heliocentric world picture were destroying the core of Revelation." After all, Scripture says that the world is established and shall never be moved (see Ps 93:1 and 96:10). Indeed, Benedict notes that many at the time of Galileo took it for granted that the ascription of the entire Pentateuch to Moses and adherence to a geocentric worldview were "indispensable conditions of the trustworthiness of Scripture and, therefore, of the faith founded upon it."

Faced with what looks like a glaring contradiction between the Bible's ancient faith and the findings of modern science, Ratzinger explained, "It became necessary fully to reconceive the relationship between the *outward form of presentation* and the *real message* of the whole, and it required a gradual process before the criteria could be elaborated" ("Exegesis and Magisterium of the Church," 134). While the phrasing here is vintage Ratzinger, this sort of distinction has a long pedigree in Catholicism, notably in St. Thomas Aquinas's contrast between matters that pertain to the essence of

Scripture (the inerrancy of its salvific message) and those features that pertain to this core only accidentally (for example, the scientific worldview of the biblical authors).

As an illustration of his genuine commitment to learn from the mistakes of history, Pope Benedict would later go so far as to lament "the Church's error in the case of Galileo Galilei." The pontiff acknowledged that censuring the Italian astronomer had damaged the Church's credibility, and he clearly wished to avoid repeating this blunder in the case of Darwin (Address to the Parish Priests and Clergy of Rome, February 14, 2013). Yet, far from scorning the Church for her past missteps, which indeed stood "in need of correction," Benedict treated this episode as a learning experience. Recognizing the Church's historical condemnation of a position now accepted as true emboldened Ratzinger to dedicate his work to demonstrating that the credibility of the Christian Tradition requires integrating the old and the new. This synthesis aims to glean the strengths of both while acknowledging their respective weaknesses.

The Logos and Benedict's Critique of Scientism

From what has been said thus far, it is evident that Benedict did not harbor any objections to scientific breakthroughs in their own right. He was always optimistic that contemporary advances in the empirical domain were only going to deepen our knowledge of reality once illumined with the light of faith. However, this is by no means to say that the pontiff believed the matter to be quite that simple, for he also perceived profound problems lurking under the surface where faith and reason come into contact.

The key issue in this regard is something so fundamental that many Christians take it for granted. Put simply, the question is whether God exists and governs the universe, or not. In other words, which of the following approaches is true to reality: Is it that of the atheist, who denies that divine power is at work in nature? Or is it rather that of the believer, who holds that divine intelligence created the universe and governs it still today? In contrast with what some prominent atheists insist, Ratzinger is adamant that this query is actually not scientific in nature. That is to say, his point is that we cannot determine the question of God's existence on the basis of the empirical disciplines of physics, biology, and the like. We are dealing here with a *philosophical* matter, and so the conversation needed to adjudicate it must take place at the level of philosophical thought.

While Christians have at times been guilty of subordinating science to theology by seeking to predetermine its conclusions, Ratzinger notes that today the opposite tendency is more common. This is the attempt to explain the whole of reality — including God — in terms of science. In this sense, for many in our day science has become a substitute for metaphysics and theology — a sort of universal "first philosophy" (*Truth and Tolerance*, 178–83). Some who are enamored by the explanatory power of science unfortunately can be led to embrace what Benedict and his predecessor John Paul II called scient*ism* — an ideology that refuses to admit the validity of any form of knowledge other than that which comes from the realms of mathematics and the empirical sciences. When scientism prevails, all other areas of knowledge — religious, theological, ethical, and aesthetic — are relegated to the realm of the mere subjective. Yet, as Benedict urged in his Regensburg Address, this widespread reduction "needs to be questioned." According to this pope, the key task before us now is how to "overcome the self-imposed limitation of reason to the empirically verifiable." To recall Galileo's memorable saying, science teaches us how heaven goes, but it cannot tell us how we go to heaven.

While he rejoices in the insights that science brings to our understanding of the natural world, Ratzinger notes that empirical science is unable to answer the most fundamental question, which is whether creation is inherently meaning*ful* or meaning*less*. Science cannot tell us whether or not divine reason stands at the beginning of all things, and neither can it tell us where everything ultimately comes from, how we ought to live in the world, or what our ultimate destiny is (*Truth and Tolerance*, 181; Meeting with Clergy of the Dioceses of Belluno-Feltre and Treviso, July 24, 2007). Remarkably, Pope Benedict threw down the gauntlet on this matter in the following homily: "Here we are faced with the ultimate alternative that is at stake in the dispute between faith and unbelief: are irrationality, lack of freedom and pure chance the origin of everything, or are reason, freedom and love at the origin of being? Does the primacy belong to unreason or to reason? This is what everything hinges upon in the final analysis" (Easter Vigil Homily, April 23, 2011). Articulating this point with a slightly different nuance, Professor Ratzinger once said that there are at bottom only two fundamental worldviews: materialism and mere chance on the one hand, and on the other, a spiritually informed worldview suffused with meaning ("Belief in Creation and the Theory of Evolution," 140–41).

Alternatively, we might pose the question in this way: Did intelligence first come online in the cosmos with *Homo sapiens* only after the universe had been blindly humming along for billions of years? Or, on the contrary, is the Christian Tradition right to affirm, "In the beginning was the Word" (Jn 1:1)? Benedict's response to this query is straightforward: "As believers we answer, with the creation account and with St. John, that in the beginning is reason. In the beginning is freedom" (Easter Vigil Homily, April 23, 2011). One of the pontiff's primary concerns here and throughout his life was to make it clear that Christianity is committed at its very core to the truth that the entirety of creation finds its basis in the divine mind, the Logos. From this perspective, it is contradictory to hold that the cosmos popped into existence without a first cause or that the evolution of man was an entirely blind and random process.

As a matter of fact, Benedict takes the proclamation of the Logos to be the "central message" of Scripture's creation narrative. It is this, he maintains, that Genesis 1 teaches when it figuratively depicts God "speaking" the cosmos into being. Although the presence of speech may seem like a trivial anthropomorphic detail within the broader story of creation, Benedict notes that it embodies a revelatory truth that ran directly counter to the worldview of other creation narratives from the ancient Near Eastern world. By describing creation arising through divine speech, Genesis definitively affirms that the world issued forth from God's mind — *not* by chance or through a cosmic struggle between different deities, as other ancient religions envisioned. And, in case this reading of Genesis is not clear enough on its own terms, Benedict reminds us that it is made explicit in the prologue to John's Gospel, which he identifies as "the conclusive and normative scriptural creation account" (*In the Beginning*, 15). When Saint John writes, "In the beginning was the Word," he is confirming what Genesis first revealed about the origin of the universe — namely, that it issued forth from God's mind. The New Testament in turn reveals the fullness of truth that the opening chapters of Genesis only foreshadowed: The Word through which God "spoke" creation into existence is none other than his son, our Lord Jesus Christ.

Faith, Evolution, and the Futility of Naturalism

To understand the rationale for Ratzinger's constant stress on the priority of the Logos in creation, we need to return to the concept of scientism and consider how it often plays out in the context of a concrete topic. As we have already witnessed, one such issue that perhaps above all others occupied his mind was life's evolutionary history. We are now in a position to add additional dimension to this conversation.

On the material level, Benedict was not perturbed by the proposition that "the entire world of living things came about ... by the accumulation of transcription errors." In fact, Ratzinger deems this "an incredibly profound diagnosis and itself an image of the human person" (*The Divine Project*, 83). Yet, even while acknowledging the role of natural selection in human origins, Ratzinger would never simply leave it at that. It cannot be that nature is all there is, as many claim the science of evolution implies. He therefore immediately probes into the issue of how we should respond to this reductive philosophy of naturalism, the view that all reality can be explained by natural causes and laws.

What ensues is the same approach that Benedict and John Paul II consistently followed over many decades. Our popes invariably begin with respect for the "principle of autonomy," which means that the natural sciences should be allowed to operate according to their respective methods without theology seeking to fix their conclusions in advance (John Paul II, *Fides et Ratio*, 13, 77). In this vein, Ratzinger tells us that it "remains the business of the natural sciences to explain the particular factors by which the tree of life grows and expands." In other words, it is the job of science to address the questions of when, where, and precisely how life arose on this planet, for these are not matters that pertain to the substance of the Catholic Faith.

What *does* touch the heart of the Faith is the issue of whether chance is all there is to this world. With this in mind, Ratzinger insists that man's evolutionary origin cannot be construed in such a way that it subtracts anything from his unique dignity. That is to say, man is indeed "a divine project and not an accumulation of transcription errors" (Ratzinger, *The Divine Project*, 83–84). The origin and life of human beings was not a happenstance occurrence but willed as the fruit of divine love. Reading this response in the context of Benedict's broader body of thought, this stands out as a shining example of his desire for reason to help theology understand its proper scope and his optimism that theology can illumine reason in the light of faith. In this case, this means distinguishing the science of biology itself from the unwarranted naturalistic assumptions that all too often accompany it.

To achieve this end, Ratzinger would sometimes direct his audience to the implications that would ensue if we were to affirm that no Logos underpins creation. One such argument assumes the form of a question: "Can reason really renounce its claim to the priority of what is rational over the irrational, the claim that the Logos is at the ultimate origin of things, without abolishing itself?" (*Truth and Tolerance*, 181). What Ratzinger is suggesting here is that our human rationality — the ability to make truth claims in the first place — would be unreliable if they were not grounded in an infinite Mind in whose truth we are all common participants. To put it another way, there is no reason to believe that any of our reasoning gives us access to the truth if our reason itself is *merely* the product of subrational evolutionary processes.

In one of his rare public pieces penned after retiring, Benedict underscored that two things would be undermined if the natural world were somehow to exist apart from God. As we have touched on, one of these is that a world without God — one in which man is merely the product of chance mutations — would be a meaningless universe: "Only if things have a spiritual reason, are intended and conceived — only if there is a Creator God who is good and wants the good — can the life of man also have meaning." Yet, as we have seen above, the question of whether or not the universe is purposeful — whether it has meaning grounded in the divine Logos — is a question that empirical reasoning on its own cannot answer.

Second, Benedict points out that a universe not grounded in God is a world without any standards of good and evil. It is one in which power — survival of the fittest — is the sole guiding principle. If this and the randomness of natural selection really are the exclusive basis of life, then it turns out that all of mankind's moral imperatives are just coping mechanisms. In other words, they would merely be means that humans concoct to try to get our way and to shield ourselves from those more powerful than us ("The Church and the Scandal of Sexual Abuse," 176).

―――――――――――― ◆ ――――――――――――

As we have just discussed, Benedict considered it irrational to deny God's existence while asserting claims to truth or morality. Indeed, the pontiff saw that holding to God's non-existence is an unprovable premise that involves more "faith" than the Christian conviction that our ordered universe proceeds from the divine Logos.

Yet, this was merely the "negative" side of the pontiff's argument. In this chapter, we have pinpointed some serious shortcomings of a naturalistic worldview, but for Benedict the "positive" side of the argument in favor of a robustly Catholic vision of the world is actually more important. In his view, the real proof for the Church's approach to the universe cannot come from arguments alone. The truth of the Faith, Benedict understood, is ultimately discovered in the *laboratory of life* when we embrace Jesus Christ and life in his Church. Although Christianity is by no means unreasonable, Ratzinger stressed that adherence to it does require an existential decision on our part: "Christian Faith represents the choice in favor of the priority of reason and of rationality. This ultimate question ... can no longer be decided by arguments from natural science, and even philosophical thought reaches its limits here. In that sense, there is no ultimate demonstration that the basic choice involved in Christianity is correct" (*Truth and Tolerance*, 181). It may sound rather odd for a man who considers reason so important to speak this bluntly about its limitations, but the fact is that Benedict was not as sanguine as many when it comes to how much he thinks we can definitively prove. Although he was a staunch theist and devout Christian, he was typically reticent to pursue definitive proofs for the Christian approach to reality. As we have already seen, however, this is by no means to say that Benedict despaired of the possibility of knowing the truth about God here below. Nor was he too shy to poke holes in materialist ideology. Indeed, the pontiff noted that the very reliability of science "presupposes the mathematical structure of matter, its intrinsic rationality" (Address at the University of Regensburg September 12, 2006).

In the end, this emphasis is one of the crucial areas where Benedict's theology continues to remain eminently relevant today. Arguably better than anyone else, this pontiff demonstrated the unity of faith and reason and the reciprocal ability of each to enhance the other. With his unwavering efforts to get to the heart of the matter in places where these domains intersect, he forged a path forward that enables us to navigate between the pitfalls of fideism on the one side and rationalism on the other. Especially when we consider how he applied his principles to concrete issues, it becomes evident that Benedict has supplied the Church with a trustworthy map by which to navigate the realms of faith and reason, a blueprint that any contemporary believer can confidently follow.

READING LIST

- ◆ Benedict XVI. Address to Representatives of British Society at Westminster Hall. September 17, 2010.
- ◆ Benedict XVI. Address to Representatives from the World of Culture in Paris. September 12, 2008.
- ◆ Benedict XVI. Easter Vigil Homily. April 23, 2011.
- ◆ Benedict XVI. "Faith, Reason and the University: Memories and Reflections." Address at the University of Regensburg. September 12, 2006.
- ◆ Benedict XVI. "The Listening Heart: Reflections on the Foundations of Law." Address to the Bundestag. September 22, 2011.
- ◆ Benedict XVI. *What Is Christianity? The Last Writings.* San Francisco: Ignatius Press, 2023.
- ◆ Ratzinger, Joseph. *In the Beginning: A Catholic Understanding of the Story of Creation and the Fall.* Grand Rapids, MI: Eerdmans, 1995.
- ◆ Ratzinger, Joseph. *The Divine Project: Reflections on Creation and the Church.* San Francisco: Ignatius Press, 2023.

CHAPTER 5

Creation

Having explored Benedict's principles for navigating issues at the meeting point of faith and reason, the next logical step is to examine how he applies them in a particular case. Toward this end, we will explore something that captured the pontiff's attention more than almost any other: the doctrine of creation. We will delve into Benedict's view that the universe is a symphony of reason and love, exploring how creatures participate in the work of God who is both Logos and Agape. As we will see, Benedict rejects the notion of a distant God who intervenes in his creation only occasionally. In its place, he highlights that God's presence permeates every aspect of the natural world.

In the second half of the chapter, we will turn our attention to unfolding the biblical basis of Benedict's vision, examining how he interprets the Book of Genesis's creation narrative. Written in a figurative style, the early chapters of Genesis do not offer scientific or historical explanations of the world's origin. Instead, they serve to convey the deepest truths about God and man, realities that transcend the purview of science. We will witness how Benedict's distinction between Scripture's essential message and its symbolic means of portrayal allows him to emphasize the core truths of creation, while acknowledging the imperfect scientific worldview of the inspired authors. We will explore how the application of Benedict's principles has a remarkable capacity to help believers make sense of biblical passages that seem to conflict with empirical science.

Creation, the Work of Logos and Agape

In the last chapter, we discussed the significance Benedict placed on perceiving the natural world's anchoring in the Logos — Eternal Reason — which is ultimately a Divine Person. The pontiff maintained that this foundational affirmation is what allows the universe to be imbued with meaning and a moral order, and he beheld in it the crucial difference between a secular and a Christian perspective on nature. Bearing this in mind, we may now highlight another central feature of Christianity's cosmic vision whose truth regrettably eludes many.

In Benedict's view, the foundation of an accurate understanding of the natural world requires wedding two dimensions of reality that are all too often separated. As we have already discussed, one of these is *reason*. Now we may add that the other is *love*. For Christians, the Triune God and the Incarnation of Jesus Christ manifest a reality that even those who are open to the divine in a more general sense may not perceive. This is the reality that the Logos or Divine Reason (see Jn 1:1) who stands at the beginning of all things is also Agape, Divine Love (1 Jn 4:16). In the fullness of time, the Lord has revealed to us that love and reason together are the fabric that structures reality.

In one of his papal audiences, Benedict attempted to capture this truth by saying, "The beginning of all things is creative wisdom, and this wisdom is love" (General Audience, November 9, 2005; "Man between Reproduction and Creation," 82). If both truth *and* love are the foundation of creation, he reasoned, this implies that we as creatures will find fulfillment only by committing our lives to the twofold vocation of pursuing the truth wherever it may be found while also pouring ourselves out in love to the other. Cardinal Christoph Schönborn, one of Ratzinger's former students who alongside him oversaw the creation of the *Catechism*, once said that this conviction is the innermost key to Benedict's account of the created world and of man's existence within it.

A crucial implication follows from the reality that love resides at the heart of being: The universe that reflects God's own love has a shape that may be described as *cruciform* (cross-shaped) or *paschal* (structured according to the pattern of the suffering, death, and resurrection of Christ). For us mortals, this entails — like it or not — that we are all actors in the life-through-death drama that is creation. Meditating on Our Lord's words in John 12:24, Ratzinger taught that the mystery of the grain of wheat is embedded in the very structure of the cosmos. Like this kernel that must die and break apart to bear fruit, so it is with every creature (1964 course on the doctrine of creation, 211).

This truth applies in an eminent fashion to the life of man. As Saint Paul taught in a vivid agricultural analogy for the resurrection, our bodies must be "sown" into the ground perishable if they are to one day be raised from the dead imperishable (see 1 Cor 15:42–54). Yet, this dynamic does not merely refer to something that transpires at the end of time. Right here and right now, we who bear God's image are presented with the opportunity to immerse ourselves in the paschal rhythm of creation by pouring ourselves out to others in love, offering our bodies as living sacrifices in imitation of our God who emptied himself to us. As disciples, Ratzinger says that we manifest the glory of Jesus Christ in the world by bringing together "two pillars of reality" in our manner of life — namely, that "true reason is love, and love is true reason" (*Truth and Tolerance*, 183). To put this in language often reiterated by Benedict, this means that the follower of Christ needs not just *orthodoxy* (right teaching — truth) but also *orthopraxy* (right practice — love).

Benedict would be the last to deny that the Christian Faith has an intellectual dimension. However, his view is that the profession of the Christian creed is not true faith — and will scarcely convince anyone else of its truth — unless it flows into life and transforms our entire existence. In his rare public statements as emeritus pontiff, Benedict stressed that to proclaim the truth that God is both reason *and* love "is the first and fundamental task that the Lord assigns to us" ("The Church and the Scandal of Sexual Abuse," 176).

How Creatures Work in Concert with God's Reason and Love

In the last chapter, we saw how Benedict's perspective on evolution differs from ideological atheism and from those whose biblical literalism or fideism leads them to repudiate the discoveries of modern science. In concert with the Church's overarching principles, Benedict holds that Christians should let the natural sciences speak for themselves, and from there we can plunder the wisdom of these "Egyptians" to better understand the Faith.

We are now well positioned to consider another topic connected with evolutionary theory in which Benedict's theological brilliance shines in an exemplary way. This centers on the issue of how God and creatures work together to choreograph the flourishing of the universe and to bring forth ever new expressions of life.

Evolutionary "Leaps" and God's Presence in the Whole of Creation

As we embark on this exploration, it is vital first to acknowledge something that Benedict never lost sight of: the necessarily incomplete nature of science as a domain of inquiry. While the fundamental truth of theories such as the Big Bang, heliocentrism, gravity, evolution, and plate tectonics have long been recognized by those in their respective fields, the fact is that no one has a full grasp of the mechanisms that underlie these pivotal dynamics. For these processes that at least currently are not fully understood, Benedict deploys the words "evolutionary leaps" and "breakthroughs."

While some Christians seek to salvage God's presence in creation by pointing to steps in the history of life that have not (at least as of now) been explained through natural causes, Benedict found significant problems in the insistence that periodic divine interventions in nature are necessary for creation to continue operating. Thankfully, as ever, on this subject he did not remain at the level of critique. The pope also proposed a more holistic path toward understanding how God operates through nature in our world — one that fully affirms the glory of God while also respecting the dignity of creatures as true agents in the unfolding of the cosmos.

At a gathering on the subject of evolution, Benedict once said to his former graduate students that it is not appropriate to "cram the dear Lord into these gaps" and that he is "too great to be able to find lodgings in such gaps" (Comments of September 2, 2006, in *Creation and Evolution*, 144). This view is consistent with that of his predecessor John Paul II, who deployed the language of an "ontological leap" to describe the origin of man in evolutionary time. According to this pontiff, there is an "ontological discontinuity" that separates us from our pre-human ancestors, yet he insisted that this does not negate the "physical continuity" by which our species arose from them (John Paul II, Message to the Pontifical Academy of Sciences Plenary Session, October 22, 1996, 6). While both Benedict and John Paul were well informed in the sciences, both were content to follow the consensus of scientific inquiry over the past two centuries, leaving the study of the precise mechanisms underlying evolution's "leaps" to the competence of the scientific community.

This perspective is echoed in the ITC's 2002 work dedicated to the nature of man and his vocation as the steward of creation. Stamped with the seal of approval of its then-president Cardinal Joseph Ratzinger, this document echoes his thought on many fronts. For instance, it notes that scientific debate will inevitably ensue at the level of particulars surrounding the mechanisms of evolution, but it stresses that the essential point remains the same regardless — namely, that the entire dynamic of evolution is guided by God. Like Benedict, this document employs the word "design" in relation to creation. It does so not in order to claim that this or that uncanny feature of the world is marvelous because it was designed by God, but rather to affirm the providential design of creation *in its entirety* (International Theological Commission, *Communion and Stewardship*, 68).

Consistent with the Christian Tradition at large, Benedict therefore perceives God's hand *everywhere* in creation. As a consequence, he affirms that the Lord's hand is manifest in things we all experience every day — even in those areas of nature for which science is able to provide a sufficiently thorough natural account. In this, the pontiff's understanding of the universe's wise ordering is much the same as Saint Paul's when he taught that all people ought to be able to know God's existence simply by looking at the things he has made: "Ever since the creation of the world his invisible nature, namely, his eternal power and deity, has been clearly perceived in the things that have been made" (Rom 1:20). Or, to take a page from the Old Testament text that underlies Romans (Wis 13:2), evidence of the Creator is not to be found primarily in minute and complex structures but rather in universally accessible phenomena — fire, wind, swift air, the circle of the stars, turbulent water, and the luminaries of heaven — for whose wonders we are now in possession of reasonably good scientific explanations.

God Works in and through Natural Processes

While many believers operate on the assumption that the existence of God precludes the mechanisms of random genetic variation and natural selection associated with evolutionary theory, Benedict held no such reservations. In response to this viewpoint, the Ratzinger-led ITC urged us to remember that "contingency [i.e., chance or randomness] in the created order is not incompatible with a purposeful divine providence." The reason for this claim is the Vatican's underlying understanding that "divine causality and created causality radically differ in kind and not only in degree" (*Communion and Stewardship*, 69). Divine providence and contingency within creation are not in competition with one another, because the causality at work within each occurs at a radically different level of being. Yet, as the ITC laments, some Christians miss this point and end up sharing some of the same problematic premises with the atheism they are trying to combat — specifically, the assumption that divine and creaturely causality are mutually exclusive, and that anything explainable by natural means is not caused by God. In other words, that what nature causes, God does not.

To spell out the meaning of this metaphysical concept in plainer language, Ratzinger proposed one of his characteristic analogies: He insists that we should not conceive of God the creator as a "craftsman" who "tinkers" with the cosmos by manipulating the world and creatures as if they were pieces of machinery ("Belief in Creation and the Theory of Evolution," 141). The problem with this picture is that it envisions God inhabiting and acting in the cosmos along the same plane of being as creatures, thus rendering him fundamentally just another being (albeit higher) among others. Whether purposefully or unwittingly, it presents a picture of the world where God creates it and then more or less leaves it on its own, occasionally dipping into the operations of the cosmos to keep the engine of nature humming. By contrast, the picture of creation held by Benedict and Aquinas is that God is present everywhere in the universe, and that creation would cease to exist if God were not continually present to it at all times.

For ancient and modern Catholic thinkers, creation does not simply mean a onetime act in the distant past. It is a single act that encompasses all time, by which God gives being to the universe and continues to maintain and govern it. Even so, Benedict would be the last to say that his grasp of the cosmos is so obviously correct that everyone will see its truth. While he was always convinced that God's action in the world typically runs through his creatures, he was also firmly aware that God can and does at times act differently — through miracles. Yet, to claim a miracle every time we cannot fully explain the operation of nature was in Benedict's mind tantamount to eviscerating nature.

In the end, in the mind of this pontiff, the pivotal question is this: "Which kind of rationality suits the Christian Faith?" Is it one in which God constantly intervenes to substitute for the functions of his creatures — an indication of poor design — or is it rather one that maximizes creaturely participation in the Lord's own work? On this front, Benedict answers the question in the same way that he does when it comes to other areas of Catholic thought and practice. As we have always seen in practices such as intercessory prayer and the power of redemptive suffering, the Catholic impulse is to magnify the creature's participation in God's action rather than be ashamed of it. In this, Benedict and Aquinas concur that it was fitting that the God who is the Good itself ennobled our creaturely state by making us his coworkers. In the words of the Angelic Doctor, it was more perfect for God to make creatures authentic causes of change than if he had remained the sole cause of new life in the universe (Aquinas, *Summa Theologiae*, I, q. 103, a. 6).

Human Persons Are More Than Their Biology
Ratzinger operates along the same lines when it comes to the creation of the first humans, which can be grasped by looking at what happens in the creation of every human today. It is a marvel, he says, that the origin of

the human soul occurs "not next to" but rather "precisely *in*" the processes of a living being, through

> the operation of nature by which a sperm and egg come together to form an embryo ("Man between Reproduction and Creation," 79). The scholastic language by which we sometimes speak of the soul's infusion, explains Ratzinger, is "just another way of saying that spirit is created and not the mere product of development, even though it comes to light by way of development" ("Belief in Creation and the Theory of Evolution," 141). As Professor Ratzinger noted, despite the fact that traditional thinkers often spoke of man being created "directly" by God, the heart of their teaching does not require that God "miraculously tinkered" with the movement of nature to prepare for the emergence of mankind. (1964 course on the doctrine of creation)

To assert that there is an ontological gap between mankind and his ancestors is not to assume some empirical gap in the course of natural history. It is to say, rather, that man's origin in the course of the natural order is not explicable merely by an appeal to nature alone. As Ratzinger points out, this same reality concerning the first humans is true of every human person of all times: "The picture that describes the origin of Adam is valid for each human being in the same way. Each human is Adam, a new beginning; Adam is each human being. The physiological event is more than a physiological event. Each human is more than a new combination of information; the origin of each human being is a creation" ("Man between Reproduction and Creation," 79).

A corollary to this can be found in Professor Ratzinger's most developed reflection on the subject. In this context, Ratzinger rejoiced in the reality that parents are "co-workers of the Creator" and true "co-causes" of their offspring who are blessed to participate in the Lord's creative love through the act of procreation (1958 course on the doctrine of creation). Ratzinger understood that a truly holistic account of man accentuates the role human parents play in the procreation of their children. While God is the ultimate cause of any new creature coming into existence, we as parents exercise true causality in the origin of our children. By the grace of God, parents truly outdo themselves when the Lord of life takes a husband's sperm and a wife's egg and from these forms an entirely new creature who bears his image in the world.

These lessons from Ratzinger's professorial days cohere well with what the Ratzinger-helmed ITC said when it described God as the "cause not only of existence but also the cause of *causes*," a teaching that it elucidated by adding that "God's action does not displace or supplant the activity of creaturely causes, but enables them to act according to their natures" (*Communion and Stewardship*, 68). Framing the dynamic in this way reflects Aquinas's understanding of God's creative activity, which the Angelic Doctor sees to consist primarily in giving being to creatures and *endowing them with natures* — the specific capacities that enable creatures to *move themselves* to their proper ends. To borrow the words through which St. John Henry Newman depicted God's operation in the world by means of evolutionary processes, the reality that God has conferred on creatures the ability to achieve their ends without his intervention need not imply his absence. Indeed, from this classical perspective, every event in nature is caused both by God and by creatures, each operating on a distinctive order of causality. In this light, Ratzinger would doubtlessly concur with Newman that human evolution appears to reflect "a larger idea of Divine Prescience and Skill."

The Biblical Basis of Benedict's Vision of Creation

We have just witnessed Ratzinger explain how God and creatures work together to bring about new life, but this is not precisely the same picture envisioned across the Christian imagination. This naturally prompts the question of how Ratzinger's claim aligns with the testimony of Scripture.

Before examining concrete biblical texts, it is first important to recall and deepen our grasp of some interpretive principles that we explored in Chapter 3. As we learned there, the literal (i.e., author-intended) sense of a passage in Scripture is not always historical in nature. On the contrary, it is often symbolic or figurative, as is the case in the Bible's opening chapters.

The reason for this is that the opening chapters of Genesis are written in what the *Catechism* calls a "figurative" mode. In this genre, the classic images of creation over seven days and man's emergence from the dust of the earth are deployed not in view of reporting raw history but rather the deepest truths about God and man that cannot be grasped by science alone (CCC 390). Accentuating the symbolic style of this portion of Scripture, Ratzinger taught,

> This does not imply that the individual passages of the Bible sink into meaninglessness and that this bare extract alone has any value. They too, express the truth — in another way, to be sure, than is the case in physics and biology. They represent truth in the way that symbols do — just as, for example, a Gothic window gives us a deep insight into reality, thanks to the effects of light that it produces and to the figures that it portrays. (*In the Beginning*, 25–26)

To extend Benedict's analogy, the biblical text can also be illumined through the lens of the early Church's iconography. Unlike much of more recent Christian art, icons are intentionally *not* physically accurate, for their purpose is to reveal truths that are *more* real than what the eye can see.

Along these lines, the pontiff frequently made it a point to clarify precisely what Sacred Scripture does and does not teach when it comes to creation. As we have already seen, this entails distinguishing a biblical text's "essential point" or "kernel" from its worldview, mode of expression, or "shell." When it comes to Genesis, Professor Ratzinger taught that its opening narrative does not seek to expand our knowledge of history into the prehistoric (1964 course on the doctrine of creation). Bishop Ratzinger would later echo this thought with his teaching that "the Bible is not a scientific textbook" and that one "cannot get from it a scientific explanation of how the world arose" (*In the Beginning*, 4). To cast this point in the language of the Angelic Doctor, empirical questions about creation touch on the substance of the faith only accidentally (Aquinas, *In II Sent.*, dist. 12, a. 2).

Bearing this in mind frees Benedict to achieve a feat that eludes many well-intentioned believers: He is able to grant the rather obvious fact that the biblical authors' scientific knowledge (the "shell" of their thought) is far from perfect, yet he also maintains that this sort of account is not necessary for the text to convey its central point. According to Ratzinger, this "kernel" lies not on the *phenomenological* level — the realm of concrete physical things studied via the scientific method — but rather on the *ontological* level. This is the proper domain of theology, which addresses subjects that transcend science: questions regarding who God is, why God made things, and what they are in their essence ("Belief in Creation and the Theory of Evolution," 133).

Anticipating any struggle that might present itself when we try to make this distinction in other areas, Ratzinger provided some valuable and concrete guidance. Specifically, he suggested that we ask ourselves the following: Does how we answer this question have an impact on anything essential concerning who God is and what he is calling us to do? Here is how Ratzinger responds to this query in the case of two important scientific matters: "The figure of Jesus, his spiritual physiognomy, does not change whether the sun revolves around the earth or the earth revolves around the sun, whether or not the world came to be through evolution." By the same token, Ratzinger affirms that some issues, such as how we answer the question of whether or not Our Lord rose from the dead, do indeed touch on the heart of who Jesus is ("Farewell to the Devil?," 202).

Now that we have a grasp of Benedict's overarching perspective on creation and the interpretive principles needed to understand Scripture's portrayal of our universe, we are in a position to illustrate how he brought all this to bear on the Bible's opening chapters. Recalling the Second Vatican Council's teaching on the need to ascertain a given passage's literary form, the pontiff consistently distinguishes the essential content Genesis intends to teach from its form of portrayal, the familiar images that Scripture's sacred authors deployed to draw their audience into higher realities (*In the Beginning*, 4–8).

Creation over Seven Days and Tending the Garden of Eden

To us today, the Bible's depiction of one God creating the world over a span of seven days might not come across as particularly compelling. In fact, this portrayal of the universe's origin strikes many of us as plainly wrong. Suppose, however, that you were an ancient Mesopotamian, or a Jew struggling to maintain your faith in the face of the overwhelming pagan culture in the midst of your exile in Babylon. In such a situation, Genesis's message would have been monumental — and not because you thought it was teaching that the universe was created over seven twenty-four-hour days.

In Genesis 2:3, we read that God "blessed the seventh day and hallowed it, because on it God rested [*shabat*] from all his work he had done." For his interpretation of this verse, Benedict stands in a long line of thinkers including Augustine and Aquinas. These greats were well aware that the "days" of which Genesis speaks here do not describe a succession of events in time but rather "denote merely sequence in the natural order" (Aquinas, *Summa Theologiae,* I, q. 68, a. 1; cf. I, q. 69, a. 1; Augustine, *The Literal Meaning of Genesis,* IV, 22, 24).

Asked by an interviewer how this passage can be reconciled with our modern knowledge of the universe's vast age of nearly fourteen billion years, Cardinal Ratzinger responded that "even then believers themselves did not think that the creation account was, so to speak, a photographic depiction of the process of creation." On the contrary, he explained, this passage "only seeks to convey a glimpse of the essential truth, namely, that the world comes from the power of God and is his creation." The sacred author's central point was that creation came from the one true God and that it was neither the source of its own existence nor the consequence of a cosmic battle among a multitude of capricious deities. When it comes to the empirical level, Ratzinger then adds, "*How* the process actually occurred is a wholly different question, which even the Bible itself leaves wide open" (*Salt of the Earth,* 31).

Benedict preached the following in an Easter Vigil homily. The full text surrounding this citation is significant, as he discusses why the Church includes Genesis's creation narrative in the liturgy:

> [The creation story] is not information about the external processes by which the cosmos and man himself came into being. The Fathers of the Church were well aware of this. They did not interpret the story as an account of the process of the origins of things, but rather as a pointer towards the essential, towards the true beginning and end of our being. Now, one might ask: is it really important to speak also of creation during the Easter Vigil? Could we not begin with the events in which God calls man,

forms a people for himself and creates his history with men upon the earth? The answer has to be: no. To omit the creation would be to misunderstand the very history of God with men, to diminish it, to lose sight of its true order of greatness. (Benedict XVI, Easter Vigil Homily for April 23, 2011)

But if the imagery of seven consecutive days in Genesis's creation narrative is not present in the Bible for scientific reasons, then why is it there? One of the highlights of Benedict's approach to creation is his understanding of the motivation behind the sacred author's structuring of the universe's origin through the metaphor of a seven-day week. Its purpose, he maintained, was to reveal the foundation and goal of creation — namely, that the Lord has entered into covenant with the cosmos and that the purpose for which the universe exists is for creatures to find rest in his Temple on the seventh day. As Benedict put it, humans enter into union with God by sharing in his Sabbath rest every seven days: "The covenant, communion between God and man, is inbuilt at the deepest level of creation. Yes, the Covenant is the inner ground of creation, just as creation is the external presupposition of the Covenant. God made the world so that there could be a space where he might communicate his love, and from which the response of love might come back to him" (Homily, April 23, 2011).

Benedict stresses that Scripture is primarily a story about Israel — which is to say every believer — being called into covenant with God to "rest" with him in the holy communion of divine worship. In particular, there is something revealing in the original text that is not obvious in modern translations — namely, that the Hebrew verb for God taking his Sabbath "rest" (*šabbāt*) is etymologically close to the number seven (*šb'*) and is often used in reference to covenant oaths. Understood in this light, the sacred author's portrayal of God having "*rested* on the *seventh* day from all his work which he had done" is a clever wordplay. It suggests that the work of creation culminated when God "sevened himself" to all creation by means of a covenantal oath.

In Ratzinger's own words, this playful structuring of creation around the Sabbath is best understood as an instance of cultic etiology, an account of creation's "why" that serves to reveal the reason for our worship. In the words of Ratzinger, the goal of this particular etiology is to convey the following message: "The goal of creation is the covenant, the love story of God and man. ... The goal of worship and the goal of creation as a whole are one and the same — divinization, a world of freedom and love" (*The Spirit of the Liturgy*, 26–28; *The Divine Project*, 48–49). This teaching is reinforced when we read Genesis in light of the entire biblical canon. By entering into covenant with God through sabbath worship, we become his adopted sons and daughters, with all the rights and privileges pertaining thereto. As the New Testament has it, we inherit "all things that pertain to life and godliness" by virtue of being made "partakers of the divine nature" (2 Pt 1:3–4).

Yet, if all creation is ordered toward Sabbath "rest," then clearly there needs to be a *place* in which this communion with God can take place — a sanctuary. Enter Eden. In line with fellow contemporary interpreters, Benedict understands that this paradisiacal garden was not meant to identify the precise physical location where humans first arose — which modern science identifies as hundreds of thousands years ago in Africa rather than six thousand years ago in the Mesopotamian garden of delights portrayed in Genesis. Like the other elements in the creation narrative, Benedict understood that this too has a figurative meaning. As the eminent theologian explained on numerous occasions, Eden unveils the cosmic foundation for human life, and as such it is an "image for the undamaged creation and for secure existence within it" (*God and the World*, 77; *In the Beginning*, 64). Eden, in other words, is a figurative way of depicting man's original state of communion with God — and thereby with all creation.

Last but not least, a noteworthy but often overlooked feature of Benedict's thought in this domain needs to be mentioned. If the Lord has sworn a covenant built into the fundamental structure of creation, then it reaches beyond the life of man alone. Indeed, a recurring theme of Benedict's pontificate was his proclamation that there exists "a covenant between human beings and the environment, which should mirror the creative love of God, from whom we come and towards whom we are journeying" (*Caritas in Veritate*, 50). The inspiration for Benedict's bold proclamation can be found in the Lord's words to Noah, "Behold, I establish my covenant with you and your descendants after you, and with every living creature that is with you, the birds, the cattle, and every beast of the earth with you, as many as came out of the ark" (Gn 9:10).

The covenantal relationship envisioned here is of the same kind that St. Francis of Assisi proclaimed seven centuries ago in his jubilant *Canticle of the Creatures*. At bottom, this great saint saw the revelation of the Lord's covenant with creation as an invitation to find joy in the knowledge that we are partners in worship with every creature that the Lord has made. As for the medieval Italian saint, so too for the modern Bavarian pontiff: The Lord's cosmic covenant is truly Catholic, which is to say universal. Texts such as Psalm 148 and Daniel 3 reveal to us that all creatures of our God and King are joined in divine praise: mother earth, brother sun, sister moon, all the powers of nature, and the endless multitude of living beings each of which declares the glory of God in its own resplendent way.

On the basis of this biblically rooted vision, Benedict developed an approach to care for creation that supplies precisely the nuance and charity that is largely lacking in our culture today. In contrast with the various forms of extremism that so often dominate discourse about the environment today, the perspective offered by the Bavarian pontiff walks the line between authorizing man's unbridled exploitation of God's good earth on the one hand and viewing human beings as a scourge upon earth on the other (*Salt of the Earth*, 134). In so doing, it gets to the heart of the matter while avoiding all the vitriol that so often prevents us from arriving at it. At its core, Benedict's environmentalism is an invitation to recognize and rejoice in the interconnectedness of all God's creatures. It encourages us to adopt a way of inhabiting creation that takes into account the good of all creatures and not just ourselves. Furthermore, it teaches us how to cultivate the virtues necessary to make a lasting difference in our world, offering the solution to what environmentalists so desperately seek, a solution that can only come from the full vision of reality that faith makes possible.

Adam and Eve

Many Christians assume that the story of Adam's creation and fall offers what we moderns would call a "video camera account" of the origin of the human beings. Benedict, however, concurs with the insights of contemporary biblical scholarship with his understanding that the narrative was rather intended to be read figuratively and archetypally. In other words, Benedict does not view the account of man's creation in Genesis as a historical chronicle of the first members of *Homo sapiens* some 200,000 years ago. From this perspective, Adam is an immensely rich figure. He is the first man, and he is the nation of Israel. He is also every one of us, for the life of every human being mirrors that of the nation of Israel in history and that of Adam in primal time. Like Adam and Israel, each of us is specially created by God and offered the gift of God's grace. Also like Adam and Israel, we all break the Lord's covenant and stand in need of a divine Redeemer.

Ratzinger's insistence that Adam stands for every man across space and time was one of the most consistent themes of his reflections on creation. Among the many texts where this conviction shines clearly, we recall these words:

> With respect to the creation of man, too, "creation" does not designate a remote beginning but, rather, has each of us in view along with Adam; *every man* is directly in relation to God. *The faith declares no more about the first man than it does about each one of us,* and, conversely, it declares no less about us than it does about the first man ... *the mystery of creation looms over every one of us.* ("Belief in Creation and the Theory of Evolution," 141; "Man between Reproduction and Creation," 79, emphasis added)

Notably, the contemporary language of Ratzinger's account unfolded here aligns remarkably well with the ancient Jewish tradition, for in Hebrew *adam* simply means "human being."

If this is how Benedict understands the creature we call "man," then what about Eve (see Gn 2:22). In line with his overall approach to Genesis 1–11, Ratzinger describes the creation of the primordial woman from Adam's rib alternatively as an "image," "myth," or "legend." The intention of this language, he explains, is to express "the most intimate reference of man and woman to each other" (*Daughter Zion*, 16). In response to an interview question, then-Cardinal Ratzinger explained that the literary figure of Eve's origin from Adam expresses the "equal dignity" and "common nature" of man and woman. It also expresses the complementarity of the two sexes, speaking to the desire of each to find wholeness through a sincere gift of self to the other. Indeed, the fact of Eve's direct origin from Adam provides a mythic rationale for God's designing marriage between one man and one woman (*God and the World*, 80).

In his university days, Professor Ratzinger had already stressed that we should be proud rather than ashamed of the Bible's symbolic depiction of Eve's creation. In this setting, Ratzinger endeavored to show how the sacred page gives access to the eminently real and answers questions that are far more important than the mere empirical. For instance, he taught that

> we have to learn to leave behind our rationalistic notion of symbols here. ... If you leave the text in its original structure and do not drag it into the mindset of rationalism, then one sees that the text itself does not want to answer the question of *how* it came to pass that a woman began to exist. Rather, it wants to answer the question of *what kind of being the woman is* and *what mystery* lies in the relationship between man and woman. (1964 course on the Doctrine of Creation, 185)

In short, like Adam and so many other elements in the Bible's opening chapters, the figure of Eve is intended to be read in archetypal fashion. Accordingly, to look at the Bible's portrait of her for empirical data surrounding the physical origin of the first female member of our species would be futile. However, if we want to know the more pressing questions of what a woman is and what her relationship with man ought to be, then there is no better place to look than Genesis's portrayal of the mother of all the living.

Dust and Breath

Now that we have covered how Ratzinger understands the figures of Adam and Eve in their own right, we can turn to a related pair of images that Genesis deploys to unveil the mystery of mankind. Whereas in Genesis 1 God creates man and woman immediately with a majestic fiat (vv. 26–27), the creation of Adam and Eve in the following chapter unfolds in more detail and in the opposite order. It is in this more anthropomorphic account that we read of the Lord molding man "of dust from the ground" and breathing into man's nostrils "breath of life" (Gn 2:7).

Ratzinger does not read these images any more scientifically or historically than he does the figures of Adam and Eve. Indeed, the very name Adam ('*adam*) is a term that Genesis connects with the ground ('*adamah*), out of which the man was said to be taken. As Ratzinger sees it, we have here once again a figurative image deployed to make a theological point about man as such rather than a historical claim about the name of the first member of *Homo sapiens* or a scientific account of human evolution: "The story of the dust of the earth and the breath of God ... does not in fact explain *how* human persons come to be but rather *what* they are" (*In the Beginning*, 50; *The Divine Project*, 77).

What, concretely, do the symbols of "dust" and "breath" then reveal about man? As archetypical images that apply to all humans, Ratzinger says that they speak to the reality that man is deeply connected to the rest of creation while nevertheless enjoying a wholly unique capacity for divine intimacy:

> I think we have here a most important image. ... The essential point in this picture is the double nature of man. It shows both the way he belongs to the universe and also his direct relation to God. The Christian faith says that what we learn here about the first man is true of every man. That each and every human being has, on the one hand, a biological origin and yet, on the other, is more than just a product of the available genes and DNA, but comes directly from God. (*God and the World*, 76–77)

To put it in another way, the essential point of these images is that man comes from both above *and* below: He is connected to the earth (dust) even as he transcends it (breath of life). As dust, we are mortals. Endowed with the breath of life, however, we are something incalculably more — bearers of the *imago Dei*, the image of God.

Not only that, but Ratzinger also observes that the reality of our creation "from the dust" drives home a revealed truth that runs contrary to the myths of many past and present worldviews. There are not different degrees of humanity in our world, he insists, and so there is no way in which it can be said that some of us have greater dignity than others. There is therefore no place in this world for slavery, racism, or any other manner of behavior that would imply the opposite of what Genesis has taught us about the inherent goodness of all human beings. From the perspective of Catholicism's revealed ethos, rather, there is only solidarity, empathy, respect, and recognition of the other's dignity. In the words of Ratzinger, emperor, beggar, master, and servant are all "one and the same man, taken from one and the same earth and destined to return to that same earth" (*The Divine Project*, 68).

———— ◆ ————

As we have seen, Benedict's vision of creation bridges the realms of faith and reason, beholding the natural world as the reflection of the divine Logos as well as the fruit of Agape. Rejecting the notion of a distant God who only occasionally intervenes in his creation, a consistent theme of the pontiff's thought was an emphasis on the divine presence in the natural order and the manner in which all creatures are ennobled as participants in Our Lord's causality within the natural order. According to this pope, creation utterly depends upon God, yet he also endows creatures with natures by which they move themselves toward their proper ends. In this — by refusing to privilege divine activity over the creaturely or vice versa — Benedict's account stands out as a uniquely balanced alternative to the opposing extremes typically on offer today.

As we have noted, another crucial point of nuance in Benedict's approach to creation is the unique basis on which he grounds the imperative to care for God's good earth. Countering the notion that man is a plague upon this planet on the one hand or that humans are authorized to exploit the planet on the other, this pope advocated an urgent retrieval of the biblical revelation that the entire cosmos is united in a bond of covenantal kindship.

Finally, we shifted gears to examining Benedict's interpretation of Genesis, and here we witnessed the great care with which the pontiff scrutinized the sacred page for truths that transcend the confines of science. As ever, he harnesses the distinction between the essential message of

Scripture from the symbolic vehicle through which they were conveyed. By delving into specific biblical themes such as the seven-day creation, Eden, Adam and Eve, and man's creation as "dust" and "breath," we saw how Benedict skillfully reconciles apparent discord between the ancient biblical text and modern scientific discoveries. In this way, Benedict's theology seamlessly unites faith, reason, and creation, offering profound insights that have long resonated with believers and which today remain as timely as ever.

READING LIST

◆ Ramage, Matthew. *From the Dust of the Earth: Benedict XVI, the Bible, and the Theory of Evolution.* Washington, DC: The Catholic University of America Press, 2017.
◆ Ratzinger, Joseph. *In the Beginning: A Catholic Understanding of the Story of Creation and the Fall.* Grand Rapids, MI: Eerdmans, 1995.
◆ Ratzinger, Joseph. "Belief in Creation and the Theory of Evolution." In *Dogma and Preaching*, 131–42. San Francisco: Ignatius Press, 2011.
◆ Ratzinger, Joseph. *The Divine Project: Reflections on Creation and the Church.* San Francisco: Ignatius Press, 2023.
◆ Ratzinger, Joseph. "Man between Reproduction and Creation: Theological Questions on the Origin of Human Life." In Vol. 2 of *Joseph Ratzinger in* Communio: *Anthropology and Culture*, 70–83. Grand Rapids, MI: Eerdmans, 2013.

CHAPTER 6
Jesus of Nazareth

A fter examining foundational biblical texts on the theme of creation through the lens of Benedict's interpretative insights, we now turn our attention to the central theme in Scripture: the life and ministry of Our Lord. The person of Jesus never faded from the Bavarian pontiff's contemplative gaze, and it became the focal point of three landmark books authored during his papacy.

Following Benedict's lead, this chapter begins by embarking on an exploration of the pivotal aspects of Christ's life portrayed in the Gospels. As we will discover, the pontiff's exegesis brings us closer to the heart of Christ while also offering a compelling strategy for countering attacks on the credibility of the New Testament that would reduce Jesus to a mere rabbi or myth.[4]

---

4. For an entire book dedicated to unfolding Benedict's understanding of Jesus, see my book *Jesus, Interpreted: Benedict XVI, Bart Ehrman, and the Historical Truth of the Gospels* (The Catholic University of America Press, 2017).

The Jesus of Nazareth Trilogy

As a Christian disciple and clergyman, Ratzinger spoke about Jesus Christ all the time. Whether it is in the form of a scholarly essay, a papal homily, or an impromptu comment, we do not have to look far to get a sense of the way he approached the mysteries of Our Lord portrayed in Scripture. However, there is clearly no better place to glimpse Benedict's perspective on Christ than in his *Jesus of Nazareth* series. A project that Ratzinger worked on for decades, Ratzinger's *Jesus* books are the fruit of his lifelong quest for the face of Christ and will undeniably be reckoned among his greatest legacies for years to come. In essence, the purpose of these volumes is to offer a compelling answer to Jesus' question: "But who do you say that I am?" (Mt 16:15). Over the course of this endeavor, Benedict constantly engages the question of how committed Christians can learn from the most serious difficulties posed by modern biblical scholarship while remaining steadfast in our profession of the Church's ancient Faith.

Benedict saw perhaps more than anyone else that the Church needs faithful who are well read in Scripture, formed in the tradition, invested in dialogue with modernity, and zealous to help other believers face the myriad obstacles that contemporary society throws their way. This is one of those prominent areas where Benedict stands out from the crowd in his ability to navigate the most difficult questions while affirming the foundations of the Christian Faith that have been cast into doubt in the modern world. At a time when many believers have the underlying fear that engaging critics might risk a loss of faith, Benedict had no such reservations. Indeed, his ability to rise and meet every challenge put before him makes this pope a model for all of us who desire to offer the world a reason for the hope that is in us (see 1 Pt 3:15).

The Call for a "Criticism of the Criticism"

As we have witnessed, the worries of Christians in relation to modern biblical scholarship are not entirely unfounded. In the popular media, it is very commonplace to hear experts allege that Jesus was merely a legend. While some may grant that he existed, the view deemed most acceptable in our society is that he was merely human and therefore did not perform any miracles, let alone rise from the dead. This view is captured well in a famous assertion by Rudolph Bultmann that Benedict knew very well: "It is impossible to use electric light and the wireless and to avail ourselves of modern medical and surgical discoveries, and at the same time to believe in the New Testament world of spirits and miracles."

In contrast with a common tendency among Christians, Benedict did not seek to counter allegations like this one by attacking the intellectual or moral integrity of those making them — far from it. Benedict felt the force of their assertions, and he took them seriously. This pope understood that helping others respond to criticism requires a real effort to understand the motivations and arguments of people who have no sympathy for the Christian Faith. In short, Benedict sought to provide a way out of problems not by avoiding but instead by meeting them on their own terms. This entailed facing obstacles head-on with the utmost confidence that the faith is strong enough to handle any and all conceivable challenges.

From this perspective, we can understand why Benedict did not pretend that the New Testament's miracles should be recognized as obviously historical by any reasonable person. As he was well aware from reading other ancient texts like the Qur'an, a story is not true simply because a book narrates it as having been revealed. On the contrary, Benedict understood that accepting the truth of Scripture rests on some more fundamental premises, such as whether or not we think God exists and does wonders in the first place. This is why Ratzinger stressed that biblical interpretation is at its core not a historical but rather a *philosophical debate*. Benedict did not doubt natural reason's capacity to corroborate Christianity. However, this way of phrasing things is a bold affirmation that we are not going to convince people of the truth of the Gospels without meeting them where they are, granting the seriousness of their questions, and digging down to the deeper and often unrecognized motivations that underlie them.

This is where Ratzinger's renowned call for a "criticism of the criticism" comes in. The conviction here is that Christians need to be prepared to respond to challenges in kind, countering those censuring the Faith with a challenge of their own — namely, calling into question the skeptic's "fundamental dogma" which is the assumption that "God cannot act in history" ("Biblical Interpretation in Crisis," 6).

Benedict often made recourse to Vladimir Soloviev's *Tale of the Antichrist* to elucidate this point. In this short story, the notorious doomsday figure tries to seduce Christians by touting his honorary doctorate in theology from the University of Tübingen. Referencing this tale, Benedict wrote:

> The fact is that scholarly exegesis can become a tool of the Antichrist. ... The alleged findings of scholarly exegesis have been used to put together the most dreadful books that destroy the figure of Jesus and dismantle the faith. The common practice today is to measure the Bible against the so-called modern worldview, whose fundamental dogma is that God cannot act in history. ... And so the Bible no longer speaks of God, the living God; no, now we alone speak and decide what God can do and what we will and should do. (*Jesus of Nazareth: From the Baptism*, 35)

What the casual contemporary reader may miss is that this was no mere theoretical point, for Tübingen was a mecca of historical-critical biblical research at the time when Benedict taught there, and there he had ample opportunity to witness the good tools of modern scholarship being deployed in the effort to destroy the Faith. Even at the time, Ratzinger found that these scholars were acting much like Satan, who tempted Jesus by twisting the words of Scripture and parroting them back at him (see Mt 4 and Lk 4).

This is the crucial background that undergirds Benedict's rebuke of scholars who study Scripture with the express purpose of dismantling the faith. Instead of naively succumbing to their assaults or retreating into a bubble to evade them, the pontiff encouraged Christians to confront them proactively by probing whether their own skeptical assumptions might only be a manifestation of their own groundless "faith."

If we have the courage to do this, Benedict suggested, then it just may happen that seemingly irrefutable arguments against the Catholic Faith will be revealed "not to be science but philosophical interpretations only apparently belonging to science." To understand just how crucial Benedict considered this point, note that this last line came from Benedict's "Spiritual Testament," published just after his death. It is remarkable that the pope dedicated the largest and culminating paragraph of this reflection on a matter that remained dear to his heart for a span of over sixty years.

Reconciling the "Historical Jesus" and the "Christ of Faith"

Understanding what Benedict was doing with his *Jesus* trilogy requires that we imitate the pontiff's example and contextualize his project against the backdrop of his larger life story. As we have already glimpsed, this includes gaining some background regarding the challenges that he had to face as an academic, prelate, and disciple inhabiting the present age. To put it differently, the most direct way to grasp the point of Benedict's meditations and arguments is by understanding his motivations in making them.

Above all, the *Jesus* books were the fruit of the pope's prayer life, the memoirs of his lifelong yearning to behold the face of the Lord. This explains in part why his interpretations seem to constantly be bouncing back and forth between two worlds. On one page, Benedict will be analyzing different exegetical hypotheses or reflecting on a passage's linguistic features, and then all of sudden he will stop and ask: "But how does this apply to our life?" At this point, he often pivots from Scripture's literal sense to engage the spiritual insights of a Church Father who challenges us to bring the Church's ancient wisdom to bear in the world of today. This is a crucial part of what we have seen Ratzinger describe as an essential component in a "criticism of the criticism" and in Method C exegesis. It brings into play a dimension of Scripture that escapes many modern interpreters but without which the Bible remains a "dead letter."

At the same time, Benedict's *Jesus* books are works of apologetics. As part of his larger endeavor to counter anti-Christian biases in the world of biblical scholarship by critiquing the critics, one of Ratzinger's main goals was to help people overcome the prevalent dichotomy between the "Jesus of history" and the "Christ of faith." In the foreword to his first volume of the *Jesus* series, the pontiff laments the widespread but uncritical assumption that much of what we profess about the life of the incarnate God is uncertain. Operating with a "hermeneutic of suspicion" propagated by the likes of Adolf von Harnack, it is frequently said that we cannot reliably get back to the historical man Jesus because the Gospels are already shrouded in the trappings of the early disciples' irrational faith commitments. The ramifications of this philosophical worldview are grave, for Benedict pointed out that unwittingly embracing it can sunder our "intimate friendship with Jesus, on which everything depends" (*Jesus of Nazareth: From the Baptism*, xii, xi–xxi).

The Pontiff's Principles Applied to Concrete Gospel Passages

To fully grasp the nature and importance of Benedict's project, however, we need to examine more concretely how he goes about defending the truth of specific Gospel texts. As we discussed in the previous chapter, the pontiff does this through a rigorous engagement with modern trends in biblical interpretation coupled with a firm belief in Scripture's truth and life-changing power handed on by the ancient Christian Tradition.

In contrast with many of his colleagues in academia, Benedict often took a firm stance with respect to the importance of the Gospels' historicity. His overall concern was to maintain the fundamental reliability of the Gospels as witnesses to Christ's life. To be sure, Benedict was willing to grant that the gospel texts underwent developments through the editorial work of the various evangelists and their redactors. However, the hallmark of the pontiff's approach to Jesus is his insistence, "Even if the details of many traditions have been expanded in later periods, we can trust the Gospels for the essentials and can find in them the real figure of Jesus" (*God and the World*, 204). Presenting a faithful portrait of the real historical Jesus, Benedict elsewhere contended, the evangelists "were practicing painstaking fidelity, but it was a fidelity that played a role in the formation process in the context of lived participation, though without influencing the essentials" (*Light of the World*, 174).

In saying this, Benedict concedes that those with whom he disagrees on many matters nevertheless have a point — namely, the Gospels do not always provide us with the *ipsissima verba* (the very words) of Jesus. Readers who have read the Gospels side by side at some point will have noticed that the evangelists frequently present two, three, or even four differently worded accounts of the very same episode. Especially when it comes to events such as the baptism, Last Supper, and crucifixion that can only have happened once, Benedict was cognizant that the Gospels cannot all be reporting on history in precisely the same way. Where the pontiff diverges from many is on the question of whether a document is trustworthy if it is not a verbatim transcript. Benedict knew that ancient people were not in possession of video cameras. Even if they were, he understood that a mere chronological account was not the kind of historical record that they sought to pass on to future generations.

The evangelists who wrote the Gospels wanted to present us with the substance of Christ's words and deeds, but their style was more that of an iconographer than a portrait painter. Icons are intentionally not physically precise, for their purpose is to reveal truths that are more real than what the eye can see. They proceed in the manner they do because they are convinced that doing so might unveil something interesting that a more literal or "realistic" approach might miss. Operating from this perspective, Benedict is comfortable acknowledging elements in the Gospels that involve a certain degree of literary license. Accordingly, the pontiff identified the genre of the Gospels as "interpreted history," historical records of what Matthew, Mark, Luke, and John deemed essential for the faithful of their communities yet conveyed in light of the evangelists' respective experiences and goals (*Jesus of Nazareth: The Infancy Narratives*, 17). Thus understood, the primary aim of the Gospels is to proclaim Jesus. Yet, to acknowledge that they are not purely historical documents is not to say that the gospels are anti-historical. In the pontiff's view, an authentic Christian appropriation of the gospels will recognize that they have a historical nucleus, yet one that is intimately bound up with the various authors' unique attempts to draw us into the mystery of Christ.

In some cases, such as the narrative of the Magi and flight of the Holy Family into Egypt (see Mt 2), Benedict regards the tradition as fundamentally historical even as he expresses openness to the possibility that it was intended more as a meditation or midrash, as we see often in the Judaism of the time. He grants, for example, that this passage has resonances with other narratives of persecuted child-kings, and he accepts that we are not in possession of evidence from outside Scripture to confirm it. In fact, he goes so far as to write the following:

> In this regard, Jean Daniélou rightly observes: "The adoration of
> the Magi, unlike the story of the annunciation [to Mary], does
> not touch upon any essential aspect of our faith. No foundations
> would be shaken if it were simply an invention of Matthew's based
> on a theological idea." ... Daniélou himself, though, comes to the
> conclusion that we are dealing here with historical events, whose
> theological significance was worked out by the Jewish Christian
> community and by Matthew. To put it simply, I share this view.
> (*Jesus of Nazareth: The Infancy Narratives*, 119)

At other times, Benedict plainly conveys his conviction that certain aspects
of a given narrative are not historical. For instance, he comments that the
second temptation of Christ where the devil sets Our Lord on the pinnacle of the Temple "has to be interpreted as a sort of vision" (Mt 4; *Jesus of
Nazareth: From the Baptism*, 34). Even so, he also argues forcefully that the
existence of the devil is not peripheral to Christianity but pertains to the
substance of the Faith ("Farewell to the Devil?," 202). Similarly, the pontiff recognized that the New Testament's presentation of the Last Supper
is informed by two distinct traditions, each of which represents a unique
memory of the words by which Jesus instituted the Eucharist (one shared
by Matthew/Mark on the one hand and Luke/Paul on the other). Benedict
takes this as a demonstration that the Church permitted "a degree of nuanced redaction" when narrating Our Lord's words, yet he also insists that
the nascent Church "was conscious of a strict obligation to faithfulness in
essentials" (*Jesus of Nazareth: Holy Week*, 127).

We have here merely a small handful of numerous instances where
Benedict brings his characteristic quest for the essential to bear on the
truth of the Gospels, but he applies it seemingly every time the opportunity presents itself. You can therefore find Benedict's fascination with the
distinctive approaches of the four Gospels in his meditations on all manner of events, including the Incarnation, crucifixion, descent into hell,
Resurrection, and Ascension. In all this, he maintained a resolute stance
with respect to the essential historicity of these episodes.

Coming Soon?

An especially rewarding area of Benedict's exegesis to explore revolves around a topic that he considered to be perhaps the most difficult in the entire New Testament: its various statements that touch on the timing of Christ's return to fully establish the kingdom of God at his Second Coming (*parousia*). What concerned Benedict was his observation that the authors of Scripture appear to have erred by expecting Christ to re-appear very soon, even during their lifetimes. For example, in 1 Thessalonians 4:13–18 Paul exhorts the faithful to hold fast, speaking in the first person: "we who are alive, who are left until the coming of the Lord." In 1 Corinthians 7:29, he likewise urges believers to bear in mind that "the appointed time has grown very short." In this same letter, he later reaffirms the imminent return of Christ by saying, "We shall not all sleep, but we shall all be changed, in a moment, in the twinkling of an eye, at the last trumpet"— at which point the dead will be raised imperishable (see 15:51–52). In the presence of such compelling evidence, Ratzinger remarked in his masterpiece on the last things, "Beyond a shadow of a doubt, the New Testament does contain unmistakable traces of an expectation that the world will end soon" (*Eschatology*, 35).

The words of Scripture were penned two thousand years ago, and yet clearly the kingdom has yet to fully materialize. This raises the question, Why did Jesus not come back quickly as he seems to have promised? Benedict provides a simple yet powerful response to this challenge by searching out the intention of Scripture's sacred authors in instances where they appear to have failed to predict the world's cataclysmic demise. For example, regarding the situation in Thessalonica, Benedict observes that "the intention" of Paul's warnings about the impending end of the world contains a "simple and profound message" that is "primarily practical" (*St. Paul*, 73). Specifically, Paul issued his apocalyptic warning about the imminent return of the Lord with a trumpet blast because he needed to correct Thessalonians who were rationalizing their neglect of worldly duties with the claim that the end was approaching soon anyway (see 1 Thes 4:13–18; 2 Thes 3:11).

Turning his attention to the Gospels, Benedict notes that the *parousia* appears to be tightly connected with the destruction of Jerusalem in AD

70. In his vision of "the Son of man coming in clouds with great power and glory," Mark reports Our Lord's warning from his great eschatological discourse: "Truly, I say to you, this generation will not pass away before all these things take place." Benedict begins his treatment of this extensive speech (Mk 13 with parallels in Mt 24 and Lk 21) by admitting the obvious difficulty it presents. However, he then immediately reminds us that the full gospel of Jesus Christ cannot be heard by looking at one text in isolation from the "quartet of the four evangelists." Hence, if Mark's account presents difficulties, the pontiff urges us to look at what the other evangelists say on the topic and evaluate Mark's essential purpose in light of that knowledge.

When considering whether the early Church erred in anticipating the kingdom's full establishment during the apostolic era, Ratzinger deploys his characteristic interpretive key to assist us in penetrating the inerrant heart of texts that echo this expectation. "The question of exact chronological succession," he says, "is not what interests them." According to Ratzinger, rather, "the governing affirmations of their message" center on something else that is the truly decisive point. In dealing with the second coming, the biblical authors subordinate the question of its *timing* to the question of *how* Christians ought to behave regardless of when Christ comes again (*Eschatology*, 41–42). Although the early Christians generally assumed the timeframe remaining until Judgment Day was very short, Benedict understood that this was a "secondary consideration" for them. Irrespective of the duration remaining in their earthly pilgrimage, the "essential point" that concerned the early Christians was something far more relevant: the need for spiritual preparation, for mission, and for endurance in the face of persecution (*Jesus of Nazareth: Holy Week*, 43).

The same distinction can be made in reference to the symbolically charged elements at work in Jesus' eschatological discourse, with his talk of wars, earthquakes, famines, stars falling from heaven, the Son of God coming on the clouds, and the like:

> While this vision of things to come is expressed largely through images drawn from tradition, *intended to point us toward realities that defy description*, the difficulty of the content is compounded

by all the problems arising from the text's redaction history: the very fact that Jesus' words here are intended as continuations of tradition rather than literal descriptions of things to come meant that the redactors of the material could take these continuations a stage further, *in the light of their particular situations and their audience's capacity to understand, while taking care to remain true to the essential content of Jesus' message*. (*Jesus of Nazareth*: *Holy Week*, 27, emphasis added)

Further, it is worth noting that Benedict also characteristically acknowledged that these challenging texts appear to have undergone a significant process of redaction, or editing, in the first few decades after they were initially composed. As elsewhere, though, this eventuality did not trouble the pope in the least, for he was convinced that the sacred author had grasped the heart of Jesus' message and conveyed it in the most fitting way possible regardless of "the extent to which particular details of the eschatological discourse are attributable to Jesus himself" (*Jesus of Nazareth*: *Holy Week*, 34–35).

And what is the core of Jesus' wild apocalyptic representations? According to Benedict, it was not primarily about the end of the world, but instead about the end of *the present order of Judaism* in the first century: "The nucleus of Jesus' prophecy is concerned not with the outward events of war and destruction, but with the demise of the Temple in salvation-historical terms, as it becomes a 'deserted house.' It ceases to be the locus of God's presence and the locus of atonement for Israel, indeed, for the world" (*Jesus of Nazareth*: *Holy Week*, 46). As Benedict indicates here, Christ's message is that, from this point onward, the divine presence would not be restricted to one central locale in the land of Israel, which meant that true believers henceforth were empowered to worship God in spirit and truth (see Jn 4:23–24). Once again, the pope did not identify Scripture's main concern with the endeavor to resolve particular matters related to the end of the world. On the contrary, the pontiff understood that it was about the implications of Christ's message in the immediate context of when the Gospels were written.

Benedict was not troubled by the likelihood that some biblical authors expected the kingdom to be fully established in their day. Yet, as we have discussed, the pope also realized that these expectations were not asserted for their own sake, any more than the author of Genesis was endeavoring to provide a chronological play-by-play of the world's creation. In this, he offers a sound alternative that falls between skeptics who deem the early Church's hope a total failure, and believers who fail to acknowledge that the biblical text presents a genuine challenge requiring a serious answer.

Jesus Christ may return today, or it may be many eons before he appears in glory. Irrespective of its timing, Ratzinger highlights that the core concern of God's word remains the same: Christians of all epochs must be awake and prepared. For even if Christ does not return to earth in our lifetime, each of us will meet him face to face at some point — and the precise moment of this meeting will likely occur most unexpectedly. It is with this in mind that Our Lord himself pronounced, "Watch therefore, for you do not know on what day your Lord is coming" (Mt 24:42).

God's Kingdom in the Flesh

What is the kingdom of God? To understand Benedict's response to this question, we must first recall something in his biography. During his early years and as a student, Joseph Ratzinger was indebted to Jewish scholars and displayed a special sensitivity to their plight in the aftermath of the Holocaust perpetrated by his nation's leaders. For this reason, he took a special interest in understanding Jesus from a Jewish perspective.

To appreciate the radicality of Christ's person and message, Ratzinger considered it crucial that Jews living at the time of Christ were not expecting the suffering savior that Christians claimed Jesus to be. Their hope, rather, was for a political figure who would usher in an everlasting kingdom *here on earth*, centered in Jerusalem. Confronting the observation that this hope never came to fruition with the coming of Jesus, Benedict voices the concern of our Jewish brethren: "It is our Jewish interlocutors who, quite rightly, ask again and again: So what has your 'Messiah' Jesus actually brought? He has not brought world peace, and he has not conquered the world's misery. So he can hardly be the true Messiah who, after all, was supposed to do just that" (*Jesus of Nazareth: From the Baptism*, 31, 116). In short, the view presented here is that a Savior who has not brought peace and not solved the problem of world hunger is not worthy of the name.

What, then, has Christ's kingdom brought if not peace among nations or bread for the world? The significance of this question cannot be over-stated, for according to Benedict the proclamation of the kingdom con-stitutes "the core content of the Gospels," and in his view "everything de-pends" upon getting this right (*Jesus of Nazareth: From the Baptism*, 47–48). In a passage that kindled Benedict's indignation, the Catholic modernist Alfred Loisy lamented that Jesus had preached the kingdom, yet what came instead was the Church. Was Loisy right? Did Jesus' kingdom fall short, leaving Christians with a disappointing human institution as paltry compensation?

Benedict willingly admits that at a very early stage the Church did in-deed shift her focus from the kingdom to Christ himself. In contrast with the critics, however, the pope saw this move as perfectly warranted, and it led him to draw a conclusion that differed sharply from theirs. The key issue, he said, revolves around the relationship between the kingdom and Christ. For those with the eyes to see, Jesus *did* bring the kingdom to earth — just not in the way that many had expected. What, then, did Jesus bring? The pope replied: "The answer is very simple: God. … He has brought God, and now we know his face, now we can call upon him. Now we know the path that we human beings have to take in this world. Jesus has brought God and with God the truth about our origin and destiny: faith, hope, and love" (*Jesus of Nazareth: From the Baptism*, 44). A dedicated enthusiast of philology, on this subject the pontiff made much of the patristic notion that Jesus is the *autobasileia*, the kingdom in his own person. In Christ, the messenger is the message. The Lord has returned to Zion, and Jesus is God in the flesh exercising his Lordship among us.

Yet, it is precisely this audacious claim that accounts for much of Ju-daism's reluctance to accept the teachings of Rabbi Yeshua of Nazareth. To be sure, part of the problem had to do with the way he subverted people's hope for an earthly political kingdom, and his allowance of alterations to the Torah (regulations concerning diet, circumcision, etc.) posed a seri-ous hurdle for strident Jews who considered such matters essential to their faith. The real issue, though, was not what he subtracted from the law but rather what he *added* by saying, "Come, follow me" (Mt 19:21).

Distinguishing himself from certain modern interpreters, Benedict demonstrated familiarity with the work of contemporary Jewish thinkers. These scholars have read the gospels, and concluded that Jesus was a man claiming to be God himself. On this score, Benedict notes, "No one would crucify a teacher who told pleasant stories to enforce prudential morality" (*Jesus of Nazareth: From the Baptism*, 186). Although the scholars in question here ultimately opted not to follow Jesus, they at least recognized that he was no mere moralist. Rather, as we find highlighted in his parables — which according to Benedict comprise the heart of his teaching — the deepest theme of Jesus' message was himself.

Benedict was sensitive to the likelihood that a Christian understanding of the kingdom may come across as a cheap response to those desperately awaiting the Messiah to deliver them from oppression and end all wars. According to the pontiff, however, it is only our hardness of heart that makes us consider the self-manifestation of Our Lord as too little. The truth of the matter is that while poverty and hunger continue to plague humanity today, man does not live by bread alone. Jesus is not indifferent to our bodily needs, but, as Benedict points out, "he places these things in the proper context and the proper order" (*Jesus of Nazareth: From the Baptism*, 32). In the end, the heart of the issue is the primacy of God — the truth that without him nothing else can be good.

Love, the Goal of Christological Doctrines

As we have just seen, Benedict dedicates considerable time to considering the Jewishness of Jesus and the biblical portraits through which his figure emerges. However, this is by no means to say that the pontiff ignores the finer points of Christology such as it developed over the ensuing centuries. In fact, the teaching of the ecumenical councils on Christ's humanity and divinity was a theme that this theological giant revisited many times over his life in the Church. For example, in his *Jesus* trilogy, Benedict lingered on this subject within a meditation on Christ's agony in the garden of Gethsemane, where Our Lord prayed to his Father, "Not as I will, but as you will" and then again, "your will be done" (Mt 26:39, 42). In characteristic form, Benedict was sensitive to the objection that this text might give the impression of Christ either being schizophrenic or lacking unity with the Father. By way of response, the pontiff offered a concise master course in Christology, beginning with the First Council of Nicaea in 325, which defined the Church's teaching on Christ's consubstantiality with the Father, and culminating in the Third Council of Constantinople in 681, when the Church arrived at her definition of Jesus' two wills (*Jesus of Nazareth: Holy Week*, 157–62).

Even when he explores defined dogmas like these, it is revealing that Benedict always found a way to bring the discussion back to the question of how the affirmation in question bears on our relationship with God. Indeed, he often stresses that merely having all the right ideas and finding satisfaction in how nicely they fit together does not qualify one as a genuine Christian disciple. As Benedict was always fond of saying, "Christianity is not an intellectual system, a collection of dogmas, or moralism. Christianity is instead an encounter, a love story; it is an event" ("Funeral Homily for Msgr. Luigi Giussani," 685–87; *Introduction to Christianity*, 205). To anticipate a point that we will return to later in this book, a life dedicated to unconditional love is the specific form of faith that the Church's dogmas seek to foster. Indeed, Ratzinger placed such a significant emphasis on this aspect of Catholicism that he often described faith and love as two dimensions of the single reality that is our lived relationship with Jesus Christ.

—————————— ◆ ——————————

In this chapter, we have discovered that Benedict's meditative approach to the life of the Lord Jesus is at once both deeply academic and profoundly personal. Penetrating the gospel narratives of Christ's life, the pontiff always endeavored to bridge the gap between modern scholarly biblical criticism and the Church's ancient, faith-based understanding of Scripture. In this connection, his writing is characterized by an unwavering commitment to face challenges head-on, which itself is a testament to his confidence in the enduring power of faith in the face of widespread skepticism in our culture. In the pope's own words, the "main implication" of his approach is that "we can trust the Gospels for the essentials and can find in them the real figure of Jesus" (*God and the World*, 204; *Jesus of Nazareth: From the Baptism*, xxi; *Jesus of Nazareth: The Infancy Narratives*, xii). Coupled with his stress on the need for a productive dialogue between tradition and modernity, Benedict paved a way for countless future Christian believers to engage the Bible with conviction and bring its message to bear in their daily lives.

As ever, the pontiff was never content to remain at the level of principles. In this light, we explored how Benedict addressed a variety of concrete topics and passages and witnessed his adamancy that faith is more than a mere set of doctrines to be accepted intellectually. At its core, this pope saw Christianity as an intimate friendship with Jesus, an encounter that shapes our very identity and destiny. As he famously said, "Being Christian is not the result of an ethical choice or a lofty idea, but the encounter with an event, a person, which gives life a new horizon and a decisive direction" (*Deus Caritas Est*, 1). With his eyes fixed on Christ, Benedict reminds us that our truest selves emerge through the selfless love embodied in Christ's life. Mindful of this, he beckons us to embrace the crosses unique to our lives, confident that in Jesus' footsteps alone lies the promise of eternal life.

READING LIST

- Benedict XVI. *Jesus of Nazareth: From the Baptism in the Jordan to the Transfiguration*. New York: Doubleday, 2007.
- Benedict XVI. *Jesus of Nazareth: Holy Week: From the Entrance into Jerusalem to the Resurrection*. San Francisco: Ignatius Press, 2011.
- Benedict XVI. *Jesus of Nazareth: The Infancy Narratives*. New York: Image, 2012.
- Benedict XVI. *Verbum Domini*. Apostolic Exhortation. September 30, 2010.
- Ramage, Matthew. *Jesus, Interpreted: Benedict XVI, Bart Ehrman, and the Historical Truth of the Gospels*. Washington, DC: The Catholic University of America Press, 2017.
- Ratzinger, Joseph. *Behold the Pierced One: An Approach to a Spiritual Christology*. San Francisco: Ignatius Press, 1986.
- Ratzinger, Joseph. "Farewell to the Devil?" in *Dogma and Preaching*, 197–205. San Francisco: Ignatius Press, 2011.
- Ratzinger, Joseph. *Introduction to Christianity*. San Francisco: Ignatius Press, 1990.

CHAPTER 7
Christian Faith in an Age of Unbelief

D o you assume that resolute faith in Christ cannot coexist alongside the experience of doubts and uncertainty? Many fear that grappling with challenging questions touching the truth of the Faith betrays a lack of that same faith. Regrettably, some people react to the presence of these doubts by giving up on the Church altogether. Others, seeking firm ground, head precisely in the opposite direction. Continuing to profess belief in Christ and his Church, they nevertheless cling to the reliability of faith so desperately that it leads them to ignore or deny the truth claims of anyone who challenges their basic — and often flawed — understanding of the Faith. In the end, however, these seemingly straightforward solutions tend to expose themselves for the shallow ideological remedies that they are. Thankfully, Benedict's thought offers the possibility of a better way forward for the countless believers who find themselves caught in an existential struggle with the perceived need to choose between equally unappealing extremes.

As Roman pontiff, Benedict wrote powerful encyclicals on each of the theological virtues of faith, hope, and charity. In these next three chapters, we will explore what this pope took to be the heart of these virtues and why they were vital for Christian living. For the time being, our task will be to showcase Benedict's distillation of the essential elements of the Faith encapsulated in the Creed. In so doing, we will see how he goes about answering the question of what it means to utter the word "Amen," what it means to follow Jesus Christ in the face of the myriad obstacles and doubts that today's believer inevitably confronts. In so doing, we will explore a number of themes that touch on the heart of faith, including Benedict's conviction that seeing the truth of the Faith requires living it and the crucial importance that he placed on the Magisterium of the Church as the sure safeguard against a "self-made" faith.[5]

What Do You Really Want: Truth or Happiness?

"If you wish to strive for peace of soul and happiness, then believe; if you wish to be a disciple of truth, then inquire." At the outset of his encyclical on faith, Benedict XVI reflected on these pointed words penned by a young Friedrich Wilhelm Nietzsche to his sister Elizabeth. Benedict judged the philosophy of this nineteenth-century German thinker, widely considered history's greatest critic of Christianity, to be the faith's most serious alternative. The pontiff's frequent engagement with Nietzsche makes it clear that he viewed answering his philosophy as a crucial enterprise for Christian believers today. But why did the pontiff refer to one of the greatest skeptics of all time at the start of a document intended to promote the Christian Faith?

This pope did not view Nietzsche's arguments solely as interesting historical artifacts. On the contrary, Benedict was so concerned with Nietzsche because he found the latter's criticisms to be representative of our present-day secular culture's default view — specifically in its assumption that there is no objective reality behind faith and that Christian morality is an oppressive relic of the past that must be jettisoned together with its foun-

---

5. For an in-depth survey of the themes that we will explore in the following chapters, see my book *The Experiment of Faith: Pope Benedict XVI on Living the Theological Virtues in a Secular Age* (The Catholic University of America Press, 2020).

dational myth. In short, for Benedict, Nietzsche was important because his challenge casts into relief a question that burns in the hearts of countless people in today's desacralized world: Is faith indeed a light of truth given to man from above, or is it an illusion that provides a sense of happiness simply by pacifying us? Even as a young priest, Father Ratzinger perceived that more and more people were leaning toward the latter answer in response to this question, and this is why he made it a priority to counter the "oppressive power of unbelief" that has largely overtaken Western society. For Ratzinger, the fundamental objective became to showcase the "real content and meaning of the Christian faith" in an age where Christianity found itself "enveloped in a greater fog of uncertainty than at almost any earlier period in history" (*Introduction to Christianity*, 31, 41).

No reader of this book will be surprised to hear that the Catholic tradition considers belief in Christ to be true in direct contact with truth, that knowing Jesus connects us with reality rather than immersing us in mere illusion. On this score, St. Thomas Aquinas went so far as to speak of theology as a science (*scientia*) whose truth claims enjoy greater certitude than those of any other area of inquiry. In the Catholic tradition, faith is known as a theological virtue, because it unites us to God (*theos*), thereby enabling us to participate in Our Lord's own knowledge of himself and his creation. For the Christian, faith is an embrace of Jesus Christ, and participating in his life enables us to behold reality with Our Lord's very eyes. In the words of Benedict's encyclical on faith published shortly after his retirement by his successor, faith is a supernatural, infused virtue that is "capable of illuminating every aspect of human existence" (*Lumen Fidei*, 4, 7, 18).

Faith's Truth is Seen Only by "Experimentation"

Given his unwavering dedication to articulating an intellectually compelling presentation of the Faith, it is obvious that Benedict viewed the rational component of Christian faith as pivotal. He therefore never shied away from defending its definitive truth claims. Having said that, a hallmark of this pope's theology is the conviction that these assertions do not even begin to exhaust the reality of what it means to believe. Indeed, Benedict was persuaded that faith cannot truly be had apart from the *experience* of faith. This he describes as occurring when we seek to incarnate God's word in our own daily lives through contemplation and charity. In Ratzinger's classic attempt to define what it fundamentally means to say *credo* ("I believe"), faith is described as a total way of inhabiting reality. According to this towering theologian, belief opens an entirely new mode of access to reality that is otherwise inaccessible to man. To this he adds,

> If this is so, then the little word *credo* contains a basic option vis-à-vis reality as such; it signifies, not the observation of this or that fact, but *a fundamental mode of behavior toward being, toward existence*, toward one's own sector of reality, and toward reality as a whole. ... What is belief really? We can now reply like this: *It is a human way of taking up a stand in the totality of reality*, a way that cannot be reduced to knowledge. ... Essentially, [belief] is entrusting oneself to that which has not been made by oneself and never could be made and which precisely in this way supports and makes possible all our making. (*Introduction to Christianity*, 50–51, 72–73, emphasis added)

As Benedict explained decades later as pope, his confident entrustment to God carries with it this important consequence: Through faith, the Lord "gives me a different certitude, but no less solid than that which comes from precise calculation or from science" (General Audience, October 24, 2012). Yet, as he had already taught for decades, the pontiff often stressed that a full grasp of Catholicism's truth is unavailable unless we commit to *living* the teachings of the Church. Drinking deeply from the well of Sacred Scripture and the wisdom of the ancients such as St. Anselm of Canterbury, Benedict would say that knowing the truth of the Faith boils down to this: "Unless you believe, you will not understand" (Is 7:9 LXX). As Ratzinger had written many decades prior in a volume dedicated to illuminating the fundamental principles of theology, "A mystery can be seen only by one who lives it. Here the moment of spiritual insight coincides of necessity with the moment of conversion" (*Principles of Catholic Theology*, 51).

As ever, Benedict was not content to state such a claim merely in abstract form, and so he turned once again to analogy from the arts for assistance. Celebrating Mass in Saint Patrick's Cathedral in New York in

2008, the pontiff gave a fascinating homily in which he described the great building as a parable for faith. Like any Gothic cathedral, he observed, this church's windows appear dark and dreary from the outside. But once one enters the church, these same windows suddenly come alive with resplendent light passing through their stained glass. This, then, is the allegory that Benedict draws: "Many writers — here in America we can think of Nathaniel Hawthorne — have used the image of stained glass to illustrate the mystery of the Church herself. It is only from the inside, from the experience of faith and ecclesial life, that we see the Church as she truly is: flooded with grace, resplendent in beauty, adorned by the manifold gifts of the Spirit" (Homily, April 19, 2008). The reality is that Catholicism's truth ultimately can be seen fully only from the inside. This is not an enterprise to be undertaken lightly, for it requires us to fast from our own preconceptions and embark upon what Benedict dubs *the experiment of faith.*

Ratzinger dedicated considerable time to developing this notion of the Faith as an "experiment," as can be seen when he describes life in Christ: "Only by entering does one experience; only by cooperating in the experiment does one ask at all; and only he who asks receives an answer." As he so often does, Ratzinger then turns to the sciences to add further depth to his point. Referencing the past century's discoveries in the realm of quantum mechanics, he continues:

> We know today that in a physical experiment the observer himself enters into the experiment and only by doing so can arrive at a physical experience. This means there is no such thing as pure objectivity even in physics; even here the result of the experiment, nature's answer, depends on the question put to it. In the answer there is always a bit of the question and a bit of the questioner himself. (*Introduction to Christianity*, 175–76)

Ratzinger's concern here is to make it clear what it is that we can and cannot expect from an apology for the truth of Catholicism. Specifically, we should not be so naïve as to assume that all rational people will inevitably draw the same conclusions we do if only we teach them the Faith with sufficient clarity. As Benedict wrote in his encyclical on faith, the reason for this is that the truth of Jesus Christ is ultimately accessible only to the one who is willing to follow him. This is because the love of God transforms us inwardly, thereby empowering us to see reality with new eyes. Citing St. Gregory the Great, the pontiff thus recalls that *amor ipse notitia est* — love is itself a source of knowledge (*Lumen Fidei*, 27–28).

To be clear, we are not talking about mere sentimentality here. In the end, Benedict knew that attaining to the fullness of truth requires charity, and that authentic charity demands commitment to the fullness of truth.

Faith, Doubt, and "Negative" Theology

Although Benedict held that faith is a supremely luminous light, he was also keenly aware of an objection that St. Thomas Aquinas addressed more than seven centuries ago. If faith is eminently certain, so the challenge goes, then why is it so easy to doubt? The Angelic Doctor's answer to this difficulty is as simple as it is profound: "It may well happen that what is in itself the more certain may seem to us the less certain on account of the weakness of our intelligence" (*Summa Theologiae*, I, q. 1, a. 5 ad 1). As Saint Thomas knew well, doubts can be of our making on account of sin, yet they can also be related to the basic fact of our creaturely finitude. This, in brief, is how the Angelic Doctor accounts for the reality that the light of faith is in itself the brightest of all lights available to us here below and yet appears "dark" in the eyes of so many. Quite simply, short of the beatific vision, our limited intellect is inadequate to the task of penetrating to the depths of supernatural truth.

Taking this into account, Aquinas was able to clearly distinguish unbelief (where one outright rejects the Church's teachings) from "movements of doubt" (engaging in serious questioning while continuing to steadfastly live the truths of the faith). The latter of these two, the experience of mental unrest, will always remain part and parcel of our existence in this vale of tears (*Summa Theologiae*, II–II, q. 4, a. 8 ad 1). This same experience was identified by one of Benedict's favorite theologians, St. John Henry Newman, who contrasted the experience of full-blown doubt with the very different dynamic of confronting innumerable "difficulties" in one's walk of faith.

Stepping back further in time, we discover that the Church has a longstanding theological tradition of reflecting on the darkness that all believers experience to one degree or another in the course of our earthly pilgrimage. This is called "apophatic" or "negative" theology, depending on whether you privilege the Latin or Greek form of the word. In essence, apophaticism stresses the unknowability of God's transcendent being and the radical limitation of every affirmation we seek to make regarding the divine. As a representative illustration of this approach, Aquinas wrote that the summit of our knowledge of God in this life consists in knowing what God is, but what he is not (*De veritate*, q. 8, a. 1 ad 8; *Summa Contra Gentiles*, III, 39, n. 2270).

For his part, Benedict takes a characteristically personalist or existential approach to negative theology, considering what the unfathomable reality of God requires of us by way of a response. In a moving answer to the question of how he dealt with darkness in his own faith life, the pontiff underscored the role that humility had come to play in his spiritual life. The fact that I do not understand something, he emphasized, does not mean that what the Church teaches is wrong. When you encounter a doctrine or biblical passage whose meaning escapes you, he counsels, "you must be humble, you must wait when you can't enter into a passage of the Scriptures, until the Lord opens it up for you" (*Last Testament*, 10).

After saying this, the emeritus pontiff immediately acknowledged the likelihood that certain vexing issues will remain with us as long as we live. This aligns well with the Catholic tradition that God at times withholds the gift of clarity from us for the sake of a greater spiritual good. In point of fact, the history of Catholic spirituality teaches us that many of the greatest saints — Mother Teresa, Thérèse of Lisieux, and Faustina, to name just a few — struggled with spiritual darkness and doubt. Moreover, the tradition informs us that this doubt was not despite their holiness but precisely *because of it*. As St. John of the Cross taught, the Lord may allow us to remain in spiritual desolation for prolonged periods with an eye toward our purification, so that we may love him for who he truly is rather than merely for his gifts.

The Dispositions of the Saints We Need to Face Uncertainty

In view of this conviction we grasp the rationale of Pope Benedict's extensive, multiyear project of leveraging his general audiences to tell the story of the Catholic Church through the lives of her saints. In these catecheses, we encounter time and again Benedict's conviction that there is no better way to manifest the truth of Catholic Faith in today's world than by sitting at the school of those who lived the experiment of faith. As the pontiff continued to maintain even in his final writings, the saints are the best interpreters of Scripture, and the reason for this is because they reveal the meaning of God's word by the way they lived their lives (*Verbum Domini*, 48; Gänswein, *Who Believes Is Not Alone*, 246).

The style and methodology of Benedict's catecheses mirrors his work in the domain of biblical exegesis. He always begins by taking note of a given person's historical context. Throughout his presentation, he then seeks to elucidate the core truths that emerge from historical enquiry. Most importantly, the pope would pause at key moments — especially at the end — to ask how the topic in question pertains to the life of the Church today. In this connection, Benedict held up a few saints in particular for our imitation. Reflecting on St. James the Greater, he exhorted us to learn from the apostle's bold and immediate response to Christ's call to leave behind the familiarity of his life as a fisherman. The pontiff encourages us to model our actions on James's "promptness in accepting the Lord's call even when he asks us to leave the 'boat' of our human securities." Like this apostle, the present-day disciple of Christ must cultivate the docility to leave the "boat" of our human securities in order to follow the Lord whenever he should call us " (General Audience, June 21, 2006).

Strikingly, Benedict signals the life of "doubting" Saint Thomas as another model for our faith life. Thomas is well known for his skepticism about the truth of Jesus' resurrection (Jn 20:25). Ironically, this apostle's frank willingness to confront the Lord is put forward by Benedict as an exemplar:

> The apostle Thomas's case is important to us for at least three reasons: first, because it comforts us in our insecurity; second, because it shows us that every doubt can lead to an outcome brighter than any uncertainty; and, lastly, because the words that Jesus addressed to him remind us of the true meaning of mature faith and encourage us to persevere, despite the difficulty, along

our journey of adhesion to him. (General Audience, December 19, 2012)

As we witness here and in many other instances, Benedict did not view doubt as something unequivocally negative. In fact, he considered it an experience that can lead to great good if we confront it with sincerity and humility.

The third saint put forward by Benedict represents another model of how to ask tough questions of the Lord, but this time it is someone whom we do not typically consider a "doubter." And, yet, this saint — the Mother of God — was nevertheless willing to ask the Lord a challenging question at the very moment of the Annunciation: "How will this be, since I do not know man?" (Lk 1:34). Importantly, Mary did not ask a brazen question looking for something from God, as can be seen in the fact that she also exhibits the willingness to reciprocate with the Lord. As Benedict writes, she "lets herself be called into question by events" in a spirit of profound humility and obedient faith. In the eyes of this pope, Mary's life reveals that faith is not so much about getting answers and grasping the truth as it is about letting the truth grasp *us*.

The emeritus pontiff captured this well near the end of his earthly pilgrimage when he meditated at some length:

> Indeed, we cannot say "I have the truth," but the truth has us, it touches us. And we try to let ourselves be guided by this touch. ... One can work with the truth, because the truth is person. One can let truth in, try to provide the truth with value. That seemed to me finally to be the very definition of the profession of a theologian; that he, when he has been touched by this truth, when truth has caught sight of him, is now ready to let it take him into service, to work on it. (*Last Testament*, 241)

We find here a theme that recurred throughout Ratzinger's life, all the way through his pontificate as Pope Benedict. Truth is a *person*, he stressed, and therefore Christianity is not merely a religion based on a book but rather the religion of the *living and incarnate Word* who is Truth itself. While seeking the truth in Scripture and official magisterial documents is certainly an essential dimension of our faith, for Benedict it is not so much that we believers are in pursuit of this truth. On the contrary, it is first and foremost the Truth who pursues us, embraces us, and guides us.

Benedict also looks to figures and events from salvation history as signposts to guide our life of faith. As we discussed above, Ratzinger always approached Scripture bearing in mind both its original meaning and how it continues to apply to our lives today. In light of this, he indicates that the divine pedagogy that unfolds over the course of the Old Testament has a twofold character, for the entire story of salvation history is an adventure that must unfold today in each of our lives: "What Israel had to do in the early days of its history, and the Church had to do again at the beginning of her career, must be done afresh in every human life" (*Introduction to Christianity*, 151). Like Israel, we as individuals do not completely understand the truths of the Catholic Faith. Although the Church may possess the fullness of truth, this does not guarantee that each of us has grasped that truth fully. In other words, we cannot rest on the laurels of the popes or Church Fathers, presuming that all is well in our own souls as if we have mastered the Faith.

In a papal discourse from his catechetical series on prayer, Benedict looked to the patriarch Jacob's nocturnal struggle with God in Genesis 32 as emblematic of our life's pilgrimage. According to Benedict, this episode speaks to the tenacity that we all must have in "the night of prayer ... the long night of seeking God, of the struggle to learn his name and see his face" (General Audience, May 25, 2011). The pontiff considered Jacob's story a paradigm for all of us who struggle to persevere faithfully in our journey with the Lord day by day amid myriad encounters with aridity, doubt, and suffering. Referring to this, he recalled a line from the *Catechism* that was the fruit of reflection on this same biblical passage: "From this account, the spiritual tradition of the Church has retained the symbol of prayer as a battle of faith and as the triumph of perseverance" (2573). With this in mind, Benedict himself describes the life of prayer as a "battle" that requires us to do "hand-to-hand combat."

But why does the Lord demand that we endure this long night of wrestling with him — especially given that it is a match we can never truly win?

Benedict explains that it is to help us come to terms with something essential about holiness, that it "cannot be grabbed or won through our own strength." That is to say, it is inevitable that we are going to face struggles in our quest for sanctity. When the dust settles, we are not going to have achieved perfect clarity or charity on this side of eternity any more than Jacob or Job did. Perhaps nowhere more fittingly is this conveyed than in the encyclical on faith that Benedict penned shortly before retiring:

> Faith is not a light which scatters all our darkness, but a lamp which guides our steps in the night and suffices for the journey. To those who suffer, God does not provide arguments which explain everything; rather, his response is that of an accompanying presence, a history of goodness which touches every story of suffering and opens up a ray of light (*Lumen Fidei*, 57).

The "Risky" Enterprise of Faith in Christ

In conjunction with his portrayal of the Christian enterprise as a life-long wrestling match with the Lord, Ratzinger was fond of deploying a number of other thought-provoking expressions to capture this dynamic. For instance, in his classic primer on the Faith we find faith referred to as "an adventurous leap" which entails the "risky enterprise of accepting what plainly cannot be seen as the truly real and fundamental" (*Introduction to Christianity*, 51–52). Decades later in one of his final audiences as pope, Benedict would go so far as to speak of believers' decision to commit themselves Christ as a "gamble for life" and an "exodus ... a coming out of ourselves, from our own certainties, from our own mental framework, to entrust ourselves to the action of God who points out to us his way to achieve true freedom, our human identity, true joy of the heart, peace with everyone" (General Audience, October 24, 2012).

Developing Benedict's image of Christian faith as a "risk," we might say that our quest for union with the Lord is an enterprise that demands we lay all our life's chips on the table. In the language of Saint Paul, this exodus out of our creature comforts may entail a certain "loss." Yet, unlike the other forms of setback that we suffer in this life, this one is of such a kind so as to be counted as nothing because of the surpassing worth of what we gain from it: perfect happiness in communion with Christ Jesus Our Lord (see Phil 3:7–8).

The same can be said with respect to Benedict's other image of faith as a "leap." Whereas charging courageously into physical darkness might end up causing a person great harm, we have nothing enduring to lose — and everything to gain — by diving headlong into our relationship with the Trinity. Moreover, unlike the caricature of faith as a *blind* leap, this is not at all the way Benedict and the broader Catholic tradition envision life in Christ. To be sure, faith requires trustful submission to the divine Other, but that submission is grounded in the truths of reason which it illumines in the light of Christ.

Part of the "risk" involved with the adventure of Christian discipleship stems from the fact that faith is a relationship. As with any deep bond, faith in Jesus requires trust, devotion, and abandonment into the hands of another who will inevitably stretch us beyond our comfort zone. As Benedict wrote in his homily inaugurating the Pauline Year in 2008, this is precisely what the apostle's theology teaches us: "Paul's faith is being struck by the love of Jesus Christ, a love that overwhelms him to his depths and transforms him. His faith is not a theory, an opinion about God and the world. His faith is the impact of God's love in his heart. Thus, this same faith was love for Jesus Christ" (Homily, June 28, 2008). In short, for Saint Paul and for Benedict who proposes him as an eminent guide, the experience of being loved by Christ forms the basis of a friendship. That friendship imbues all areas of our life with divine charity, and by it we are progressively "changed into his likeness from one degree of glory to another" (2 Cor 3:18).

With this in mind, Benedict underscored that Christian moral living is not merely intellectual and that it is "not born from a system of commandments but is a consequence of our friendship with Christ" (General Audience, November 26, 2008). The pontiff's words here resonate remarkably well with Fr. Servais Pinckaers' classic statement that Catholic moral teaching is "not a mere code of prescriptions and prohibitions" but rather "a response to the aspirations of the human heart for truth and goodness." While such a vision by no means dispenses one from living in accordance with the Church's clear moral teachings, the point is that adherence to doctrines does not constitute genuine faith unless it is ordered toward communion with the person of Jesus Christ.

Obedience to the Church Saves Us from a "Self-Made" Faith

We have already seen how Benedict sets out to meet the challenge of Nietzsche's criticism that faith is for weak souls who cannot handle the cold reality of a universe without God. We are now in a position to explore how Benedict's encyclical engages another classic critic of Catholicism: Jean-Jacques Rousseau. The specific complaint lodged by Rousseau that concerns us here comes from a speech by one of the characters in his *Émile*: "So many men between God and me!" Put differently, why does the Catholic Church so stubbornly insist on mediating the Faith to her people? Why not simply let each believer engage God directly? Is God not capable of reaching us without the help of other finite and fallen human beings?

Benedict finds in Rousseau's faultfinding an occasion to showcase some of the Christian Faith's deepest wisdom, and this is connected with his understanding of faith as a response to a reality that precedes us. Reflecting on Saint Paul's Letter to the Ephesians, the pope had this to say to those who consider mediated faith to be an immature faith. Whereas these individuals might say that Catholics need to grow up and think for themselves with an "adult faith," Benedict incisively notes that those who seek to choose what they want to believe in an entirely autonomous fashion end up with a "do-it-yourself faith." While this alleged faith may present itself as courageous in its willingness to dissent from the teaching of the Magisterium, Benedict retorts that in fact "no courage is needed for this because one may always be certain of public applause." Where real courage and true "adult faith" lies, he continues, is in a different kind of nonconformism — one by which we adhere steadfastly to the teachings of the Church in the face of a culture that gives us every reason not to follow Christ (Homily, June 28, 2009).

Yet, Benedict's criticism of abandoning Christ's Church in the name of courage penetrates even more deeply. If we as individuals are the final arbiter of what should and should not be believed, then our faith is indeed no faith at all. In other words, in this instance what we call "faith" is merely a ratification at every turn of what we had already assumed to be true beforehand. Nowhere is this stated more succinctly than in an essay penned by Ratzinger on the question of why he remained Catholic despite all the problems he encountered: "A faith of one's own devising," he says, "would only vouch for, and be able to say, what I already am and know anyway" ("Why I am Still in the Church," 147). As Ratzinger said elsewhere, "Meaning that is self-made is in the last analysis no meaning. Meaning, that is, the ground on which our existence as a totality can stand and live, cannot be made but only received" (*Introduction to Christianity*, 72–73).

What is more, Benedict finds particular significance in St. Leo the Great's saying, "If faith is not one, then it is not faith." Commenting on this line, the pope explained, "Since faith is one, it must be professed in all its purity and integrity." Because all the articles of faith are interconnected, the pontiff continued, "to deny one of them, even of those that seem least important, is tantamount to distorting the whole" (*Lumen Fidei*, 48). For Benedict as for St. John Henry Newman whose theology is reflected in this passage, the Catholic Faith is by its very nature comprehensive. On the positive side, this means a simple believer who assents to the Magisterium embraces the whole deposit of revelation, even if grasping all its details eludes him. The corollary of this, though, is that refusing to accept one of the Church's core defined teachings undermines the very foundation of one's faith, for it makes the whole enterprise an exercise in reaffirming what we already thought anyway irrespective of Christ and his Church.

Benedict carried these reflections with him for the entirety of his life. For instance, in one of his final essays dedicated to this very subject, the emeritus pontiff wrote that faith is "a profoundly personal contact with God," yet at the same time he insisted that it "inseparably pertains to the community." Here again, in the autumn of his life, Benedict underscored that the Church "does not create itself" and that it is not merely "an assembly of men who have some ideas in common and who decide to work for the spread of such ideas." If Church doctrine were determined by majority rule, the emeritus pope continued, then everything "ultimately would be based on human opinion" and therefore could not be "the guarantor of eternal life or require me to make decisions that cause me to suffer and are contrary to my desires" ("Faith is Not an Idea," in *What Is Christianity?*, 101–02).

We can find the same train of thought in Benedict's final encyclical, published after he retired. In this setting, the pontiff bluntly asked, How can we be certain, after all these centuries, that our faith puts us in touch with the "real Jesus"? His response follows along the precise lines we have just witnessed: "Were we merely isolated individuals, were our starting point simply our own individual ego seeking in itself the basis of absolutely sure knowledge, a certainty of this sort would be impossible" (*Lumen Fidei*, 38). As an individual, I cannot possibly prove all the truths of the Faith for myself. Thanks be to God, however, membership in the community of the Church saves us from the superhuman task of personally verifying every last proposition of the Catholic Faith. In this light, embracing that which precedes us in the form of Holy Mother Church's magisterial authority is an eminently liberating enterprise.

To be sure, a commitment to follow Christ does not cause all our doubts to evaporate or make all our problems go away, and it should be no excuse for intellectual laziness. And yet, entering into the "ecclesial existence" described by Benedict reveals a particular way of life whose very beauty is a testimony to its truth. Like the grandeur of the Gothic cathedral's stained-glass windows, the fulfillment that comes from life in the Catholic Church is something that one can only see *from the inside*. Here, too, this is not to say that everything in the Church is all roses and butterflies, because dealing with the imperfections of other believers can be a real cross. Benedict therefore enjoins us not to forget that the exodus from our own ego and incorporation into the Mystical Body of Christ requires something much more radical than the revision of a few opinions and attitudes. Indeed, in his words, it is nothing less than a "death event" (*Nature and Mission of Theology*, 51).

For many believers, when coming across a teaching of the Church that challenges their former preconceptions or way of life, an occasion for dying to self presents itself. In this connection, Benedict stresses the pivotal reality that Catholic doctrine is not determined by majority vote but has been divinely revealed and safeguarded by the Magisterium of the Church comprised by her pope and bishops. Benedict takes great pains to emphasize that this authority is not "something extrinsic" to the Faith or a limitation of our freedom, but rather one of Christianity's essential features insofar as it "provides the certainty of attaining to the word of Christ in all its integrity" (*Lumen Fidei*, 36). For instance, there would be no definite way to resolve ambiguous texts in the Bible without the Magisterium of the Catholic Church. For that matter, without this authority we would never have had a definitive canon of Sacred Scripture in the first place. It is hard to think of a better expression of this truth than the way Benedict put it in a homily delivered to the "little family" of religious friends who accompanied him in retirement.

> Faith is not of our own invention; it is a gift of God to safeguard and to live. Hence, it is not something at our disposal. We cannot change it however we want. It is a gift of God and only in this way will it grow and deepen. Even the pope is not an absolute monarch. He cannot do whatever he wants. He is rather the guarantor of obedience to the gift of God, which is a true treasure for the world (Homily, June 29, 2014, in Gänswein, *Who Believes Is Not Alone*, 248).

We have covered a lot of ground in this chapter's survey of Benedict's teaching on the virtue of faith. I hope to have shown that the pontiff's approach provides a nuanced alternative that can help us walk the narrow path between fideism and skepticism, offering a window into the full depth of Christian Faith amid myriad temptations to doubt. Against Nietzsche, Benedict affirmed that faith yields true and certain knowledge. However, as we have witnessed, he also understood that grasping this requires a healthy dose of humility, the recognition of our intellectual limits, and a total dedication to running the "experiment" of faith in our lives.

Responding to Rousseau's charge that Catholicism involves too many mediators between us and God, Benedict pointed to the providence of having the Magisterium of the Catholic Church to save us from a "self-made" faith and the examples of the saints to guide us along the path to holiness. If not for these gifts of God, we would have no guarantee that what we profess reflects the mind of Christ rather than our own preconceptions. Yet, seeing as we do have access to this great good, Benedict sees it as our task as Christians to embrace it to the fullest and to gradually let the truth of Christ possess us ever more fully.

In concluding this chapter, then, it is instructive to hear Ratzinger one more time on what he thinks it means to carry out this enterprise with the declaration "I believe":

> It means affirming that the meaning we do not make but can only receive is already granted to us, so that we have only to take it and entrust ourselves to it. ... Christian belief — as we have already said — means opting for the view that what cannot be seen is more real than what can be seen. It is an avowal of the primacy of the invisible as the truly real, which upholds us and hence enables us to face the visible with calm composure — knowing that we are responsible before the invisible as the true ground of all things. ... Belief means: the trustful placing of myself on a ground that upholds me, not because I have made it and checked it by my own calculations but, rather, precisely because I have not made it and cannot check it. (*Introduction to Christianity*, 73–75)

Of course, to say that we cannot "check" the Faith does not imply that we should not be vigilant to confirm its truth inasmuch as we are able. Much less does it imply that we should adopt the ideology of fideism, which requires embracing assertions that our reason knows to be false. To reinforce what we discussed above, we can say that Benedict views true faith not as a blind surrender to the irrational but rather a movement toward the Logos. All the same, the pope's words provide a salutary corrective for those of us who tend to think we have more or less figured out God.

READING LIST

- Benedict XVI. *Deus Caritas Est*. Encyclical Letter. December 25, 2005.
- Benedict XVI. *Spe Salvi*. Encyclical Letter. November 30, 2007.
- Benedict XVI. *The Transforming Power of Faith*. San Francisco: Ignatius Press, 2013.
- Benedict XVI. *What Is Christianity?: The Last Writings*. San Francisco: Ignatius Press, 2023.

◆ Benedict XVI and Francis. *Lumen Fidei*. Encyclical Letter. June 29, 2013.

◆ Ramage, Matthew. *The Experiment of Faith: Pope Benedict XVI on Living the Theological Virtues in a Secular Age*. Washington, D.C.: The Catholic University of America Press, 2020, chapters 4, 5, 10, and 11.

◆ Ratzinger, Joseph. *Credo for Today: What Christians Believe*. San Francisco: Ignatius Press, 2009.

◆ Ratzinger, Joseph. *Introduction to Christianity*. San Francisco: Ignatius Press, 1990.

◆ Ratzinger, Joseph. *What It Means to Be a Christian*. Translated by Henry Taylor. San Francisco: Ignatius Press, 2006.

◆ Ratzinger, Joseph. *The Yes of Jesus Christ*. New York: Crossroad Publishing Company, 2005.

◆ Rausch, Thomas. *Faith, Hope, and Charity: Benedict XVI on the Theological Virtues*. New York: Paulist Press, 2015.

CHAPTER 8
Hope and Eschatology

In the last chapter, we devoted a considerable amount of time probing the question of what it means to live the "experiment" of Christian Faith in our secular age. But faith is not the only theological virtue essential to the Catholic experience. The virtues of hope and love are inextricably bound up with faith, and it is to these that we now turn our attention.

With an eye toward illuminating the nature of Christian hope, we will need to begin on a rather sober note by listening to Benedict about the inclination within our society to place all our aspirations for fulfillment within the horizon of the present world. In what follows, we will hear Benedict's take on how the desire for heaven has faded away and been replaced with an unending quest for technological and political progress. Having witnessed how hope has undergone this transformation in our contemporary world, we will examine Benedict's articulation of what Christian hope is and why it is so essential for us and our society, especially at a time when so many are plagued by disillusionment and despair.

We will then turn our attention to pondering human life in the heavenly realm and the enchanting beauty that lies beyond this vale of tears. Rectifying the common misconception that heaven is a disembodied state completely disconnected from here and now, from here we will probe Benedict's teaching that the entire cosmos will somehow be restored and transfigured at the end of time. Finally, as we discovered in the case of faith, we will learn that this pontiff envisions Christian hope as a reality that suffuses our life with meaning but which is only available to those willing to embark on "the experiment" of Christian discipleship.

The Relationship of Faith and Hope

Benedict frequently spoke on the theme of hope and even devoted an entire wide-ranging papal encyclical to the subject. In combination with his commentary on the creed in *Introduction to Christianity*, this document provides us with an apt outline of what this pope thinks it means to hold Christian hope.

The title of Benedict's letter *Spe Salvi* is drawn from Romans 8:24: "For in this hope we were saved." A moving biblical text, this line from Saint Paul nevertheless raises some important questions that Benedict insists we address: How certain is the hope that we are dealing with here, and what precisely does this hope refer to in the first place? As Paul says in the second half of the above verse, "Hope that is seen is not hope. For who hopes for what he sees?" Hope's confidence is not the same as the certitude we have regarding things that lie right before our eyes. On this score, it is revealing that Benedict viewed faith and hope as practically interchangeable with one another.

In the Catholic tradition, the theological virtues of faith, hope and charity are understood to be intimately united while nonetheless remaining distinct from one another. The virtue of faith that we have already examined is said to perfect the intellect by enabling us to participate in God's own knowledge of himself while also endowing us with the power to behold all things through Jesus' eyes. Moreover, Benedict emphasizes that faith is not primarily an intellectual matter but a holistic way of life that is best thought of as a relationship of complete trust and undying faithfulness. As in the case of faith, the object of the theological virtue of hope remains God himself, yet the tradition makes a distinction between the two. Whereas faith perfects our intellect to know and trust God in this life, the virtue of hope perfects our will to trust in God's promise of eternal life — a promise whose confidence originates not in our own strength but on account of the unfathomable mercy and grace of God. Like all virtues, hope is a sort of mean between two vices. While one who truly has a virtue cannot have "too much" of it, our tradition further informs us that two very different sins oppose every virtue: an excess and a defect. In the present case, the sin of despair militates against hope (as a defect of trust in God's mercy), while with the sin of presumption we excessively trust in our own power, not acknowledging our need for God's mercy.

Given what we just said regarding the distinction between the virtues of faith and hope, it is noteworthy that the first major heading of Benedict's encyclical on this topic reads "Faith is Hope." The basis for this statement is Hebrews 11:1, "Faith is the assurance (*hypostasis*) of things hoped for; the conviction of things not seen." Benedict takes issue with modern translators who render the word *hypostasis* here as "assurance." Instead, he thinks that the Latin Vulgate gets it right when it translates this verse so as to make it clear that faith is the "substance" (*substantia*) of things hoped for and the "proof" (*argumentum*) of things not seen. Benedict finds it significant that the Latin word *substantia* does a better job of rendering the original Greek *hypostasis* than we find in the English "assurance" or the German *feststehen* ("standing firm"). But why does this pope place such great stress on what seems to be a minor translation issue?

The reason is that speaking of faith as the *substantia* of things hoped for signifies that there is a profound relationship — in some sense even identity — between faith and hope. In saying this, Benedict does not imply an outright rejection of the traditional distinction between the two, but he does wish to add another angle from which to understand their connection. To articulate his precise understanding of this dynamic, Benedict again turns to an analogy from the sciences. Through faith, he maintains that we already possess the substance of all the things that we hope for "in embryo" (*Spe Salvi*, 7). In other words, hope "gives us even now something of the reality we are waiting for," a share in the fullness of divine truth and life for which we hope to enjoy in heaven when the "embryo" of our faith is at last born. At the foundation of this statement lies the Church's teaching that a human being maintains his same identity and dignity from the moment of conception until death. Just as personhood endures amid the myriad changes that he undergoes during that time, so too through hope we already hold within ourselves the same reality that will be fully unveiled at the end of time in its heavenly fullness. To borrow the language of St. Thomas Aquinas, amid the inevitable variations in the "accidents" of our life that change over time, at this very moment we possess in part the substance of what we will one day attain and know fully in the beatific vision.

False Assurances and the Achievement of True Hope
If faith grants believers right now a participation in the reality that they hope to possess fully in eternity, the next logical question to ask is this: What, exactly, do we mean when we speak of eternal life? Since we tend to appreciate a thing better by way of contrast with its opposite, it will be helpful to consider briefly the alternative versions of hope offered by our culture. To put it simply, we will make it clear what the object of our hope is *not*.

For the Christian, it goes without saying that our ultimate fulfillment is not something that can be achieved in this present age. However, Benedict sees two major ways in which our society nonetheless strives in vain to accomplish this task. First, many people look to scientific advancements to cure all our ills. This "faith in progress," says Benedict, is part and parcel of the ideology that fall under the banner of *scientism*. As we have discussed, the scientific enterprise itself is a great good. Yet, granted the countless contributions that empirical research has made to the betterment of life on earth, Benedict stresses that science will never be able to provide us all the deepest answers that we seek, and whatever progress we make will never bring about a world of complete perfection. In the words of Benedict, "Francis Bacon and those who followed in the intellectual current of modernity that he inspired were wrong to believe that man would be redeemed through science. ... It is not science that redeems man: Man is redeemed by love" (*Spe Salvi*, 25–26).

People today also substitute politics for religion to make up for a lack of true hope. As Benedict points out, the central historical figure who brought about this transformation was Karl Marx and his notion of "all-encompassing change" (*Spe Salvi*, 20). Marx knew how to overthrow an existing order, the pope acknowledged, yet what the revolutionary lacked was a correct grasp of how matters should proceed thereafter. In the end, he failed to comprehend that no totalizing political system can enforce justice without destroying freedom. Furthermore, absent from his philosophy was the Church's understanding that no system can fulfill man's need for love and human connection. This is where Catholic social teaching's doctrine of *subsidiarity* comes in. Contrasting an authentic Christian perspective on societal justice from the prevailing secular approach of our day, Benedict identified subsidiarity as "the most effective antidote" against a Marxist regime that would wield "dangerous universal tyrannical power." Shedding light on the significance of this term, the pontiff described subsidiarity as the ideal pathway to establishing solidarity with those in need. It involves honoring people's personal dignity by offering them the freedom to discover the truth and shape their own destiny, rather than imposing a presumed truth upon ordinary citizens perceived as incapable of knowing better (*Caritas in Veritate*, 57).

According to Benedict, the common denominator between Marx's wrongheaded political philosophy and Bacon's scientism is that both limit their horizon to this world. As we have seen, it is not that this pope found science and politics to be irrelevant or that he opposed efforts to improve the human condition in the present moment. As we so frequently find in various heresies, the problem here is not so much in what is affirmed as in what is denied. Benedict identifies the central error here as *materialism* — the delusion that man is made only for this world and that we can live by bread alone. While Benedict certainly appreciates the importance of having good social structures, the pontiff reminds us that these are not enough, for "progress, in order to be progress, needs moral growth on the part of humanity." Put differently, if advancements in our society are to become fully human, they must be integrated through the transformative healing power that comes only with faith. In his characteristic manner, Benedict summarizes everything we have said thus far in the most straightforward way possible: "Let us put it very simply: man needs God, otherwise he remains without hope" (*Spe Salvi*, 23).

As this pope's mentor Saint Augustine famously said, "Our hearts are restless until they rest in [God]." Moved by this conviction, both great Christian thinkers nevertheless underscore that none of us quite fully understands the thing that we are striving for in hope. As we witnessed Aquinas teach in the last chapter, we can know *that* God exists and even speak about his nature as love, truth, and the like. Yet in the end those of us who have yet to achieve the beatific vision cannot fully know *what* God is. With this in mind, Benedict says that the intention of the words "eternal life" is to give a name to this "known unknown" (*Spe Salvi*, 12). In this connection, he admits that the expression "eternal life" is "inadequate" and even "creates confusion," for it can easily lead to the mistaken impression that eternity is merely an unending succession of days on the calendar. Against this overly simplistic notion, Benedict underscores the human person's innate desire for the infinite, stressing that our hearts' deepest desire is not merely for longer life but for total union with him who is Life itself.

Shifting our perception of eternity from a timeline to something more holistic, Benedict suggests that we instead meditate on heaven as "the supreme moment of satisfaction, in which totality embraces us and we embrace totality." Adopting language reminiscent of some of the greatest mystics of Church history, such as St. John of the Cross and St. Francis de Sales, the pontiff hints at the experience of the beatific vision in these terms:

> It would be like plunging into the ocean of infinite love, a moment in which time — the before and after — no longer exists. We can only attempt to grasp the idea that such a moment is life in the full sense, a plunging ever anew into the vastness of being, in which we are simply overwhelmed with joy. ... We must think along these lines if we want to understand the object of Christian hope, to understand what it is that our faith, our being with Christ, leads us to expect. (*Spe Salvi*, 12)

Or, if we prefer a different image, Cardinal Ratzinger suggested our communion with Christ can also be profitably expressed in spousal terms. From this perspective, our love relationship with the Lord is one in which "two subjects are fused in such a way as to overcome their separation and to be made one," meaning that we become one with Christ analogous to the way "in which man and woman are one flesh" (*Called to Communion*, 39).

Eternal Life and the Resurrection of the Body

From the very beginning, the Church has professed the resurrection of the body on the Last Day as an essential feature of the Faith. The importance of this hope, which we reaffirm each week in the liturgy, cannot be overstated. In the apostolic era, Saint Paul went as far as to assert that the entire Christian enterprise would be futile if Jesus had not been raised bodily from the dead (see 1 Cor 15:13–17). In this same vein, two millennia later Benedict upheld the truth that Christianity "stands or falls with the truth of the testimony that Christ is risen from the dead" (*Jesus of Nazareth: Holy Week*, 241–42). Ratzinger elsewhere has written that the Christian message "is basically nothing else than the transmission of the testimony that love has managed to break through death" (*Introduction to Christianity*, 307).

Having confidently proclaimed this hope, Benedict's approach to the resurrection nevertheless contains some important nuances that might surprise the average believer. Paramount among these is the pontiff's conviction that the notion of bodily resurrection leads people to misconceive what it means. Specifically, Ratzinger was concerned to highlight that the "real heart" and "the real content" of hope in the resurrection is not for the reassembling of earthly bodies at a time in the distant future when their atoms will have long since been scattered to the four winds:

> The awakening of the dead ... is thus concerned with the salvation of the one, undivided man, not just with the fate of one (perhaps secondary) half of man. It now also becomes clear that *the real heart of the faith* in resurrection does not consist at all in the idea of the restoration of [ordinary physical] bodies, to which we have reduced it in our thinking; such is the case even though this is the pictorial image used throughout the Bible. (*Introduction to Christianity*, 349–50, emphasis added)

Following immediately upon these words, Ratzinger continues, "What, then, is the real content of the hope symbolically proclaimed in the Bible in the shape of the resurrection of the dead?" By way of an answer, he contrasts it with the dualistic conception of man prevalent both in ancient philosophy and among modern Christians. In essence, Ratzinger's point is that Christianity's hope for resurrection does not involve the reunion of an ordinary material body with an entirely separate and immaterial soul. Yet, this is not to say that our eternal destiny involves being bodiless. It is not less than an earthly experience of the body — it is more.

Ratzinger was aware of how difficult it is, despite our best efforts, not to picture the soul as a quasi-physical entity that God "places in" a body made purely of matter. Cognizant of this challenge, he reminds us that the human soul does not refer to a "thing" that "enters" our bodies but rather to that fundamental dimension of our being that is not reducible to the material. In this context, he says, "What we call in substantialist language 'having a soul' we will describe in a more historical, actual language as 'being God's partner in a dialogue.'" Underscoring that man is not a mere soul connected with a body, he promotes the Bible's more holistic and unified view, preferring to speak of the resurrection of *entire persons*. Bringing this discussion to a close, he then adds the following in characteristic language:

> The foregoing reflections may have clarified to some extent what is involved in the biblical pronouncements about the resurrection: *their essential content* is not the conception of a restoration of bodies to souls after a long interval; *their aim* is to tell men that they, they themselves, live on; not by virtue of their own power, but because they are known and loved by God in such a way that they can no longer perish. (*Introduction to Christianity*, 354–55)

For his perspective on this subject, Ratzinger is deeply indebted to Saint Paul's teaching that "flesh and blood cannot inherit the kingdom of God, nor does the perishable inherit the imperishable" (1 Cor 15:50). Ratzinger emphasized that passages like these make it clear what Saint Paul did and did not have in mind. His hope was not for the return of the "fleshly body" in the sense of our present biological structure. Indeed, the above passage expressly describes this as impossible and in its place proposes that Christians look forward to an unfathomably loftier form of life. In this eternal state, the physical body will neither be left behind nor simply reconstituted but rather *transformed* and *elevated* to the status of the "spiritual body." In this state, our bodies will differ from earthly ones in the way that a mature tree or flowering plant differs from its seed. While the two are substantially the same, in another sense there is almost no comparison between them. And, yet, both the apostle and Our Lord taught that the same entity sown into the ground and broken apart in the winter of death is what will rise again on the Last Day (see Jn 12:24; 1 Cor 15:36–44; *Introduction to Christianity*, 349–51, 357–58).

The Transformation of All Creation

The theme we have been discussing is a common thread in Christian preaching and spirituality, but another prominent feature of Benedict's understanding of heaven is not so frequently emphasized. This concerns the reality that heaven is not just a communion between humans and God, but the glorious union and transformation *of all creation* in God. This vision is not of the pontiff's own making. Like all good theology, it is grounded in Sacred Scripture. For example, Saint Paul tells us in one pivotal text that the whole creation is "groaning in travail" as it waits to be "set free from its bondage to decay and obtain the glorious liberty of the children of God" (Rm 8:19–23). Highlighting the same concept in slightly different terms, Saint John envisions "a new heaven and a new earth" that will be fully revealed at the end of time (see Rv 21:1; 2 Pt 3:8–14). To drive home this point, John goes on to report the Lord saying, "'Behold, I make *all things* new'" (Rv 21:5). With their exalted expectations for the future of the created world, Scripture's sacred authors share with one another the deep conviction that the cosmos we inhabit is fundamentally good and destined in some way to share with us in eternal glory.

In his landmark volume on the Last Things, Ratzinger boldly defined this future state as a "pan-cosmic existence." Making his own the words of Saint Paul, he then added, "Only where creation achieves such unity can it be true that God is 'all in all'" (*Eschatology*, 192; 1 Cor 15:28). As an indication of just how dear this theme was to his heart, it is telling that the emeritus pontiff chose to expand upon it in one of his rare postretirement writings. He boldly declared, "[I]f we really wanted to summarize as succinctly as possible the content of the faith established in the Bible, we could say: the Lord has started a love story with us and wants to sum up all creation in it" ("Faith Is Not an Idea," in *What is Christianity?*, 175).

Creation's Final "Evolutionary Leap"

As part of his endeavor to capture the dynamic of creation's eschatological transformation, Benedict was especially fond of describing the final transfiguration of the cosmos through his characteristic medium of analogies drawn from the sciences.

One of the pontiff's favorite comparisons was to describe creation's ultimate telos as an eschatological (i.e., end of time) "evolution." With this image, Benedict sought to unveil something profound in the dynamic of evolutionary history on earth, the long story of life and death by which God orchestrated the emergence of new and ever greater forms of life in preparation for the advent of man and the incarnation of Christ. According to the pontiff, this natural dynamic is deeply connected with the definitive heavenly transfiguration of the cosmos at the end of time — where, passing through death, all life will be transfigured and conformed to the image of Jesus Christ. In the words of Ratzinger, the transformation of all in Christ, or *Christification*, is the ultimate goal of history and "the real drift of evolution": "Faith sees in Jesus the man in whom — on the biological plane — the next evolutionary leap, as it were, has been accomplished; the man in whom the breakthrough out of the limited scope of humanity, out of its monadic enclosure, has occurred" (*Introduction to Christianity*, 236–39).

Yet, in contrast with earlier stages of life's development, Ratzinger underscores that this definitive "leap" will not occur naturally within the current physical universe. On the contrary, it involves elevation to a quite different plane of existence altogether: that of definitive and eternal life, one in which the blessed have transcended the rule of death. Departing the present temporal "realm of biological evolutions and mutations," Ratzinger teaches that the saints will undergo a "last stage of evolution," a final "leap" into resurrected life on the Last Day (*Introduction to Christianity*, 238–39, 304). As Benedict preached in his inaugural Easter homily as pope, this "mutation" encompasses not only humanity but further entails the definitive transformation of the entire cosmos in Christ, "a new world, which, starting from Christ, already continuously permeates this world of ours, transforms it, and draws it to itself" (Homily, April 15, 2006). Crucially, this transformation is neither the kind of thing that will simply happen if we leave nature to itself nor something that we can achieve through technological progress on this side of eternity.

Nuclear Fission in the Heart of Being

As a further signpost to the mystery of creation's eschatological transfiguration, Benedict advances another scientific analogy that seeks to capture the role that the Blessed Sacrament plays in this drama. Specifically, the pontiff draws a parallel between the transformative effects of the Eucharist and the unfathomable energy unleashed in an atomic event. In brief, "The substantial conversion of bread and wine into his body and blood introduces within creation the principle of a radical change, a sort of 'nuclear fission' … which penetrates to the heart of all being." As the pontiff proceeds to add, this transformation "penetrates to the heart of all being, a change meant to set off a process which transforms reality, a process leading ultimately to the transfiguration of the entire world, to the point where God will be all in all" (*Sacramentum Caritatis*, 11).

As an indication of just how powerful he found this analogy to be, Benedict would revisit this same imagery many times, including shortly before his death. Yet perhaps the most notable occurrence of this message came during a remarkable homily delivered at World Youth Day. In this setting, the pope asked the young worshipers to contemplate what precisely is taking place in the consecration of the Eucharist. By transforming his violent death into a complete self-offering of love, the pontiff explained that Jesus enacted a "substantial transformation" which "set in motion a series of transformations leading ultimately to the transformation of the world when God will be all in all." Once again, Benedict turned to the realm of physics to find an analogy for Christ's transformation of violence and death into love and life:

> To use an image well known to us today, this is like inducing nu-
> clear fission in the very heart of being — the victory of love over
> hatred, the victory of love over death. Only this intimate explosion

of good conquering evil can then trigger off the series of transformations that little by little will change the world. All other changes
remain superficial and cannot save. For this reason we speak of
redemption: what had to happen at the most intimate level has indeed happened, and we can enter into its dynamic. Jesus can dis-
tribute his Body, because he truly gives himself. (Homily, August
21, 2005; *Caritas in Veritate*, 11; The Meaning of Communion," in
What Is Christianity?, 156–57)

In the words of Benedict's biographer, this pope saw Eucharistic love as
"the core and energy of creation, in a sense its operating system" (Peter
Seewald, *Benedict XVI: A Life: Volume 1*, 217). In short, the pontiff's analogy
of nuclear fission reveals that the sacrificial love unleashed in the Eucharist
is unfathomably more powerful than anyone would guess, given the humble elements involved in the process.

Our Role in Creation's Transfiguration

Alongside the scientific imagery Benedict deploys, another analogy holds
a special place in his heart. This one, however, takes its inspiration not
from empirical observations but rather from the sacramental realm: the
belief that creation is called to a telos so sublime that it can be compared
to a "transubstantiation." Additionally, something remarkable about this
perspective is that it envisions human beings playing pivotal roles in this
drama through their priestly vocations to "consecrate the world to God"
(Second Vatican Council, *Lumen Gentium*, 34).

Significantly, Benedict returned to this theme a number of times as he
approached the end of his earthly life. In one posthumously published essay on the meaning of communion, for example, he wrote that the priestly
"service of transformation … is always ordered to the great transformation
of the entire creation" ("The Meaning of Communion," in *What Is Christianity?*, 158). Relatedly, in a brief address delivered on the sixty-fifth anniversary of his ordination, the emeritus pontiff boldly proclaimed,

The cross, suffering, all that is wrong with the world: he transformed all this into "thanks" and therefore into a "blessing." Hence

he fundamentally transubstantiated life and the world. ... We wish to insert ourselves into the "thanks" of the Lord, and thus truly receive the newness of life and contribute to the "transubstantiation" of the world, so that it might not be a place of death, but of life: a world in which love has conquered death. (Address, June 28, 2016)

Notably, the emeritus pontiff preached along the same lines in his final homilies to the small community of religious that accompanied him in his twilight years. In one meditation on the dignity of work, Benedict described care for creation as man's most ancient calling. Refuting a common misinterpretation according to which this work is merely a result of sin, Benedict characterized labor as man's capacity to participate in God's own life by positively transforming the earth (Homily, November 17, 2013).

Connecting the transformation of the cosmos with man's vocation of divinization, Benedict often identified the Eucharist as the bridge that unites the two. Emphasizing that "the rhythm of the universe is governed by worship," this pontiff saw that our reception of the Eucharist endows believers with the power to extend the transforming love of God to the whole world. In this way, he says, the faithful contribute to the transfiguration of the cosmos: "I myself become part of the new bread that he is creating by the resubstantiation of the whole of earthly reality" (*Pilgrim Fellowship of Faith*, 78). As the pontiff proceeds to explain, the transubstantiated host at Mass is the first fruit of the renewed creation — "the anticipation of the transformation and divinization of matter in the Christological fullness," which in turn "provides the movement of the cosmos with its direction; it anticipates its goal and at the same time urges it on" (*Spirit of the Liturgy*, 29). On the solemnity of Corpus Christi, Benedict expounded on this concept:

This little piece of white Host, this bread of the poor, appears to us as a synthesis of creation. In this way, we begin to understand why the Lord chooses this piece of bread to represent him. Creation, with all of its gifts, aspires above and beyond itself to something even greater. Over and above the synthesis of its own forces, above and beyond the synthesis also of nature and of spirit that, in some way, we detect in the piece of bread, creation is projected towards divinization, toward the holy wedding feast, toward unification with the Creator himself. (Homily, June 15, 2006)

In yet another homily, the pontiff taught that the role of the priesthood is "to consecrate the world so that … the world itself shall become a living host, a liturgy" (Homily, July 24, 2009).

What, concretely, does it mean for mankind to exercise a priestly role in the transfiguration of the created world? Although Benedict's language may strike us as fanciful or perhaps even irreverent, his notion of cosmic transubstantiation is in fact deeply traditional and quite simple. At bottom, it asserts that the things of this world achieve their telos when human beings sacrificially transform them into something greater than their original state, a goal achieved when we receive God's gifts wisely and in a spirit of contemplative gratitude.

With regard to the Eucharist in particular, Benedict highlights that the consecrated species are no longer ordinary bread and wine but the body and blood of Jesus Christ. Having been mystically elevated, they no longer give nourishment to our earthly life, or *bios*. Paradoxically, in being mystically transformed they have become more themselves. In this way, they attain the end for which all things were created, providing *supernatural* nourishment for the life of man's soul, or *zoe*. Notably, this is what Benedict endeavored to explain in his final essay on Eucharistic communion. Even in the autumn of his earthly life, the retired pontiff continued to approach subjects with elegant simplicity and substantial depth. In response to the question, "What happens to the bread and wine in the celebration of the Holy Eucharist?" he explained, "Something is not added to them temporarily, but rather bread and wine are snatched away from the things of this world so as to enter into the new world of the risen Jesus Christ." In brief, Benedict pronounces that the bread and wine "are no longer created realities of this world that consist in themselves, but are bearers of the mysteriously real form of the risen Lord" ("The Meaning of Communion," in *What Is Christianity?*, 156–57).

Recognizing that all analogies fall short of reality at some point, Benedict sought to illuminate his image of the Eucharist at the heart of creation by considering further what happens when the bread and wine are offered at Mass. As is the case with the Eucharist, so too he recognized that the "transubstantiation" of creatures does not necessarily entail a change in their outward appearances. Nor does this transformation cause the daily existence of the human creature to lose its apparently mundane character. For instance, no matter how much we might offer up a hectic day at work, disappointment at school, strife within our family, or struggle with an illness, the "accidents" of our sufferings do not simply go away. And yet, the very act of offering up such things — bearing the cross joyfully — can change the inner character of these experiences from one of anguish and rebellion to one of joy and sanctification.

So it was with the passion of Jesus Christ. The victory of Our Lord on the cross did not immediately destroy suffering, but endowed it with redemptive power. In his life, death, and resurrection, Christ *began* the work of transubstantiation. In the words of Benedict, "The presence in our midst of the Creator, who gives himself into our hands and transforms us as he transforms the bread and wine, thus transforms the world" (General Audience, September 2, 2009). Once again invoking his image of Jesus' Eucharistic presence as nuclear fission within the heart of being, Benedict elsewhere added: "He is within us, and we are in him. His dynamic enters into us and then seeks to spread outwards to others until it fills the world, so that his love can truly become the dominant measure of the world" (Homily, August 21, 2005). Having changed bread and wine into his body and blood, Christ now wishes to transform us into his nature through grace. And we, in turn, have the joyful duty of bringing his work to completion by consecrating our joys, our sorrows, our work, our families, and all creation to God.

So much for how man can lead other creatures to a higher end here and now. But what, exactly, will the new heaven and new earth look like when the entire cosmos and its sufferings are transformed in Christ? With respect to the eschaton, Benedict did not delve into details regarding the concrete culmination of this process beyond hinting that the Eucharist plays a central role in the movement of all creation toward God. This is for a very simple reason. While he professed that a great cosmic transformation will take place at the end of time, the pontiff was aware that comprehending *what it means* is another thing. As Scripture teaches, no eye has seen, no ear heard, and no heart conceived what God has prepared for those who love him. Yet what those who dare to hope do know is that what awaits us on the other side of death is infinitely more glorious than we could ever imagine. In his landmark book on the theme of eternal life, Ratzinger summed up the matter as follows:

> In conclusion: the new world cannot be imagined. Nothing concrete or imaginable can be said about the relation of man to matter in the new world, or about the 'risen body.' Yet we have the certainty that the dynamism of the cosmos leads towards a goal, a situation in which matter and spirit will belong to each other in a new and definitive fashion. This certainty remains the concrete content of the confession of the resurrection of the flesh even today. (*Eschatology*, 194)

Ratzinger revisited this theme in the final paragraph of his book on the Last Things. In those closing remarks, we find him eagerly anticipating "the salvation of the cosmos … in which, forgetful of self, the individual will break through the limits of being into the whole, and the whole take up its dwelling in the individual" (*Eschatology*, 238). Daring as this climactic passage may be, it is ultimately just an extension of Saint Paul's teaching that "the creation itself will be set free from its bondage to decay and obtain the glorious liberty of the children of God" (Rom 8:21).

Purgatory and Christ's Return as Judge

While the Bible paints a sweeping vision of creation's transfiguration at the end of time, this leaves unresolved a crucial question about the fate of human beings who have not rejected the Lord but who nonetheless fail to prepare themselves fully for this transformation by the time they reach the end of their earthly pilgrimage. Enter Catholicism's belief in purgatory.

From the very beginning — and tracing its roots back to ancient Judaism — Christians have spoken of an intermediate state between death and resurrection for those who die yet need to be perfected in holiness.

This is the stage where we are fully purified of our sins and purged of our imperfections so as to be able to see God face to face in heaven. Moreover, not only have we believed in the existence of such a state, from her beginning the Church has had a constant tradition of praying for the faithful departed to be freed from it (see, for example, 2 Mc 12:39–45). Despite popular misconstruals to the contrary, Catholicism teaches that our life-choice becomes definitive upon death. Purgatory is therefore not a "second chance" that gives us "additional time" to change our minds about God after we die. The only people going to purgatory are people who will one day be in heaven, and yet this interim state is often described as painful and painted with the imagery of fire (see 1 Cor 3:12–15).

Once again, despite a common misconception, the fire of purgatory is not a punishment in the sense that it is a place where the Lord locks people up in order to torture them for their past faults. In lieu of this, Benedict suggests that a healthier way to think about the "fire" of purgatory is that this represents the burning and refining power of Christ's love: "His gaze" the pontiff says, "heals us through an undeniably painful transformation 'as through fire.' But it is a blessed pain, in which the holy power of his love sears through us like a flame, enabling us to become totally ourselves and thus totally of God." Portrayed through the metaphor of purification by fire, purgatory is indeed excruciating justice, yet it is very different from the sort of pain that Jesus associates with the fires of hell (*Spe Salvi*, 47; see Mt 13:42).

This is what Dante captured seven centuries ago in his *Purgatorio*, where souls sing through their trials. According to this poet's vision, those in purgatory even remain in their suffering voluntarily when given the chance to leave their time of purification early. The reason is that these individuals do not wish to secure God's mercy at the expense of rejecting his justice. From this perspective, purgatory serves as a demonstration of the truth that God's grace does not cancel out his justice, or vice versa. The fact that purgatory exists means that the way we live our lives is not irrelevant. God does not merely look past our sins as if they never happened. And, yet, Benedict adds, the beautiful part of purgatory is that it means "our defilement does not stain us for ever if we have at least continued to reach out towards Christ, towards truth and towards love." For this reason, the pontiff could say paradoxically that "faith in the Last Judgment is first and foremost hope" (*Spe Salvi*, 43, 47).

As a testament to the incalculable wideness of God's mercy and his belief in purgatory's ability to transform sinners, Benedict commented, "For the great majority of people — we may suppose — there remains in the depths of their being an ultimate interior openness to truth, to love, to God" (*Spe Salvi*, 46). Indeed, in his catechesis on Judas Iscariot the pontiff reminded us that we cannot even say for certain which particular people are in hell. To say that Judas's sin was grave would be an understatement of incalculable proportions. On the other hand, Benedict reminds us that Christ's betrayer did indeed "repent" of his decision (see Mt 27:3–5). All the same, the nature of this repentance remains questionable given that Judas violated Christian moral principles by proceeding to hang himself. And yet, Benedict also stressed that none of us has full knowledge of the circumstances under which Judas performed this act. It is in this light that the pope taught that claiming to have certitude concerning another person's eternal fate is tantamount to "substituting ourselves for the infinitely merciful and just God" (General Audience, October 18, 2006). That said, it was not Benedict's aim to weigh in on the perennial debate over the size of hell's population. Regardless of how many souls reside there, Benedict would urge us not to lightly dismiss the possibility of our own eternal damnation. And when it comes to the greatest of sinners, he would urge us to pray, "Save us from the fires of hell. Lead all souls to heaven, especially those most in need of thy mercy."

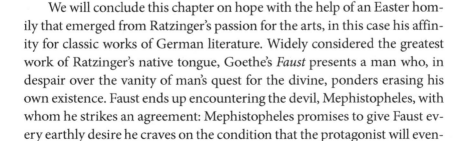

We will conclude this chapter on hope with the help of an Easter homily that emerged from Ratzinger's passion for the arts, in this case his affinity for classic works of German literature. Widely considered the greatest work of Ratzinger's native tongue, Goethe's *Faust* presents a man who, in despair over the vanity of man's quest for the divine, ponders erasing his own existence. Faust ends up encountering the devil, Mephistopheles, with whom he strikes an agreement: Mephistopheles promises to give Faust every earthly desire he craves on the condition that the protagonist will eventually serve him in hell. It turns out, though, that even these great pleasures fail to satisfy Faust. In fact, they only increase his despair. It is in this story that Benedict finds an image of hope's transformation in the modern era. Our society stands in the place of Faust, he says. Ironically, modern man's quest to find happiness by liberating himself from God under the guise of scientific and political progress has led to precisely the opposite outcome (*Images of Hope*, 37–39).

So how does one break free from Faust's despair? The answer of the ancient Church, continues Ratzinger, is that we find freedom only by walking the path of the crucified Christ, immersing ourselves in his way of being. This is precisely the same proposal we saw Benedict make in the last chapter on the virtue of faith. To see the truth of the Christian Faith, we must commit to living it fully, from the inside. In relation to the virtue of hope, Ratzinger thus adds that the truth of the Christian longing is indeed verifiable, yet only by "entering into the experiment of life with God." When we cease being disinterested spectators and begin to live an authentically Christian existence, doors of apprehension open that are otherwise beyond man's reach. As Ratzinger says, some things in life are understood only through the "higher ways of perception" that consist in faith, hope, and love" (*Images of Hope*, 37–42).

With that, our survey of Benedict's insights into the reality of hope come to a close. Having seen how hope has undergone a substantial transformation in our contemporary secular world, we have explored the profound implications of Benedict's take on the nature of authentic Christian hope. All the while, the goal has been to tease out this pope's essential insights into how we can find fulfillment and even thrive in a world where disillusionment and despair are so commonplace. In particular, we fleshed out some key analogies by which the pontiff sought to point us toward the reality of eternal life, which consists in the resurrection of human persons and the transfiguration of all creation in the new heaven and new earth. Finally, we examined Benedict's thoughts on the penultimate state of purgatory and why the Catholic tradition sees it as so essential to the perfecting of persons as they make pilgrimage toward their heavenly homeland. With that, we can now direct our attention to considering the pivotal factor that makes this transformation possible: the theological virtue of charity.

READING LIST

♦ Benedict XVI. *Caritas in Veritate*. Encyclical Letter. 2009.

♦ Benedict XVI. *The Garden of God: Toward a Human Ecology*. Edited by Maria Milvia Morciano. Washington, DC: The Catholic University of America Press, 2014.

♦ Benedict XVI. *Jesus of Nazareth: Holy Week: From the Entrance into Jerusalem to the Resurrection*. San Francisco: Ignatius Press, 2011.

♦ Benedict XVI. *Spe Salvi*. Encyclical Letter. November 30, 2007.

♦ Ramage, Matthew. *The Experiment of Faith: Pope Benedict XVI on Living the Theological Virtues in a Secular Age*. Washington, DC: The Catholic University of America Press, 2020, chapters 6 and 7.

♦ Ratzinger, Joseph. *Eschatology: Death and Eternal Life*. Washington, DC: The Catholic University of America Press, 1988.

CHAPTER 9
Charity and the Trinity

"God is love, and he who abides in love abides in God, and God abides in him" (1 Jn 4:16). In this letter of Saint John, we are presented with an entirely distinctive truth about love that is inaccessible to mankind in the absence of divine revelation. As Benedict affirmed in his first papal encyclical dedicated to this theme, the Christian understanding of love dramatically differs from everything else on offer in the world. Christian love, or charity, is not merely an emotion. Nor is it sufficient to affirm the traditional definition of love as the act by which we will the good of others. While this is a good start, the ultimate nature of love unveiled by Jesus Christ is something more stunning and unexpected — namely, that God himself is charity (Latin: *caritas*; Greek: *agape*), a communion of persons bound in love.

With this in mind, in this chapter we turn our attention to the Trinity, examining Benedict's core insights into the meaning of our faith's affirmation that God is three in one. In particular, we will discover that this pontiff privileged an approach to the doctrine of the Trinity that affirmed all the

Church's traditional theology while stressing the limitations of our ability to comprehend God and placing a renewed focus on the centrality of the revelation that relationship lies at the heart of reality.

Apophaticism: The Doctrine of the Trinity as Negative Theology

Benedict's episcopal coat of arms features a peculiar image that may initially seem out of place: a gold scallop shell. Yet, as we have now come to expect, an unusual representation like this was quite deliberate on the part of the Bavarian pontiff. The shell recalls a specific episode from the life of the pope's spiritual and intellectual mentor Saint Augustine. As legend has it, the saint was once on the seashore pondering the Trinity, when he caught sight of a child trying hopelessly to pour the entire ocean inside a shell. Bemused, Augustine asked the lad why he would think it possible to pull off such an absurd feat. The child's unexpected retort was directed to Augustine personally: a hole in the sand can no more hold the waters of the ocean than your finite intellect can comprehend the mystery of God! This story is essential to grasping Bendict's approach to the Trinity and to the nature of love, which is the heart of both divine and human life.

What does the doctrine of the Trinity actually mean? While Benedict clearly operates on the premise that belief in the Trinity is perpetually normative for our understanding of the Faith, he was always keen to stress the limitations of man's knowledge with regard to this doctrine. The preface to *Introduction to Christianity* concisely captures the attitude that this theological giant considers necessary for theologizing about the Trinity: "The fact that we now acknowledge him to be triune does not mean that we have meanwhile learned everything about him. On the contrary, he is only showing us how little we know about him" (*Introduction to Christianity*, 25). To recall a term that we encountered in Chapter 7, Benedict privileges an approach to the Trinity that is informed by "apophatic" or "negative" theology, stressing our inherent inability as finite creatures to make full sense of the dogmas we rightly profess.

It is not that Benedict found traditional terminology unhelpful or that he considered non-Christian conceptions of the divine equally truthful to the revealed ways by which our tradition points to God. On the contrary, Ratzinger dedicated significant space in his work to explaining why rival approaches to the nature of God were rejected by the early Church as heretical. In the end, however, he winds up following the wisdom of Saint Augustine, urging us to exercise modesty when it comes to the question of how fully we can *understand* the Trinity. The great thinkers of the medieval period also maintained a healthy apophaticism, but Ratzinger takes this to the next level. Whereas Aquinas meticulously crafted logical proofs for God's existence and attributes, Ratzinger favored a personalist approach. Following the example of Saint Augustine, he tended to emphasize finding God through experience of a faith seeking understanding, especially in the experience of beauty, holiness, and love that comes through living the gospel of Jesus Christ within the bosom of the Catholic Church.

In any event, Benedict's apophaticism — like that of his ancient Christian forebears — differs markedly from that of Asiatic traditions like Taoism in which all discourse about the divine nature is discouraged. The *Tao Te Ching* quips, "Those who know don't say, and those who say don't know." As a Christian, Ratzinger is not so extreme as to hold that we cannot affirm anything whatsoever about God, but he did stress that the revealed truth of the Trinity functions primarily in a "negative" way:

> If one surveys the whole question it is possible to observe that the ecclesiastical doctrine of the Trinity can be justified first and foremost on the negative side, as a demonstration of the hopelessness of all other approaches. Indeed, perhaps this is all we can really accomplish here. The doctrine of the Trinity would in that case be essentially negative — the only remaining way to reject all attempts to fathom the subject, a sort of cipher for the insolubility of the mystery of God. (*Introduction to Christianity*, 171–72)

Strange as it might seem at first blush, this is not an admission of failure but rather a profound exercise of divine praise. Confessing our finitude in the face of the ineffable divine mystery is an act of humble homage; we prostrate ourselves before the God whose nature infinitely outstrips the limitations of man's finite understanding.

Ratzinger draws an analogy from the sciences to drive home this point. As the physicist is aware of the tensions inherent in his defining light as both a particle and a wave, so too in Trinitarian theology we must learn to hold two realities together in a paradox: God is three, and yet God is also one. Yet, this by no means implies a disregard for the philosophical principle of noncontradiction. Given Ratzinger's steadfast belief in the harmony of faith and reason, he clearly cannot countenance the absurd notion that the mathematical number three equals the number one — far from it. Christian orthodoxy holds that the Trinity refers to three *persons* in communion within one divine *nature*. Even so, this is not to say that the distinction amounts to a total explanation. As Ratzinger explains, even the Church's official language is necessarily "provisional" and subject to "the restrictions implicit in our point of view" (*Introduction to Christianity*, 173).

Benedict would be the last to conclude that the dogma of the Trinity must change or that it needs to be radically reinterpreted. What is required is not a reversal of the doctrine but rather a *renewal* of its understanding, which harnesses the best of ancient and modern Christian thought. We need, in other words, to deepen our appreciation of the paradox that the dogma of the Trinity is a *normative* yet *nonexhaustive* signpost to the inscrutable mystery of God. Thankfully, he indicates that there is something we can indeed do if only we have the patience for it: "By circling round, by looking and describing from different, apparently contrary angles," Ratzinger says that we can finally "succeed in alluding to the truth, which is never visible to us in its totality" (*Introduction to Christianity*, 174).

The Trinity: Relationship as the Foundation of All Being

Even as Ratzinger encouraged modesty with respect to the question of how much we can definitively affirm about the ineffable divine nature, there are some things that he definitively and repeatedly insisted upon. Paramount among these is his conviction that the heart of reality — both created and uncreated — is *relationality*.

The Christian Faith distinguishes itself from every other religious tradition in history with its foundational claim that the one true God is not solitary, but a *communion of persons*. Ratzinger frames this in a number of different ways throughout his corpus, as when he writes that "the highest mode of Being includes the element of relationship." This truth was unknown even to the greatest classic philosophical thinkers whom Christians have esteemed from time immemorial. In Aristotle's thought, for instance, God is eternal self-thinking thought and the Unmoved Mover. Yet, divine revelation informs us of something previously unknown even to Plato and Aristotle: "The *logos* of the whole world, the creative original thought, is at the same time love," or, in other words, "truth and love are originally identical" (*Introduction to Christianity*, 148; *Truth and Tolerance*, 182).

Whereas the philosophers considered relationality a property belonging only to finite, lowly creatures, the dogma of the Trinity proclaims that "dialogue, the *relatio*, stands beside substance as an equally primordial form of being" (*Introduction to Christianity*, 183). According to Ratzinger, the Incarnation of Christ has "shattered" the classical paradigm of understanding reality primarily through the lens of substance and accidents, for we now know that being "does not belong to itself" but exists only in relation to another (*Introduction to Christianity*, 190). Crediting Saint Augustine for distilling this revelatory transformation into a succinct formula, Ratzinger affirms, "In God, there are no accidents, only substance and relation" (*Introduction to Christianity*, 184). Richard DeClue has eloquently summarized this dynamic: "God as personal is God as inter-personal and not merely as an absolute individual unrelated to everything or anyone else. Far from being a sign of imperfection, relation is part of the perfection of personhood." The foundation of all Benedict's teaching is rooted in this Trinitarian conviction, particularly in the notion of the person as relation (DeClue, *The Mind of Benedict XVI*, 87, 91).

The intra-Trinitarian life does not consist in just any form of relationality whatsoever. It reaffirms the truth that God's supreme unity is "not rigidly static," for it is a *relationship of love* (*The True Europe*, 81). If the Scriptures are to be believed in their proclamation that "God is love" (1 Jn 4:8–16) then something crucial follows. God cannot be love if he is a solitary monad. "If he is love in himself," Ratzinger elaborates, "he must be 'I' and 'Thou,' and this means that he must be triune" (*The God of Jesus Christ*, 37). Following in the footsteps of Augustine and Thomas Aquinas, Ratzinger further underscores the astonishing truth that the divine persons not only *have* relations, but *are* their relations, each being distinct from the others solely by the unique relationship that exists between them (Aquinas, *Summa Theologiae*, I, q. 40, a. 2). Ratzinger puts it this way: "In God, person means relation. Relation, being related, is not something superadded to the person, but it *is* the person itself" ("Concerning the Notion of Person in Theology," 444).

Ratzinger expounds on how this applies in the case of each divine person. Regarding the Father, he explains that "it is just as essential to the Father to say 'Son' as it is essential to the Son to say 'Father'" (*The God of Jesus Christ*, 34). A father cannot be a father except in relation to his son, nor can a son be a son without his father. The Father, then, is distinct from the Son insofar as he possesses the divine nature as the origin or principle within the Trinity, the one *from whom* the Son is begotten. The Son, meanwhile, is distinct within the Trinity as the one who is begotten of the Father (and, importantly, not created or made).

This dynamic also applies among human beings. Benedict nevertheless stresses that the analogy does not run from human fathers to God, but vice versa. "God's fatherhood is more real than human fatherhood," he says, echoing Saint Paul's naming God the Father as the one "from whom every fatherhood in heaven and on earth is named" (*Jesus of Nazareth: From the Baptism*, 141; see Eph 3:14–15). In other words, even as other religious traditions throughout history have imagined their gods as father figures, the Christian revelation of God is not simply a projection of human fatherhood onto the divine. Indeed, although we can find a "kernel of truth hidden in the mythical religions" with their imagery of gods that die and rise and divine fathers who behave (and misbehave) just like human fathers, Ratzinger insists that the biblical revelation of God the Father is something new — "a divine critique of human fatherhood" (*Jesus of Nazareth: From the Baptism*, 141; *Truth and Tolerance*, 19–20). In this way, Christianity stands in both positive and negative relationship with other religions. For on the one hand, the good among them is looked upon by the Church as a preparation for the gospel, and Ratzinger even goes so far as to affirm that Christ's work among these traditions is such that in every age Christ has worked invisibly through them to produce "pagan saints." On the other hand, the Jewish faith revealed itself to be an "anti-religion" in comparison with what came before it, as the advent of divine revelation introduced the concept of false worship — idolatry — for the first time in history (*Truth and Tolerance*, 207–212).

Returning to the Trinity, what Ratzinger said above applies also when it comes to the Holy Spirit. As the bond of love between Father and Son, the Spirit's existence is inseparable from that of the other divine persons. Accordingly, the Holy Spirit is distinct within the Trinity as he who proceeds from the Father and the Son, their mutual gift of love toward one other. To this, Ratzinger notes something else regarding the Holy Spirit's identity. Aware that the terms "holy" and "spirit" also apply to the Father and Son, and that this might lead to the impression that the Holy Spirit is not unique, he explains that the name of the Holy Spirit — the bond of unity between Father and Son — is perfect because it enshrines what the Father and Son have in common: "The particularity of the Holy Spirit is evidently that he is what the Father and the Son have in common. His particularity is being unity" ("The Holy Spirit as Communio," 326). In any event, while it took centuries for the Church to articulate all the intricate nuances of Trinitarian theology, its foundation is very simple. The doctrine of the Trinity is not a construct that theologians came up with in the library, or even in the chapel. No, the doctrine of the Trinity arises directly from deep, sustained meditation on the saving words and deeds of Our Lord in history, which culminate in the revelation that the name of the one true God is "Father, Son, and Holy Spirit" (Mt 28:19).

The Gradual Unveiling of the Trinity in History

To say that the revelation of the Trinity is the pinnacle of the Lord's self-manifestation in history implies that this truth was not always known among men. Indeed, in a masterful chapter that maps out how Israel's knowledge of God gradually developed over the course of salvation history, Ratzinger notes, "In the Old Testament … there is certainly no kind of revelation of the Trinity," although "there is latent an experience that points toward the Christian concept of the triune God" (*Introduction to Christianity*, 125). In this context, Ratzinger refers to the progressive revelation of God's nature in the Old Testament as a "process," a significant word choice because it conveys the idea that the people of Israel did not arrive at the fullness of revelation overnight but rather over the course of many centuries of preparation. On this score, Ratzinger emphatically insisted, "Anyone who wishes to understand the biblical belief in God must follow its historical development from its origins with the patriarchs of Israel right up to the last books of the New Testament" (*Introduction to Christianity*, 116).

Ratzinger would revisit this theme many times throughout his life, endeavoring to capture the dynamic in a slightly different manner each time. In the above work, he begins by recalling that Israel's God was primarily referred to as 'El' or 'Elohim' prior to the Exodus. Within the context of the ancient Near Eastern world, 'El' was a personal god and the God of a particular people: the God of Abraham, Isaac, and Jacob. Ratzinger elaborates, "The God of its fathers had not, it is true, been called Yahweh; when we meet him he bears the names El and Elohim. The patriarchs of Israel were thus able to use as their starting point the El-religion of the surrounding peoples, a religion that is characterized chiefly by the social and personal character of the divinity denoted by the word El" (*Introduction to Christianity*, 122).

In concert with other biblical scholars, Ratzinger writes that, at this early date, Israel's God "certainly does not yet appear as making the monotheistic claims of the only God of all mankind and of the whole world" (*Truth and Tolerance*, 146). Over many centuries, however, the people of Israel were gradually opened to the revelation that their God was not only the God of Abraham or the God of Israel. Eventually, it would be understood that he is not merely the *highest* God, but indeed the *only* God.

This deepening of Israel's faith occurred at what might strike one as a highly unlikely moment: the crisis of the Babylonian Exile. This period, the lowest in Israel's history, could easily have spelled the demise not only of her nationhood but her entire faith. Yet, as Ratzinger explains, this is not at all what occurred:

> In the normal way of things, a God who loses his land, who leaves his people defeated and is unable to protect his sanctuary, is a God who has been overthrown. He has no more say in things. He vanishes from history. When Israel went into exile, quite astonishingly, the opposite happened. ... The faith of Israel at last took on its true

form and stature. ... He could allow his people to be defeated so as to awaken it thereby from its false religious dream. (*Truth and Tolerance*, 148)

Up to this point, Israel had been hoping for a fulfillment that would be fully achieved in this world, and she viewed her God as one, albeit the greatest, among many deities. As Ratzinger explains, God's people needed the experience of exile to be shaken from the illusion that perfection can be achieved in this world. Along the way, their continued experience of Yahweh's saving presence enabled them to realize that the God of Israel is not tied to a particular land. As Benedict put it in his famous 2006 Regensburg Address, the process of God's centuries-long revelation "came to new maturity at the time of the Exile, when the God of Israel, an Israel now deprived of its land and worship, was proclaimed as the God of heaven and earth."

Even then, it is not until a few centuries later — after Israel had returned from Babylon and suffered at the hands of yet another nation — that we arrive at "the most important step" of the divine pedagogy. This is the diaspora, when the Israelite thought world came face-to-face with Greek culture, resulting in the translation of the Hebrew Bible into Greek as early as the third century BC (*Truth and Tolerance*, 152). The Septuagint (abbreviated LXX) is more than just a translation. In this inspired reinterpretation and development of Israel's ancient faith at the end of the Old Testament period, we encounter texts that serve as a perfect bridge to the New Testament.

This momentous work includes books such as Sirach and Wisdom, where the figure of Lady Wisdom rises to prominence as one who "came forth from the mouth of the Most High, the first-born before all creatures" (Sir 24:3). Indeed, many lines from these final books of the Old Testament could easily be mistaken for statements of Saint Paul or the Nicene Creed in relation to Jesus Christ. For example, the Book of Wisdom describes *Sophia* as follows:

For she is a breath of the power of God,
and a pure emanation of the glory of the Almighty;

therefore nothing defiled gains entrance into her.
For she is a reflection of eternal light,
a spotless mirror of the working of God,
and an image of his goodness. (Wisdom 7:25–26).

Other texts, like sections of Proverbs redacted during the Hellenistic period, portray Wisdom as present before God created heaven and earth, even
playing a role in the work of creation (see Prv 8:22–30). In reading passages like these, it is hard not to think of Saint Paul's description of Christ as
"the image of the invisible God, the first-born of all creation," adding that
"in him all things were created, in heaven and on earth" (Col 1:15–23).

Yet, it is significant that Wisdom in the Old Testament is still understood as a creature, even if she was considered to be the first and greatest
of God's works (see Prv 8:22). It is not until the Second Person of the Trinity becomes flesh that the divine pedagogy at last reaches its true climax,
wherein we learn that the Wisdom (*Sophia*) of God is identical to the Word
(*Logos*) of God and is none other than Jesus Christ (Jn 1:1; 1 Cor 1:24).
In light of this, Pope Benedict said that the revelation of Jesus Christ as
consubstantial and coeternal with the Father marks "the last step" in God's
long process of self-revelation throughout human history. In the Gospels,
we learn that the divine name "I am" is "no longer merely a word, but a
person: Jesus himself" (*Introduction to Christianity*, 132–33).

To connect this with our earlier discussions regarding Ratzinger's understanding of Divine Revelation, let's pause for a moment to appreciate
the dynamic interplay of continuity and novelty at work in the definitive
revelation of Jesus Christ as the Word made flesh. In his apostolic exhortation on the Word of God, Benedict wrote the following:

The New Testament itself claims to be consistent with the Old
and proclaims that in the mystery of the life, death and resurrection of Christ the sacred Scriptures of the Jewish people have
found their perfect fulfillment. It must be observed, however,
that the concept of the fulfillment of the Scriptures is a complex
one, since it has three dimensions: a basic aspect of *continuity*
with the Old Testament revelation, an aspect of *discontinuity* and

an aspect of *fulfillment and transcendence*. ... The paschal mystery of Christ is in complete conformity — albeit in a way that could not have been anticipated — with the prophecies and the foreshadowings of the Scriptures; yet it presents clear aspects of discontinuity with regard to the institutions of the Old Testament. (*Verbum Domini*, 40)

For example, even as it builds on what immediately preceded it, in the Incarnation we encounter something totally new with respect to the wisdom literature of the Old Testament. Although the final books suggest some kind of plurality within God, this concept remains unclear on the basis of these books alone. We are almost there, but not fully there. If the divine pedagogy were to have stopped at the Book of Wisdom, we might have been left with something like Arianism: Wisdom being perceived as almost divine, and yet still a creature, and feminine at that. Thanks be to God, the revelation of Jesus Christ not only resonated with the figure of Wisdom but moreover transcended and fulfilled it.

What the Trinity Reveals about the Meaning of Christian Identity

As we have seen, Benedict's theology of the Trinity is deeply rooted in the witness of Scripture and the Church's ancient Catholic dogmatic tradition. But, because much of what we have just discussed has centered on the historical foundations of our faith, for some it might be difficult to see its present-day relevance. Benedict, however, believes that understanding our spiritual heritage — knowing where we have come from — will always be of importance for helping to point us the correct way forward. Having said that, he does not stop there but consciously introduces a fresh perspective by emphasizing the implications of Trinitarian doctrine for contemporary Christian living.

As Ratzinger preached throughout his ordained life, the Christian religion is not merely an idea, but an experience. Thus understood, the doctrine of the Trinity is not merely a proposition that fits within a system of knowledge but is ordered above all to a *total way of life* (*Introduction to Christianity*, 99–100; see Acts 9:2). In Ratzinger's view, the anchor of all

Christian thought is the affirmation that the primordial heart of reality is an intimate relationship of love. This implies that creatures find fulfillment to the degree that their lives mirror this love in the world (*Introduction to Christianity*, 184, 187–88).

Pondering this truth in relation to the only creature that God made in his own image, Ratzinger took the following stab at what it fundamentally means to believe in the Trinity. Being a Christian, he contends, involves a radical transformation in our manner of life, a shift from living for oneself to being entirely for others. Summing up this perspective, he says that to believe essentially signifies "I hand myself over" in a total gift of self (*Introduction to Christianity*, 88). This is no trite moralism, a suggestion that we ought to behave as nice people. On the contrary, the Christian creed thus understood is an all-encompassing and lifelong movement of detachment, suffering, and sacrifice. As Benedict wrote in his encyclical on charity, "Love is … an ongoing exodus out of the closed inward-looking self towards its liberation through self-giving, and thus towards authentic self-discovery and indeed the discovery of God" (*Deus Caritas Est*, 6). In his last major speech to the Roman Curia before retiring, the pontiff would put a fine point on this and connect it with one of his most cherished thoughts, proclaiming that the paschal mystery lies at "the center of what it is to be Christian" (Meeting with the Clergy of Rome, February 14, 2013).

The Trinitarian Structure of Creation, Suffering, and Death

As we have just seen, Benedict's conviction that Trinitarian love constitutes the heart of reality implies that creatures achieve their end to the extent that they mirror and incarnate this love in their lives. We have addressed briefly what this looks like in the case of humans who are called to offer their lives in a free gift of self, but an underappreciated facet of the pontiff's Trinitarian worldview is that it also illuminates something profound about the wider natural world. Notably, it offers a uniquely compelling account of why suffering and death have been a part of life in our world from the very beginning. Nature was already "red in tooth and claw" billions of years before *Homo sapiens* arrived on the scene of history. Benedict was aware that this fact has played an essential role in the development of life from bacteria to the myriad flora and fauna that grace our planet today. But how can this be reconciled with the Christian claim that the structure of the universe bears the stamp of the God who is love?

Benedict's contribution toward answering this question lies in his claim that the deepest enigmas of our cosmos are unlocked only in the light of Jesus Christ — the Logos who bears the meaning of creation within himself (see Col 1:16; Jn 1:3) and whose self-emptying *kenosis* represents the definitive path to creaturely fulfillment (Phil 2:6–8). Seen in this light, the structure of creation and our finite creaturely existence may be described as *cruciform* (cross-shaped), *paschal* (configured according to the pattern of Christ's suffering, death, and resurrection), or *Trinitarian* (modeled after the nature of the Triune God). As a biblical theologian, Ratzinger found confirmation of this in Jesus' own words: "Truly, truly, I say to you, unless a grain of wheat falls into the earth and dies, it remains alone; but if it dies, it bears much fruit" (Jn 12:24).

Crucially, Ratzinger grasped that the application of this teaching extends well beyond cereal crops and the life of man, as it is a fundamental law of creation that the death of organisms is what makes possible the rebirth and flourishing of life (Ratzinger, *The Divine Project*, 76). This is a thought that Ratzinger held dear from his time in the academy. Indeed, in Professor Ratzinger's lecture notes we find his most daring statements about the world's cruciform shape. In these courses, the young priest explained that suffering and death are not peripheral to life but rather the "foundational principles upon which the whole interplay of the world is built" (*Schöpfungslehre* 1964, 215).

While it is clear from a scientific point of view that the long history of biological evolution on this planet necessitated death and decay, Benedict would later write as pope that the mystery of suffering cannot be fully understood by virtue of reason alone. Indeed, he professed that it is only from the perspective of the Word-made-Flesh who died and rose again that "we can manage to glimpse on the basis of a groping reconstruction of the fundamental reasons for nature" (*Creation and Evolution*, 115–16). In other words, the *raison d'être* of creation — its fundamental meaning and purpose — lies in the love of the Triune God and the paschal mystery of the Word-made-Flesh. When it comes to the unfathomable sweeping generosity of God's love, Ratzinger's thought is perhaps nowhere better glimpsed than in these poignant words about the "fundamental structure" of creation:

> Generosity is, at the same time, the divine trademark of creation: the miracle of Cana, the miracle of the multiplication of the loaves are signs of God's superabundant generosity, which is the essential mark of his activity, of that activity that squanders millions of seeds in order to save *one* living thing; that activity that squanders a whole universe in order to prepare a place on earth for the mysterious creature that is man; that activity that, in a last unheard-of generosity, goes himself to save that "thinking reed," man, and to lead him to his goal. (*Co-Workers of the Truth*, 330)

In this chapter, we have examined several interrelated facets of Benedict's teaching on the theological virtue of charity. Each of these represents a significant contribution that the pontiff's theology makes toward helping Christians navigate life amid the turbulent waters of the modern world. Beginning with his emphasis on the biblical revelation that God is love, we explored what is unique to the Christian understanding of love, or charity. In line with the Catholic tradition writ large, this pontiff stressed something crucial about man's creation in the *imago Dei*: we find fulfillment in imitation of and communion with the Triune God who himself is a communion of persons. Regarding the doctrine of the Trinity itself, we nevertheless saw that the past century's greatest expositor of the Faith emphasized the necessity of an apophatic approach in relation to our human ability to circumscribe the divine mystery.

READING LIST

♦ Benedict XVI. *Creation and Evolution: A Conference with Pope Benedict XVI in Castel Gandolfo.* San Francisco: Ignatius Press, 2008.
♦ Benedict XVI. *Deus Caritas Est.* Encyclical Letter. 2005.
♦ Benedict XVI. *The God of Jesus Christ: Meditations on the Triune God.* San Francisco: Ignatius Press, 2018.

♦ DeClue, Richard. *The Mind of Benedict XVI: A Theology of Communion.* Word on Fire Academic, 2024, chapter 3.

♦ Ramage, Matthew. *Dark Passages of the Bible: Engaging Scripture with Benedict XVI and Thomas Aquinas.* Washington, DC: The Catholic University of America Press, 2013, especially chapter 5.

♦ Ramage, Matthew. *The Experiment of Faith: Pope Benedict XVI on Living the Theological Virtues in a Secular Age.* Washington, DC: The Catholic University of America Press, 2020, chapters 8 and 9.

♦ Ratzinger, Joseph. "Concerning the Notion of Person in Theology," *Communio* 17 (1990): 439–54.

♦ Ratzinger, Joseph. *The Divine Project: Reflections on Creation and the Church.* San Francisco: Ignatius Press, 2023.

♦ Ratzinger, Joseph. *Introduction to Christianity.* San Francisco: Ignatius Press, 1990.

♦ Ratzinger, Joseph. *Truth and Tolerance.* San Francisco: Ignatius Press, 2003.

CHAPTER 10

The Gift of Human Nature in the Divine Image

In the last chapter, we delved into Benedict's approach to the central mystery of the Christian Faith, the affirmation that the God who is love exists in an eternal Triune communion of divine persons. Following in the footsteps of past theological giants, the Bavarian pope saw the Trinity as the bedrock of all else. In light of this, our next task will be to draw out some key implications of this foundational Christian claim as we turn our gaze to Benedict's insights in the realm of anthropology: the nature and vocation of the human person.

Sacred Scripture reveals that mankind has been made in the image of God, but as Christians we know that this must be understood as a reflection not just of an abstract divine nature but rather of the Trinitarian communion of divine persons. Musing on the reality of man's creation in the image of the Trinity, we will explore the revelation that Christ's *kenosis* (self-emptying) is the foundation and model for human *theosis* (divinization). For a Christian, holiness is not some vague process of becoming like God, but rather conforming entirely to the crucified God-man through *Christosis*. At this point, we will reflect on Benedict's vision of how the created world mirrors the Trinitarian dynamic of self-giving manifest in the life and ministry of Jesus Christ. This, in turn, will help us to see how the pontiff seeks to make sense out of suffering with his understanding of the cosmos as having a kenotic or paschal structure, modeled after Christ, the one by whom and for whom the world was made.

Indispensable to this point is Benedict's oft-repeated claim that human nature is not something that we can make for ourselves but rather something that is prior to us. The pontiff underscores that our humanity is a gift from God to be received with joy, even as it inevitably draws us to share in Christ's cross. As we will see, an important contention in this regard is that conformity to Christ requires a correct understanding of freedom, which entails the willingness to commit ourselves in obedience to the teaching of the Church as the path to full freedom, holiness, and happiness. Contemplating this vision, we will discover that Benedict offers a uniquely balanced approach to life and an incisive corrective to the widespread confusion in our society over the right way to live.

Christ the True Adam Who Reveals Man to Himself

What, ultimately, does it mean to say that human beings have been created in the image of God? Benedict locates the answer in Jesus' identity as the exemplary man, the second and definitive Adam. While these linguistic permutations are characteristically Ratzinger's, the fundamental idea derives from Saint Paul, who contrasted the "first man Adam" through whom death entered the world (see Rom 5:12–14) with Christ the "last Adam," who undid the curse and opened to us the way to everlasting life (1 Cor 15:22, 45).

To grasp the essence of what Paul and Benedict are teaching here, we need to revisit a key concept from the worldview of Sacred Scripture. As we saw in Chapter 5, *adam* in Hebrew means "human being." In that context, we observed that "Adam" in Genesis was not a proper name, like "Joseph" or "Peter." From the biblical perspective embraced by Ratzinger, Adam is the archetypal human being, the representative of mankind as a whole.

Fast forward to the New Testament, and we discover that the True Adam is actually not the first human being — frail and sinful natural man — but rather the incarnate second person of the Trinity who represents the telos or "end" of history. As Ratzinger mused on many occasions, Jesus is the "index" for what it means to be a human person, the long-awaited manifestation of what we are all called to become by the grace of God:

> What is disclosed in [Christ] is what the riddle of the human person really intends. Scripture expresses this point by calling Christ the last Adam or "the second Adam." It thereby characterizes him as the true fulfillment of the idea of the human person, in which the direction of meaning of this being comes fully to light for the first time. ("On the Understanding of 'Person' in Theology," 114, 192; *Principles of Catholic Theology*, 156; *In the Beginning*, 48)

Historically speaking, the Incarnation indeed came relatively late in the game. The universe is almost fourteen billion years old, *Homo sapiens* has walked this earth for at least a couple of hundred thousand years, and yet God became man only two millennia ago. Nonetheless, Scripture reveals to us that Christ was "in the beginning" (Jn 1:1), the "first-born of all creation" *in* whom and *for* whom all things were made (see Col 1:15–16). In the words of Ratzinger, "From the standpoint of Christian faith one may say that for *history* God stands at the end, while for *being* he stands at the beginning" (*Introduction to Christianity*, 242). Or, if we wish to cast this in Thomistic language, it can be said that Christ the Last Adam is also the "Final Adam" in the sense of being creation's goal or *final cause*. The Incarnation may have come late in time, but it was always first in God's intention. In the words of Ratzinger, "the Alpha is only truly to be understood in the light of the Omega" ("The Dignity of the Human Person," 121).

But what, precisely, does it mean for Christ to be the perfect man and pinnacle of history? On this front, Ratzinger's approach closely mirrors that of the Second Vatican Council. Teaching that "Christ, the final Adam … fully reveals man to man himself and makes his supreme calling clear," the council specified the heart of this revelation: the reality that "man … cannot fully find himself except through a sincere gift of himself" (*Gaudi-

um et Spes, 22, 24). This teaching takes its inspiration from Saint Paul, who taught that the son of God emptied himself of his divine prerogatives in order to become totally one with us (see Phil 2:5–11). In so doing, he tore down the dividing wall between humanity and divinity and bound God and man into one (*Introduction to Christianity*, 234–40).

In his own effort to capture this dynamic, Ratzinger says that Jesus, as the definitive man, is "pure relation," the "completely open man" who pours himself out in a complete gift to others (*Introduction to Christianity*, 234–40). If this striking way of describing Jesus sounds familiar, it is because this is precisely the same way that we witnessed Benedict speak about the Trinity in the previous chapter. In this context, it is worth recalling an important line from that discussion: "In God, person means relation. Relation, being related, is not something superadded to the person, but it *is* the person itself" ("Concerning the Notion of Person," 444). Since man is the image of God where person means relation, it stands to reason that our personhood should mirror this reality. This leads Ratzinger to say that man "is God's image in his concrete reality, which is relationship" (*The God of Jesus Christ*, 30). Jesus Christ can therefore be called "pure relation" because he has perfectly exemplified — indeed, incarnated — the divine image on earth through his life, death, and resurrection.

Ratzinger contends that the heart of Christ's life is captured in the notion of *exodus* — literally, a "going out" of oneself — which the pontiff identified as "the definitive fundamental law of revelation" (Ratzinger, "Gratia Praesupponit Natura," 161). This, in turn, is the hermeneutic with which he answers critics like Friedrich Nietzsche, who thought that Christian morality "poisoned" love with all its rules and that its ethos amounts to the "crucifixion of man." Ratzinger counters this assertion by demonstrating how Christ's self-abandonment in favor of total love represents the true fulfillment of our deepest yearnings. One of the greatest paradoxes of reality is that man finds true healing through suffering, and that by "losing himself" he gains everything (see Mt 10:24). As we saw in the last chapter, this truth about man reflects the nature of God in eternity, where the identity of each divine person is found precisely in the unique self-donating relationship of love that he has with the others.

With this comes a crucial implication for our own lives: We become truly human and find sanctification in the carrying of whatever cross Christ has chosen to bestow upon us. "Only the humanity of the second Adam is a true humanity, only the humanity that endured the cross brings the true man to light" (Ratzinger, "Gratia Praesupponit Natura," 159). This cross will look different for each person. For some, it is prolonged physical suffering. For others, it is the tragic untimely loss of a loved one. In other instances, it might be a professional failure, loneliness, or depression. Quite often, such trials occur simultaneously, compounding their difficulty. No matter the issue, Ratzinger reminds us that the path forward is fundamentally the same. We will always find our way when we seek Jesus Christ, not merely adhering to a theory but "following his steps from day to day in patient love and suffering" (*In the Beginning*, 58; *The Divine Project*, 85–86).

"There Can Be No Love Without Suffering"

The life of Jesus Christ reveals that suffering is an integral component in our walk toward union with God in this life. Presumably, however, God could have created a world without pain and death had he so decided. Why didn't he?

In response to this question, it is instructive to turn to Benedict's encyclical on hope, where he distinguishes two reasons for suffering's presence in human life: First, he recalls the traditional teaching that much of our pain is explained by "the mass of sin which has accumulated over the course of history." Second, he observes that suffering "stems partly from our finitude" that no human is able to "shake off" (*Spe Salvi*, 36). In other words, our existence in this world was never going to be entirely free of pain because we are finite creatures modeled after the image of the Triune God, called to divinization but not able to fully achieve it on this side of eternity. In the words of Ratzinger, suffering's ineluctability in this life flows from the "logic of self-giving" at the heart of Trinitarian life and is "written into creation and into the hearts of men" ("Man Between Reproduction and Creation," 82). To a greater or lesser extent, each one of us participates intimately in the experience of the Church's great mystics like St. John of the Cross, whose painful "dark night" stemmed from his deep yearning for a total union God that cannot be attained in this vale of tears.

Furthermore, Benedict stressed that human beings are part of nature and therefore not exempt from its rules and rhythms. Yet, paradoxically, he considered the suffering inherent to our world's evolutionary dynamic the medium by which creatures are conformed to the love of Jesus Christ and enabled to share in the life of the Triune God. In this connection, the pontiff not only viewed the suffering "essential to the structure" of the cosmos as providential, but remarkably he went so far as to suggest that suffering and death are *necessary* for human flourishing. Indeed, so strongly was he persuaded of this metaphysical stance that Professor Ratzinger said, "A person without suffering in the world in which we live would be a monster and impossible" (*Schöpfungslehre* 1964, 215).

Following this train of thought, Ratzinger would later add that, even as we should of course do our best to alleviate suffering, "the will to do away with it completely would mean a ban on love and therewith the abolition of man" (*Eschatology*, 103). In one of his revealing book-length interviews, Cardinal Ratzinger said that suffering is precisely what enables us to complete the "exodus" out of ourselves, which is necessary if we are to be fully formed into the image of the Triune God:

> Pain is part of being human. Anyone who really wanted to get rid of suffering would have to get rid of love before anything else, because there can be no love [*Liebe*] without suffering [*Leiden*], because it always demands an element of self-sacrifice, because, given temperamental differences and the drama of situations, it will always bring with it renunciation and pain.
>
> When we know that the way of love — this exodus, this going out of oneself — is the true way by which man becomes human, then we also understand that suffering is the process through which we mature. Anyone who has inwardly accepted suffering becomes more mature and understanding of others, becomes more human. Anyone who has consistently avoided suffering does not understand other people; he becomes hard and selfish. (*God and the World*, 322)

It turns out, then, that suffering for Ratzinger is simply "the inner side of love." As if this were not a clear enough indication of how dearly he held this conviction, Pope Benedict went so far as to affirm "the inseparability of love and suffering, of love and God," adding that "there can be no love without suffering, because love always implies renouncement of myself" (Meeting with the Clergy of the Dioceses of Belluno-Feltre and Treviso, July 24, 2007).

Lessons from the Life of Christ and the Blessed Virgin

Having said all of this, Benedict sought to comfort the faithful with the reminder that the Lord did not create this earth with a view toward us living indefinitely upon it. In line with this, he professes a steadfast hope for that state where God will wipe away every tear from our eyes, and death shall be no more (*Spe Salvi*, 10–11; see Rv 21:4). Moreover, even as we experience all manner of trials, the pontiff encouraged believers to be bold in their hope that suffering is a pathway to meaning: "It is not by sidestepping or fleeing from suffering that we are healed, but rather by our capacity for accepting it, maturing through it and finding meaning through union with Christ, who suffered with infinite love." In sum, Benedict's position is that bearing our pain in closeness with the cross of Christ means that our pain, "without ceasing to be suffering becomes, despite everything, a hymn of praise" (*Spe Salvi*, 37).

As we saw in Chapter 8, this is what the poet Dante captured in his *Purgatorio* by having souls sing the glory of God amidst excruciating trials. Whether before or after death, the experience of transformative purgation reveals that there is indeed such a thing as sanctified suffering:

> His gaze, the touch of his heart heals us through an undeniably painful transformation "as through fire." But it is a blessed pain, in which the holy power of his love sears through us like a flame, enabling us to become totally ourselves and thus totally of God. In this way the inter-relation between justice and grace also becomes clear: the way we live our lives is not immaterial, but our defilement does not stain us forever if we have at least continued to reach out towards Christ, towards truth and towards love. (*Spe Salvi*, 47)

To shift images to one developed by Benedict's successor based on Romans 8, a proper perspective on life reveals that "many of the things we think of as evils, dangers or sources of suffering, are in reality part of the pains of childbirth which he uses to draw us into the act of cooperation with the Creator" (Francis, *Laudato Si'*, 80).

As we discussed above, nowhere is the blessed character of suffering revealed than in the person of Jesus. The paschal mystery of Our Lord reveals that suffering and death are the definitive vehicles for resurrection and eternal life. Christ suffered in unimaginable ways for the sake of our salvation, and by his life and death he manifested the supreme act of which there is no greater love (see Jn 15:13). To draw out this point, Ratzinger reminds us of Pilate's infamous words in John 19:5: "Behold, the man!" The irony of the procurator's unwitting prophetic *Ecce homo!* is that to gaze upon Christ is to behold the perfection of man himself, which consists in his death and resurrection. Like the grain of wheat that Ratzinger was so fond of recalling, the crucified and risen Christ is "the ultimate manifestation of the human project," so that, "as we gaze on the Pierced One, we are gazing at God's project with regard to man" (*The Divine Project*, 84). Towering intellectual that he was, Benedict nonetheless saw this theological musing as more than a mere theoretical affair. Indeed, the pontiff's own manner of life manifested his profound conviction that the ultimate answer to the meaning of man is not found in a theory, but rather in the person of Jesus Christ and a commitment to a lifetime of following in his footsteps (*The Divine Project*, 85–86).

It is no accident that this dynamic revealed in the person of Jesus Christ is also mirrored in the trials experienced by the Virgin Mary, who is also known as "Our Sorrowful Mother." Pausing briefly to consider what Ratzinger has to say about Our Lady's embrace of suffering — and possibly death — offers a privileged lens into their relationship with love and can therefore serve as a guide to help us face them in a more Christlike manner in our own lives.

A number of statements from Professor Ratzinger's Mariology course take for granted that suffering and death were essential features in the life of this creature who, while free from all sin, nevertheless had her soul pierced (see Lk 2:35) and even "matured as Mother of God" in such a way that "her merits increased until her death" (*Mariologie*, 1957, 47–48). Unlike the rest of us, though, with the help of God's grace, Mary made the perfect response when she chose to accept the gifts of suffering and death, which led to greater conformity to Christ. Accordingly, Ratzinger taught that the Blessed Virgin's death was not merely a passive affair. On the contrary, it was the definitive outpouring of love in a grand *fiat*. "Mary's death," he thus explains, was not due to sin but rather "the self-giving away of love, or the overwhelming power of love, which broke the outer shell and prepared the way for [its] true form" (*Mariologie*, 1957, 51). If mystics such as St. Teresa of Ávila and St. John of the Cross could speak of "dying because I do not die," from this perspective the Blessed Virgin's yearning for union to be reunited with her Son was the catalyst that led her to depart this earth and be taken up into heavenly glory.

This leads us to an existential lesson of paramount importance. Taking into account Ratzinger's understanding of Mary combined with the integral role of suffering and death in the design of the cosmos, it can be seen that the ultimate problem that each of us must face in life is not physical hardship and death per se, but rather our resistance to accepting these crosses as our path to union with the Triune God. To put it in Ratzinger's personalist language, the ultimate problem is not pain per se but rather our orientation toward the trials through which we all must pass. The question is whether we will play the victim, raging and rebelling against them, or rather whether we will overcome them with love by choosing to receive them as gifts. From this perspective, the grace lost by our first parents does not prevent us from experiencing physical pain and death. Notwithstanding the notable exception of the Blessed Mother, we are all born into the condition of original sin. And, yet, the Lord offers us the grace that allows us to suffer and die well — with Christ and like his Blessed Mother — in a loving gift of self-abandonment to the Father's will. A hallmark of Benedict's theology was his call to embrace this invitation to love, confident that our eternal happiness will be achieved not *despite* but precisely *because of* the hardships that we must face in this life.

Freedom's Fulfillment in Love

The affliction that inevitably accompanies our existence in this world assumes a multitude of forms, but one instance of it occupied prime real estate in Benedict's mind. This is a universal experience that derives from man's existence as a free creature who is nevertheless finite and frail.

We who bear God's image sometimes have trouble remembering the fact that we are not divine. As Benedict would say, we all face the same temptation that the archetypal man faced in the garden. The Lord gives us some very basic laws to follow ("Don't eat from that tree!"), but the temptation is to make our freedom an idol and deem anything that we do not choose for ourselves as an unnatural — and therefore non-binding — imposition (*Church, Ecumenism, and Politics*, 255; "Conscience and Truth," 536). As with Adam, so for all of us, the root issue here is sin — a lack of love. It is the quest to become like God without God, entirely on our own terms ("Truth and Freedom," 28). In one of his meditations on the Gospels, the pontiff explained, "Through sin, man comes to sense that his freedom is compromised by God's will and that consenting to it is not an opportunity to become fully himself but as a threat to his freedom against which he rebels" (*Jesus of Nazareth: Holy Week*, 160). In another, he added, "God himself is constantly regarded as a limitation placed on our freedom that must be set aside if man is ever to be completely himself. God, with his truth, stands in opposition to man's manifold lies, his self-seeking, and his pride" (*Jesus of Nazareth: The Infancy Narratives*, 86).

Benedict understood the allure of pitting external authority against genuine human freedom, and he observed that this underpins our society's increasing indifference — and, in some cases, hostility — toward the Christian Faith. Indeed, if we take a look around outside or in the depths of our own hearts, it is very easy to confirm the truth Benedict observed: It is transparent that the God who is love is often hated when he challenges people to transcend themselves (*Jesus of Nazareth: The Infancy Narratives*, 86). This is especially obvious with respect to Church teachings on matters related to sexuality. These days, people are often told that they should feel free to act upon this or that sexual proclivity because they did not, after all, freely choose to have the urge in question. Yet, as Benedict saw, we miss something very important about the human person when our actions are governed by feelings irrespective of input from broader channels of wisdom.

Preeminent among these is the testimony of Sacred Scripture, specifically Saint Paul's understanding of *eleutheria*. This term, which is typically translated "freedom," is a concept that can only be understood in light of its opposite: slavery. As the apostle says, the mere capacity to do whatever we want can lead to servitude when it is used against its true purpose — which is to become "servants of one another" through love (see Gal 5:13). Commenting on Saint Paul's letter, Benedict explains that the apostle has taught us "what freedom is — namely, freedom in the service of good, freedom that allows itself to be led by the Spirit of God" (*Jesus of Nazareth: From the Baptism*, 100). The pontiff treated this later in a text that almost reads like a textbook definition of authentic freedom, "This is true freedom: actually to be able to follow our desire for good, for true joy, for communion with God and to be free from the oppression of circumstances that pull us in other directions" (General Audience, May 16, 2012). The point here is that the moral truths of the Church, which guide us in making a sincere gift of self, are good news. They lead us to true freedom and, consequently, to genuine *happiness*.

Of course, Benedict was well aware that the prospect of making our lives an offering of obedient love is easier said than done. For this reason, he finds wisdom a few verses later in Galatians where the apostle teaches us that true freedom requires "crucifying the flesh" (Gal 5:24) — in light of which the pontiff adds that true freedom "constrains to such an extent that it can be called a 'crucifixion'" (*Church, Ecumenism, and Politics*, 188). He then applies this principle to the question of how we can live the Church's teachings with courage in a society where it is considered strange or even hateful. It is absolutely crucial, says Ratzinger, to bear in mind a lesson exemplified especially well in the life and work of Saint Paul:

> Suffering and truth belong together. Paul was resisted because he was a man of truth. His words and life still have meaning today because he served truth and suffered on its behalf. Suffering is the necessary authentication of truth, but only truth gives meaning to suffering. … Whoever commits himself entirely to the truth … will always approach the vicinity of martyrdom. (*Images of Hope*, 26–27)

Yet, if we as disciples will be persecuted for living the truth, the good news is that this martyrdom brings about conformity with Jesus Christ. As Our Lord said, "If they persecuted me, they will persecute you" (Jn 15:20). This is what the Fathers of the Church had in mind with the concept of *theosis* or *divinization*, which is the same reality Saint Peter pointed to when he spoke of our vocation to become "partakers in the divine nature" (2 Pt 1:4). In the words of Benedict, "The pedagogy of freedom is guidance in onto-logical dignity, education for being, education for love, and thus guidance in divinization." Connecting this point to our exploration we have made before, we should note that the pope then adds, "To be like God means to be like the *Trinitarian* God. Therefore, it means to be like Christ cruci-fied. The pedagogy of divinization is necessarily a pedagogy of the Cross" (*Church, Ecumenism, and Politics*, 188). In other words, the life and ministry of our Lord Jesus reveal that authentic *theosis* inevitably comes only by way of *kenosis* and therefore coincides with *Christosis*.

This can all sound quite romantic, and this is why Benedict wishes to emphasize from the start that the process of being conformed to Christ's love will not always *feel* good. Indeed, it often comes at the price of immense and prolonged agony, "the anguish of the Cross" (*Jesus of Nazareth: The In-fancy Narratives*, 86). Yet, to those who find themselves floundering in a world whose narrow horizon is confined to the here and now, Benedict was convinced that the Church had something truly unique and transformative to offer. Specifically, this entails holding up for today's man the noble aspi-ration to become sharers in the divinity of Christ by humbling ourselves to share in his humanity — especially by bearing our share in his cross.

The message that Ratzinger wished to convey is best summarized in these words: "We all thirst for the infinite: for an infinite freedom, for hap-piness without limits. ... Man is not satisfied with solutions beneath the lev-el of divinization" (Address to Catechists and Religion Teachers, December 12, 2000). As Saint Augustine famously wrote the better part of two millen-nia ago, our hearts are restless until they rest in God. Every human person harbors the yearning for an infinite perfection that can only be found in the love of the God in whose image we have all been made. As usual, we find here once again that Benedict's teaching is at bottom nothing new. Indeed, more than anything else, it is a *ressourcement* and an *aggiornamento* — a retrieval of the Church's ancient wisdom, proposed anew for disciples living in the world of today.

Embracing the Gift of Human Nature

One particularly valuable aspect of Benedict's fresh presentation of the Faith lies in how he connects freedom with law in the Church's moral principles. Above all, this is where our present society sees Catholic teaching as retrograde and repressive. Yet, especially here, Benedict was keen to stress that freedom requires law, which "is not the opposite of freedom, but rather its prerequisite" (*Church, Ecumenism, and Politics*, 183). Indeed, he firmly maintains that the absence of obligation does not lead to freedom but rather its destruction (Address to Representatives from the World of Culture in Paris, September 12, 2008). Against the "dictatorship of relativism" that dominates our modern mindset, Benedict proclaimed that truth and freedom belong together, insisting that "constraints are an essential, formal part of human freedom" (*Church, Ecumenism, and Politics*, 182). In short, fidelity to our human nature "requires fidelity to the truth, which alone is the guarantee of freedom" (*Church, Ecumenism, and Politics*, 190; *Caritas in Veritate*, 9; Homily to the College of Cardinals for the Election of the Roman Pontiff, April 18, 2005).

And what is this truth that we must all respect? Broadly speaking, it is the entire Deposit of Faith revealed by God. When it comes to the ethical realm specifically, Benedict teaches that it means the human person has a nature that has been given to him by God. This nature, which is prior to him, is a "fundamental gift" to be received with joy (Homily, April 28, 2013,;in Gänswein, *Who Believes Is Not Alone*, 247). To spell out what it means to respect human nature, the pontiff connects this imperative to the Church's teaching on the need to respect nature more broadly, fulfilling our "duties toward the environment." Building on this vision, the pontiff echoes his predecessor Pope St. John Paul II by stressing the need for something typically absent in secular environmentalism: respect for "human ecology" (*Caritas in Veritate*, 51).

The idea here is fundamentally very simple: If nature is to be respectfully received as a gift from its Creator, then the same goes for human nature. This perspective therefore implies that neither human nature nor the environment more broadly is something to exploit as man sees fit:

> The importance of ecology is no longer disputed. We must listen
> to the language of nature, and we must answer accordingly. Yet I
> would like to underline a point that seems to me to be neglected,
> today as in the past: there is also an ecology of man. *Man too has a*
> *nature that he must respect and that he cannot manipulate at will.* Man
> is not merely self-creating freedom. Man does not create himself.
> He is intellect and will, but he is also nature, and his will is rightly
> ordered if he respects his nature, listens to it, and accepts himself
> for who he is, as one who did not create himself. In this way, and in
> no other, is true human freedom fulfilled." (Address to the Bunde-
> stag, September 22, 2011)

Persuaded that "the book of nature is one and indivisible," Benedict therefore insists that the indiscriminate exploitation of the environment that we
are witnessing today is just part of the picture. Catholicism's doctrine of
human ecology exhorts us to challenge our society's prevailing habit of manipulating human nature according to its whims. Seen in this light, it is not
only harmful to contaminate our waterways, destroy our crops, and disrupt
our local ecosystems — but it is equally detrimental to inflict damage on
man's ecosystem through such practices as artificial contraception, embry-
onic stem cell research, abortion, and gender transition surgery (Christmas
Address to the Roman Curia, 2012).

═══════════ ◆ ═══════════

Building upon our earlier examination of the Trinity, in this chapter we
have delved into some key implications of man's creation in God's image. In
particular, we have considered how Benedict retrieves the traditional vision
of Christ as the True Adam as well as the concepts of *kenosis* and *theosis*. As
we discussed, the pontiff saw the created world mirroring the Trinitarian
dynamic of self-giving, and this outpouring of self he offers as a framework
for understanding how to find meaning in the midst of suffering.

Finally, we considered an important source of affliction for finite rational creatures, the tension that we all experience between our God-given

freedom and the limited dimensions of the divinely bestowed gift of our human nature. Here, too, we witnessed Benedict's emphasis that points of tension and trials afford us opportunities for love, to share in Christ's sacrifice that is alone the medium by which we attain full freedom and happiness. In a word, to become fully human is to be conformed to the definitive Adam, our Lord Jesus Christ. From the perspective of the God who became obedient to death on a cross, Benedict would have us know that the disciplines in the Church that might appear to constrain our freedom are in fact gifts essential to its attainment.

READING LIST
◆ Benedict XVI. Address to the Bundestag. September 22, 2011.
◆ Benedict XVI. Address to Representatives from the World of Culture in Paris. September 12, 2008.
◆ Benedict XVI. *Caritas in Veritate*. Encyclical Letter. 2009.
◆ Benedict XVI. Christmas Address to the Roman Curia. December 21, 2012.
◆ Ramage, Matthew. *The Experiment of Faith: Pope Benedict XVI on Living the Theological Virtues in a Secular Age*. Washington, .C: The Catholic University of America Press, 2020, chapters 2 and 3.
◆ Ratzinger, Joseph. *Church, Ecumenism, and Politics*. San Francisco: Ignatius Press, 2008.
◆ Ratzinger, Joseph. "Concerning the Notion of Person in Theology," *Communio* 17 (1990): 439–54.
◆ Ratzinger, Joseph. "Conscience and Truth." *Communio* 37 (2010): 529–38.
◆ Ratzinger, Joseph. *The Divine Project: Reflections on Creation and the Church*. San Francisco: Ignatius Press, 2023.
◆ Ratzinger, Joseph. "Gratia Praesupponit Natura: Grace Presupposes Nature." In *Dogma and Preaching*, 143–61. San Francisco: Ignatius Press, 2011.
◆ Ratzinger, Joseph. *Introduction to Christianity*. San Francisco: Ignatius Press, 1990.
◆ Ratzinger, Joseph. "Truth and Freedom." *Communio: International Catholic Review* 23, no. 1 (1996): 16–35.

CHAPTER 11

Prayer, Worship, and the Call to Holiness

W e now turn our attention to Benedict's wisdom on another facet of Catholicism that "precedes us" and thus is to be received in gratitude. This is the universal call to holiness, especially through the liturgical worship of the Church, which is singularly capable of elevating modern man's horizon to God. Probing Benedict's captivating teaching on the central importance of the Eucharist, we will also delve into the pontiff's efforts to evangelize our world through the enterprise of authentic liturgical reform. We will discover that Benedict applied his trademark hermeneutic of renewal and reform to the liturgy, which involved embracing the best of both ancient and modern liturgical devotion in the quest to present a new synthesis that is capable of transforming the lives of men and women in our age. As we will discover, Benedict's preeminent ability to penetrate the heart of Catholicism offers a privileged path by which to enter more deeply into the sacred mysteries and to chart a compelling way forward through controversies in the life of the Church today.

Which missal should we be using for the liturgy? What should be its language? What of the direction of prayer? How to receive communion? Benedict has thoughts on all these and many more issues, but the more important point we will discover is that his fundamental principles reveal the proper way to address all of them. Lest we get caught up in the details and lose sight of the end toward which all the liturgy is directed, we will begin by exploring Benedict's wider perspective on prayer and holiness.

Prayer and the Call to Holiness in the Simplicity of Ordinary Life

Liturgy — the celebration of divine worship, and in particular the Mass — is the preeminent instance of prayer in Catholicism. It is the Church's participation in Christ's own life and work in which our pursuit of holiness finds its source and summit (CCC 1069–73). Yet, for many, a fundamental obstacle presents itself when we begin to think about the life of holiness and prayer more generally. The concept of "the spiritual life" can be rather vague, evoking images of a disembodied existence detached from the nitty gritty affairs of daily life. Indeed, when we hear talk of holiness, it is common to think of it as something lofty that primarily takes place in a chapel and not out in the world. Without discounting the value of liturgy, which we will return to shortly, we will first discover that Benedict's understanding of holiness is applicable everywhere and at all times. It also flows directly from his thoughts that we explored in the last chapter.

In his characteristic down-to-earth manner, Benedict poses the question without hesitation: What does sanctity mean in the first place? The pontiff's answer, informed by the words of the Second Vatican Council, is straightforward: "Christian holiness is nothing other than charity lived to the full" (General Audience, April 13, 2011). If even this language sounds too solemn or formal, the pope suggests that we might frame the question slightly differently. As ever, he gets to the heart of the matter: What really is essential to holiness, to living Christian spirituality in our world?

> The essential means never leaving a Sunday without an encounter
> with the Risen Christ in the Eucharist. ... It means never begin-
> ning and never ending a day without at least a brief contact with
> God. And, on the path of our life it means following the "signposts"
> that God has communicated to us in the Ten Commandments, in-
> terpreted with Christ, which are merely the explanation of what
> love is in specific situations. (General Audience, April 13, 2011)

The pontiff's perspective on sanctity is concise and simple, something that
every human being can live realistically. We encounter the risen Lord every
Sunday, we take time to meet him at the beginning and end of each day, and
we follow his commandments. These uncomplicated practices are simply
"forms of charity," habits by which to live as Christ in specific situations.

While emphasizing the importance of the commandments, Benedict
adds that continual reliance on the law is not necessary for the person who
loves to the full. As Augustine has it, *Dilige et fac quod vis*: Love and do
what you will. Far from claiming that noble intentions suffice to justify
our actions, this classic statement speaks to the great freedom that comes
when we pursue a life of holiness. Christians need not be discouraged if
our actions sometimes fail to adhere precisely to the letter of the law, for
we know that sometimes we are going to be wrong. Yet, this is no excuse
for moral laxity. When we discover our error, we repent and seek to amend
our lives in the continued quest to live in ever greater conformity with the
love of Jesus Christ.

Is a life lived completely in love even possible? Benedict follows up
with a resolutely affirmative response to this question. His answer derives
not from theoretical speculations but from the experience of real people:
the saints. By their lives, the saints (*sancti* in Latin means "holy ones") declare that it is indeed possible to walk the path of holiness. And, yet, the
prospect that we might manage to successfully emulate a legend like Padre
Pio or Mother Teresa can sound daunting, if not downright ludicrous.

Anticipating this concern, Benedict clarifies that the "saints" he has in
mind are not merely the canonized men and women of history. Sanctity is

not reserved exclusively for those who have worked miracles, experienced extraordinary mystical phenomena, or won the Nobel Peace Prize. Who is it that this humble soul from Bavaria considers the most important witnesses of faith?

> Actually, I must say that also for my personal faith many saints, not all, are true stars in the firmament of history. And I would like to add that for me not only a few great saints whom I love and whom I know well are "signposts," but precisely also the simple saints, that is, the good people I see in my life who will never be canonized. They are ordinary people, so to speak, without visible heroism but in their everyday goodness I see the truth of faith. This goodness, which they have developed in the faith of the Church, is for me the most reliable apology of Christianity and the sign of where the truth lies. (General Audience, April 13, 2011)

Conformity to Christ: Divine Adoption and Divinization

With his commonsense approach to holiness, Benedict was mindful that many modern people have trouble seeing the relevance of the great mystics from the Church's past. Cognizant of this difficulty, the pope posed the following question point-blank in a catechesis on the life of St. John of the Cross: Does this saint have anything to say to the ordinary Christian today, or is Saint John just a model for a few elect souls?

To arrive at an answer, Benedict urges us to bear in mind that John's existential journey was anything but a "float on mystical clouds." This saint had an incredibly hard life. As a religious reformer, John came under such opposition that he was imprisoned and abused both physically and mentally by his own confreres. So what is it that Benedict wanted to highlight about this saint's doctrine of the spiritual life? For John, the audacious end game of spiritual perfection is *theosis*, or *divinization* — the transformation of the creature into God. Long before him, a veritable host of Church Fathers wrote on this topic. As Saint Athanasius famously put it, the Son of God became man so that the sons of men might become God. In the words of St. Maximus the Confessor, by a "blessed inversion" God became man through hominization, in order that we may be made

God by divinization.

This, indeed, is what Benedict identifies as "the essence of God's will": that we be drawn out of ourselves and into Christ's divine nature so that the entire cosmos may in turn be drawn to him (General Audience, December 5, 2012). He elsewhere described divinization as the "mutual compenetration between Christ and the Christian," whereby we are immersed in Christ and he dwells in us (General Audience, November 8, 2006). However, to steer us clear of a possible misunderstanding, the pope clarified that *theosis* does not lead us to become absorbed into a divine abyss. In contrast with many other religious traditions, the Christian doctrine of divinization upholds the distinction between man and God. As creatures united with God, we never lose our individuality. The person nuptially conjoined to Christ remains distinct from him in the same way that two spouses become "one flesh" even as each retains his or her identity.

Put differently, for the ancient doctors becoming by grace what Christ is by nature meant becoming adopted children of God, or "sons in the Son" (see Rom 8:14–17; Gal 4:4–7; General Audience, May 23, 2012). Importantly, by the death and resurrection of Jesus Christ, we are ennobled to become God's adopted sons and daughters. In other words, it is through the will and testament of Our Lord transferred upon his death that we inherit all that he has, with every right and privilege pertaining thereto. Divinization, then, can also be called *Christification*. In Pauline language, it occurs to the extent that we enter into Christ's way of inhabiting the world, imitating Jesus not only in his life but also in his manner of death. It means letting ourselves be "crucified with Christ" so as to rise with him (Rom 6:3–11). Like the quest for holiness in general, this is a very simple doctrine and achievable by everyone, but by no means is it easy. Conformity to Christ does not just happen. For this journey, the requirements are constant vigilance, perseverance, and the humility to get back up when we find ourselves desperately in need of divine mercy.

A vivid analogy from St. John of Damascus illumines this reality. Just as the red-hot iron takes on the properties of fire when it is plunged into a raging pyre, so the human who participates in God takes on his very wisdom, love, and life. The creature is not simply equivalent to God in this analogy. In "becoming fire," the iron is not identical to that in which it is enveloped. The two are distinct, yet not separate. Similarly, the divinized person is distinct but not separate from God — at least so long as he or she perseveres in God's grace. The oneness of the human person with God, then, is best understood not in terms of the solitary atom but rather in light of the higher form of unity that we know as *relationship* (General Audience, May 6, 2009).

With all this talk of becoming God, have the Church Fathers perhaps strayed too far afield from the word of God with its constant stress on man's creaturehood? Benedict's teaching here is crucial. As with every other Catholic dogma, the Church's belief in man's sublime calling "is by definition nothing other than an interpretation of Scripture ... which has sprung from the faith over the centuries" ("Crisis in Catechesis," 8). Among the many biblical texts that point to man's divinization, we can easily recall 2 Peter 1:3–4 (we are called to "become partakers of the divine nature"), 1 John 3:1–3 ("when he appears we shall be like him, for we shall see him as he is"), Ephesians 3:19 (a prayer that we will "be filled with all the fullness of God"), and 1 Corinthians 15:28 (God will one day be "all in all"). Alongside Scripture, the liturgy also offers an unrivaled treasury of insight into the reality of divinization. Among the many prayers that revolve around the hope for *theosis*, the words of the offertory rite stand out. Pouring water into the chalice, the liturgy presents us with this daring petition: "By the mystery of this water and wine may we come to share in the divinity of Christ who humbled himself to share in our humanity."

Yet, majestic as the goal of divinization may be, it never hurts to recall that the way we get there is in many ways quite mundane. It doesn't require the ability to cite the Bible by chapter and verse. Nor is it a club for those who have the leisure to spend extensive hours in the chapel or those who have completed some Herculean task. According to Benedict, "purification and inner self-emptying" are the fundamental requirements "to be transformed into God" (General Audience, February 16, 2011). While the pontiff certainly praises devotional practices such as the Rosary and Eucharistic adoration, he wants us to understand above all that a life of sanctity is very simple — something that anybody of any time, place, or circumstance can achieve.

Praying with Scripture: *Lectio Divina*

The preceding sketch makes it evident that Benedict's conception of the spiritual life is not complicated. The pontiff encourages us to focus our attention on finding God in the ordinary events of life, and he stresses that this enterprise of charity is a virtue achievable by all. At the same time, he underscored the crucial importance of concrete devotional practices, among which prayer with Scripture holds pride of place.

In particular, Benedict's multivolume body of catechetical works on the wisdom of the saints are a tour de force of how to interpret the Bible according to its fourfold sense. As we have seen in this book, the pontiff dedicated a significant portion of his work to helping Christians discover the meaning of Scripture's literal sense, the meaning that the sacred author intended to convey to his original audience. However, an attentive engagement with Benedict's writings makes it clear that he was equally concerned with leading the faithful into a personal encounter with Christ through Scripture's spiritual sense. Toward this end, Benedict strongly advocated for a retrieval of the ancient Church's spiritual discipline known as *lectio divina* or "divine reading."

In a striking move, the pontiff set aside time in his apostolic exhortation on the word of God to offer a tangible demonstration of how to carry out the key steps of *lectio*. Though these stages admit of some variation in the thoughts of Catholic spiritual masters across the centuries, they essentially boil down to five. We begin our prayer with *lectio* itself, the reading of a text with an eye toward determining the content of its literal sense. Next comes *meditatio*, in which we "chew" on a passage to ascertain its meaning. Along the way, we are to bear in mind *oratio*, in which we take time to converse with the Lord and respond to his word. Fourth comes *contemplatio*, where we step back to embrace our divine Beloved in silent communion. Finally, Benedict echoes the wisdom of the great doctor St. Francis de Sales when he insists that our prayer should ultimately translate into *actio*. In other words, we conclude by asking God what kind of concrete conversion of life or practical resolution he wants us to carry out (*Verbum Domini*, 86–87). Of course, the pope was aware that prayer is not ultimately a collection of procedures, and he considers these traditional steps as guidelines rather than hard and fast rules. Even so, they go a long way toward capturing the essence of Christian prayer and how each of us can make it a vibrant habit in any season of life.

We should note that these descriptions could easily be amplified or approached from different angles. For example, in his catechesis on St. Anthony of Padua, the pontiff mentions that the first step of prayer should really be *obsecratio*. Echoing the way our other relationships work, we place ourselves in the Lord's presence before beginning to talk to or read about him. In Saint Anthony's schema, this initial step is followed by *oratio*, the affectionate dialogue between our soul and God. Last but not least, he discusses the *postulatio*, in which we place our needs before God, and *gratiarum actio*, where we thank God for all the benefits we have received from him.

As the reader begins to see, the number of steps to *lectio* can easily add up to eight or more. But, here again, we must remember that Benedict is offering these steps as a means to simplify our lives, not complicate them. The pope's overarching concern is that Christians develop the habit of reading the Scriptures with a prayerful disposition, which alone makes the engagement transformative. No matter what form it ends up taking at any given time in our lives, the aim of Christian prayer is to give ourselves "increasingly to the hands of God, with trust and love, certain that in the end it is only by doing his will that we are truly happy" (General Audience, August 17, 2011).

As a final matter related to *lectio*, it is worth mentioning that Benedict saw this as something that we should be practicing within the liturgy itself. This pontiff was especially persuaded that worthy liturgical celebration involves prayer that is punctuated with periodic moments of meditative silence. Pauses at opportune moments — such as after the homily or during the offertory — make it possible for our liturgical worship to turn into a conversation with God. After hearing Scripture proclaimed in the Liturgy of the Word, he taught that we are called to offer a response to the Almighty. Put differently, the sacred liturgy offers us God's words, and our task is to attune ourselves to them and make them our own. To drive home this point, the pope cited a favorite line from the Rule of his patron St. Benedict of Nursia, stressing that the words offered by Mother Church in the liturgy gradually train our minds to accord with our voice (*mens concordet voci*).

Liturgy Grants Us a Share in Heaven Even Now

If Benedict emphasizes the need for routine meditation on the word of God, then there is something else about seeking holiness whose importance the pontiff even more emphatically accentuated. This is no private devotion but the very prayer of the Catholic Church herself: sacred liturgy. As Benedict said in an audience dedicated to the subject, the Church's public prayer is "a privileged context in which God speaks to each one of us, here and now, and awaits our answer" (General Audience, September 26, 2012). This is in line with the teaching of the Second Vatican Council, which described the Eucharistic Sacrifice as the "source and summit of the whole Christian life" (*Lumen Gentium*, 11).

In his book dedicated to recovering the heart of Christian worship, Cardinal Ratzinger identified worship as essential for human flourishing. He even went so far as to affirm that the very purpose of the creation of the world was to provide creatures with a space for divine adoration. In this connection, Ratzinger memorably suggested that we think of liturgy in terms of "play." By this concept, he did not mean to characterize liturgy as a mere performance, but rather "an oasis of freedom" in which humans participate for the sake of the thing itself and not for some ulterior end. For Benedict, the importance of worship is that it takes us beyond everyday life with its inevitable pragmatic concerns. Yet, in keeping with Benedict's metaphor, we might say that there is an eminently "practical" upshot of the Church's divine worship, for it is a dress rehearsal for eternity. But, as all analogies must ultimately fall short of reality, there is a pivotal distinction to be made here. In the liturgy, we are not merely *anticipating* heaven, for at Holy Mass *we are present there*. Indeed, a cornerstone of Ratzinger's liturgical theology is his profession that the Church's worship grants us even now "a share of heaven's mode of existence in the world" (*Spirit of the Liturgy*, 21).

A running theme across Benedict's writings was his fascination with the reality that Jesus Christ comes in glory to his people on earth every single day even now. Without abandoning the expectation of Christ's definitive return at the end of time, this perspective holds that there is another coming between his incarnation in the flesh and his *parousia* in the eschaton. Following the language of St. Bernard of Clairvaux, this is what Benedict calls the *adventus medius,* Our Lord's "middle coming." Jesus' presence in today's world occurs through a variety of modes. He comes through his word in Scripture, and he enters into the events of our lives. Above all, though, Benedict underscores his coming "in the sacraments, especially in the most Holy Eucharist" (*Jesus of Nazareth: Holy Week,* 291). This dynamic is perhaps captured best in Ratzinger's book dedicated to the Last Things, where he writes of Christ's glorious return:

> The cosmic imagery of the New Testament cannot be used as a source for the description of a future chain of cosmic events. All attempts of this kind are misplaced. Instead, these texts form part of a description of the mystery of the Parousia in the language of liturgical tradition. ... The Parousia is the highest intensification and fulfillment of the Liturgy. And the Liturgy is Parousia, an event taking place in our midst. (*Eschatology,* 202–03, emphasis added)

In this light, the plea of the Spirit and the Bride "Come, Lord Jesus!" (Rv 22:20) were not only meant for those early Christians who anticipated an impending martyrdom or the imminent destruction of the physical universe. On the contrary, this petition may equally be prayed by every believer who is blessed to partake in the marriage supper of the Lamb (see Rv 19:7–9).

As we hear in one of Benedict's final papal audiences, Jesus' repeated proclamation that he is coming soon "does not only indicate the future prospect at the end of time but also that of the present" (Rv 22:7–12; *A School of Prayer,* 270). Along these lines, the emeritus pontiff wrote in one of his last essays that the bread and wine consecrated at Mass "are no longer created realities of this world that consist in themselves, but rather are bearers of the mysteriously real form of the risen Lord" ("The Meaning of Communion," in *What Is Christianity?,* 156–57). An unexpected gift published only after his death, this text reveals Benedict's constant preoccupation with the eschatological dimension of Eucharistic communion. In other words, our reception of the Holy Eucharist does even more than take us up into the reality of Christ's death on Good Friday, for the sacrament of sacraments is the same *risen* body of Christ who came back from the dead on Easter Sunday.

Worship As a Corporate Act

The liturgy's primary end is rooted in its vertical dimension, characterized by its divinizing power that we have just discussed. However, Benedict also emphasized that our worship has a profoundly human or horizontal element. Liturgy not only unites us to God but by virtue of that union also incorporates us into Christ's mystical body, the entire communion of saints who share in his sacrifice. The classic formulation of this truth is found in Saint Paul's words, "We who are many are one body, for we all partake of the one bread" (1 Cor 10:17). It is also captured well in musical form, as exemplified in the hymn "Lord, Who at Thy First Eucharist," where our prayers find expression in the supplication, "O may we all one bread, one body be, / through this blest Sacrament of Unity." For Catholics, then, the Christian spiritual life is not a disembodied, esoteric affair that occurs "just between me and Jesus." Certainly, we are meant to experience a profound intimacy with the ineffable Triune God, yet Scripture maintains that this is not possible without the love of our brothers and sisters (see 1 Jn 4:20). In this, as in other areas, Christian spirituality is a balancing act. The liturgy is Christ's sacrifice, but it is also a communal meal. It is about my soul's relationship with God, but it also concerns my relationship with other believers, the entire human race, and by extension all creation.

On the subject of liturgy's horizontal dimension, Benedict highlighted one particular point time and time again. Like the deposit of faith as a whole, the liturgy is a gift of God. It is prior to us and greater than us — not something that we have created in our own image (*Spirit of the Liturgy*, 165). As the faithful, our job is therefore to enter into its rhythms handed on to us by the Catholic tradition, remembering that worship is above all about *God*. In this connection, a notable feature of Benedict's liturgical theology is his rejection of the widespread trend in which liturgy becomes a matter of "do-as-you-please." Much as we might be convinced that our views about the right way to worship represent God's desired approach, this pontiff constantly reminded us that worship is not about our own preferences. Drawing a powerful lesson from the Golden Calf episode (see Ex 32), he warned the faithful against turning their prayer into a "closed circle":

> The worship of the golden calf is a self-generated cult. When Moses stays away for too long, and God himself becomes inaccessible, the people just fetch him back. Worship becomes a feast that the community gives itself, a festival of self-affirmation. Instead of being worship of God, it becomes a circle closed in on itself: eating, drinking, and making merry. The dance around the golden calf is an image of this self-seeking worship. It is a kind of banal self-gratification. The narrative of the golden calf is a warning about any kind of self-initiated and self-seeking worship. Ultimately, it is no longer concerned with God but with giving oneself a nice little alternative world, manufactured from one's own resources. Then liturgy really does become pointless, just fooling around. Or still worse it becomes an apostasy from the living God, an apostasy in sacral disguise. *(Spirit of the Liturgy, 21–23)*

We must be on guard against making liturgy into an idol that turns our direction inward and serves merely to reinforce our preconceived notions about the way things must be. As this pontiff saw it, liturgy's role is the same as that of God's word and of prayer in general: to call us out of ourselves into an ever-greater gift of self in imitation of him who laid down his life for us (General Audience, October 3, 2012).

Central to Benedict's liturgical spirituality is another conviction that permeates his approach to all the other topics explored in this book. This is the belief that the life of the Church allows for a legitimate degree of freedom within defined limits. Indeed, for this humble servant of the servants of God, the key to navigating challenges in the Church is to cultivate "mobility in small things and firmness in the essentials" (Abbot Dom Louis Blanc of Triors, February 2, 2022). In this way, Benedict reaffirms the wise prescription of St. John XXIII and Saint Augustine long before him: "In essentials, unity; in doubtful matters, liberty; in all things, charity" (John XXIII, *Ad Petri Cathedram*, 83).

This foundational principle was the guiding force behind Benedict's 2007 *motu proprio* in which he advocated for the integration of the best elements from both ancient and modern liturgical practices. Seeking to broaden the range of liturgical practice that had been narrowed since the restriction of the Church's 1969 missal, Benedict championed an embrace of the "two usages of the one Roman rite" (*Summorum Pontificum*, 1). These he referred to as its "ordinary expression" (the *Novus Ordo* that most Roman parishes have been celebrating for the past several decades) and its "extraordinary expression" (known popularly as the "Traditional Latin Mass" or "Tridentine Mass," the liturgy approved by the Council of Trent in 1570).

The pontiff's language here is precise and significant. Benedict sought to showcase the catholicity of the Church by making her older liturgy more accessible than it had been in prior decades. Yet, at the same time, his identification of the *Novus Ordo* as the "ordinary expression" of the Roman rite sent another unmistakable signal. To those who would doubt the validity of the missal approved by Pope St. Paul VI, this pope wished to underscore that this form of worship is just as valid as the liturgy approved by Rome five centuries prior. On this front, many decades ago Ratzinger had already witnessed the seeds of ecclesial division and mistrust that have become so widespread today. Addressing those whose love of the Tridentine Mass had caused them to reject the *Novus Ordo*, this serene theologian provided the following analysis:

There is a passion of suspicions, the animosity of which is far from the spirit of the Gospel. There is an obsession with the letter that regards the liturgy of the Church as invalid and thus puts itself outside the Church. It is forgotten here that the validity of the liturgy depends primarily, not on specific words, but on the community of the Church; under the pretext of Catholicism, the very principle of Catholicism is denied.

In the end, Ratzinger concluded that renewal in the Church is only indirectly related to having the right texts and organizations. While these are by no means irrelevant, he maintained that the real key is of a different kind — namely, "whether there are individuals — saints — who, by their personal willingness, which cannot be forced, are ready to effect something new and living" (*Principles of Catholic Theology*, 377).

This pope's decision to open the way for a wider use of the Roman rite's more ancient expression was just one of the many ways that he sought to promote a vibrant unity amid variety in the Church. In this respect, the reader may have noticed that Benedict's appeal for a mutual enrichment of the old and the new is not unlike his call for a rapprochement between time-honored and contemporary forms of biblical interpretation. As in the case of biblical scholarship, Ratzinger appreciated that ancient and modern expressions of worship both have their distinctive strengths.

For example, Benedict sought to reinforce the Second Vatican Council's stance on the centrality of the Latin tongue in the liturgy of the West (*Sacrosanctum Concilium*, 36, 54). Toward this end, he suggested that a renewed appreciation for this language could introduce another dimension of beauty to our worship while also showcasing its continuity with the ancient tradition of the Church. Similarly, even as Benedict's public papal liturgies were celebrated "versus populum" with a crucifix on the altar facing the priest, he advocated for a rediscovery of the theological richness underlying the Church's normative worship *ad orientem* ("facing East"). In this regard, he was keenly aware that this enterprise requires dispelling the widespread misconception that the priest praying to Christ in the same direction of the laity at pivotal junctures in Mass is equivalent to him "turning his back against the people."

Even in retirement, Benedict continued to remain concerned with the question of liturgical prayer's physical orientation. Notably, the emeritus pontiff sought to illumine the rationale for *ad orientem* liturgical celebration in one of the final remarks he ever penned on the liturgy. Why is it fitting that the clergy and laity face each other only at certain points during the liturgy rather than for the duration of Mass? The reasons for this are many, explains Benedict. For example, by tradition both people and priest collectively face East because from antiquity the East has been "a cosmic symbol" for the coming of the Lord, the Sun of Justice. While this is part of the explanation, one rationale above all stood out to Benedict as a fitting basis for the traditional practice of priest and faithful facing the same direction when addressing God: "After all," he explained, "priest and people pray, not to each other, but to the one Lord" ("On the Inaugural Volume of My Collected Works," xvii).

Along the same lines, Benedict offered words of correction and counsel to those who have deep affection for the Tridentine liturgy. On this score, the pontiff echoed the Second Vatican Council by emphasizing the advantages of being able to celebrate Mass in the language of the people (English, Spanish, etc.). Alongside other key features of more recent liturgical revival, the pontiff regarded the audible participation of the faithful in liturgical prayers as a practice that aligns well with the Church's most ancient practices, and he saw it as an avenue to foster genuine "active participation" in the Mass today. Additionally, Benedict lauded the more abundant offering from the treasury of Sacred Scripture made accessible to the faithful in the *Novus Ordo* liturgical cycle. All the while, the pontiff not only imparted these principles but also demonstrated by his reverent celebrations that the liturgical practices authored by Paul VI are a valid and nurturing expression of the one Roman rite. Indeed, the way Benedict put his theology into practice in the celebration of the ordinary form of the Roman rite offered incontrovertible proof that "intelligibility does not mean banality" (Meeting with the Clergy of Rome, February 14, 2013).

And this, by definition, is to speak only of *Roman* Catholicism. Benedict was of course a Roman Catholic, as most Catholics worldwide are. Yet, he never tired of informing those unfamiliar with traditions outside their own that there is more to the Catholic Church than Rome. As Cardinal Ratzinger explained at length, the universal Church is blessed with an abundance of ancient rites that profess the Faith in communion with the Roman pontiff. A historical consequence of the apostles' dissemination of the one Gospel to the four corners of the earth, each of these practical liturgical arrangements manifests the splendor of Christ in its own unique way (*Spirit of the Liturgy*, 159–70). From the Byzantine to the Maronite to the Syro-Malabar and beyond, in these traditions we find unique customs, spiritualities, juridical structures, and ways of doing theology. Each also has its own musical and artistic patrimony that emerged from the inculturation of the Gospel into each of the world's myriad cultures. Taken together, these manifestations of the Church's faith offer a full taste of the Church's venerable heritage and allow the catholicity of the Church to shine resplendently. Consistent with the Second Vatican Council's declaration on the Eastern rites, Benedict encouraged the revival of these time-honored liturgical forms, steering clear of any intent to absorb them into the Roman rite.

Ratzinger regularly emphasized the very modest level of ingenuity required for liturgical renewal. Simply put, he taught that "the primary way to foster the participation of the People of God in the sacred rite is the proper celebration of the rite itself." Crucially, this pope underscored that the *ars celebrandi*, or "art of celebration," does not require creative ingenuity on the part of the clergy. On the contrary, he maintained that it is "the fruit of faithful adherence to the liturgical norms in all their richness" (*Sacramentum Caritatis*, 38). As ever, the Bavarian pontiff's answers to theological and pastoral problems are at bottom very simple and unifying. Somehow, Benedict always managed to take the best of the old and the new, threading the needle between ideological extremes that hinder so many from grasping the profound breadth and depth of the Catholic tradition.

Combating misguided currents that try to involve the laity at Mass by dumbing it down, Benedict believed that the path to renewal lies in mining the treasury of resources that the Church already has at her disposal. Take sacred music, for example. In the decades since Vatican II, it became increasingly evident that the council's call for the use of solemn liturgical music — especially Gregorian Chant and the use of the organ — had been almost entirely neglected in most ordinary parishes ("Music and Liturgy," in *What Is Christianity?*, 48; *Sacrosanctum Concilium*, 114). Whereas many view this as a matter of taste, Benedict knew that not all song is created equal, and he considered genuinely Christian music crucial for the evangelization of culture. As the emeritus pope divulged in *What is Christianity?*:

> The great and pure response of Western music developed in the encounter with the God who, in the liturgy, makes himself present to us in Jesus Christ. That music, for me, is a proof of the truth of Christianity. Where a response develops in this way, the encounter with the truth has occurred, with the true Creator of the world. For this reason, great sacred music is a reality of theological rank and of permanent significance for the faith of all Christendom, even though it is not at all necessary for it to be performed always

and everywhere. On the other hand, though, it is also clear that it cannot disappear from the liturgy and that its presence can be an altogether special way of participating in the sacred celebration, in the mystery of faith. (49–50)

As is evident throughout his body of work, by this the pontiff did not have in mind any sort of music whatsoever. "As far as the liturgy is concerned," he declared, "we cannot say that one song is as good as another." Rather, he stressed that everything in the liturgy — including texts, music, and execution — "ought to correspond to the meaning of the mystery being celebrated" (*Sacramentum Caritatis*, 42).

To be sure, Benedict affirmed the importance of faithfulness in other liturgical matters, especially a solid, biblically informed homily. However, above all he taught that "the best catechesis on the Eucharist is the Eucharist itself, celebrated well" (*Sacramentum Caritatis*, 64). Whether it takes place on the altar of a humble country church or in a majestic Gothic cathedral, the proper celebration of the Mass is a testimony to the splendor of Jesus Christ. And beauty, Benedict maintained, is "not mere decoration, but rather an essential element of the liturgical action, since it is an attribute of God himself and his revelation" (*Sacramentum Caritatis*, 35). Once again, however, nothing elaborate is required for splendid liturgy. Like knowing Jesus, praying with authenticity, and grasping the Trinitarian heart of Christianity, it is accessible to the faithful, provided we submit ourselves in love to the truths and practices bequeathed to us by Mother Church. Authentic liturgy is therefore celebrated by any priest who reverently follows the rubrics entrusted to him by Holy Mother Church.

In summary, Benedict was adamant that the immense riches of the Church's liturgy should be opened more widely to everyone, and that this must be done with great urgency. As the emeritus pontiff accentuated as he neared the end of his earthly pilgrimage, to prioritize liturgy in our lives is to proclaim the primacy of God. God always comes first ("On the Inaugural Volume of My Collected Works," xv). The importance of this point cannot be stressed enough. It appears even in the pontiff's final writings, where he observes that it has become "increasingly clear that the existence of the Church is vitally dependent on the correct celebration of the liturgy and that the Church is in danger when the primacy of God no longer appears in the liturgy."

Persuaded that the renewal of our liturgy is "a fundamental prerequisite for the renewal of the Church," Benedict urged an examination of conscience in which the clergy and faithful alike reflect on whether we ourselves have contributed to "the eclipse of God's priority in the liturgy." Not content merely to criticize, Benedict then identified how each of us can respond to liturgical renewal in a way that accords with our specific vocation. Pointing to his patron St. Benedict of Nursia, the Bavarian pontiff taught that we all must learn how to live this master's Rule in our particular circumstances. Even those of us without a monastic calling must learn to imitate the readiness of the consecrated brother as he hears the ringing of the bell calling him to prayer. Saint Benedict said that the monk is to "leave whatever he may have in hand and make great haste, but with due gravity." As we face myriad temptations and distractions, the pope's point is that we too must learn again to prioritize liturgical prayer in the daily rhythm of our lives ("Theology of the Liturgy," in *What Is Christianity?*, 53).

The essence of Benedict's thought on liturgy and the life of holiness can be summarized as follows: Holiness is love grounded in our encounter with Christ in prayer and the Eucharist. Benedict places a special emphasis on the sublime telos of the Christian life, which the Church's ancient faith identifies as divine adoption and divinization. To guide us in our passage toward union with God, the pope highlighted the importance of prayer with Scripture. Indeed, he felt so strongly about this that he took the unusually concrete step of walking the faithful through the steps of *lectio divina*.

Above all, this pontiff underscored the unrivaled importance of Sacred Liturgy. The Church's worship grants us a share of heaven on earth, uniting believers with Jesus himself while simultaneously incorporating us into the mystical body of his Church. In the quest to impart renewed vigor to the faith of Catholics, Benedict promoted a balanced approach to the Church's liturgical practices, calling for unity amid variety while emphasizing the evangelizing power of simple gestures, including adhering to the Church's liturgical norms. With this eminently sensible approach, this pope offers a corrective to the errors found on both extremes in our present culture. In so doing, he provides us with a path toward unity amid the great division that characterizes the experience of so many believers today. As the emeritus pontiff wisely reminded us in his final years, many of the issues that divide us today do not merit the consternation to which they give rise. In the end, the emeritus pontiff identified even the dear question of the proper direction of liturgical prayer as "actually only a detail." When delving into the subject of liturgical worship, Benedict always kept his eyes on "the essential purpose" of the investigation, which he said "was to go beyond the often petty questions about one form or another and to place liturgy in its larger context" ("On the Inaugural Volume of My Collected Works," xvii).

In the final analysis, Benedict's theology reminds us that the Church's worship, just like the word and laws of Our Lord, is a gift from the Almighty that cannot be subordinated to our personal preferences. Thanks be to God, Jesus entrusted the Magisterium with the responsibility of safeguarding the treasury of his wisdom throughout the ages. Through his Church, Christ ensures that the riches of Christianity are within reach for all who would boldly follow in his footsteps.

READING LIST

♦ Benedict XVI. *Church Fathers: From Clement of Rome to Augustine.* San Francisco: Ignatius Press, 2017.
♦ Benedict XVI. *Church Fathers and Teachers: From Saint Leo the Great to Peter Lombard.* San Francisco: Ignatius Press, 2010.
♦ Benedict XVI. *Holy Men and Women of the Middle Ages and Beyond.* San Francisco: Ignatius Press, 2012.
♦ Benedict XVI. *Jesus, the Apostles, and the Early Church.* San Francisco: Ignatius Press, 2012.
♦ Benedict XVI. *Sacramentum Caritatis.* Apostolic Exhortation. February 22, 2007.
♦ Benedict XVI. *A School of Prayer: The Saints Show Us How to Pray.* San Francisco: Ignatius Press, 2012.
♦ Benedict XVI. *St. Paul.* San Francisco: Ignatius Press, 2009.

◆ Benedict XVI. *Summorum Pontificum*. Motu Proprio. July 7, 2007.
◆ Ramage, Matthew. *The Experiment of Faith: Pope Benedict XVI on Living the Theological Virtues in a Secular Age*. Washington, DC: The Catholic University of America Press, 2020, chapter 2.
◆ Ratzinger, Joseph. "Crisis in Catechesis." *Canadian Catholic Review* 7 (1983): 7–9 at 8.
◆ Ratzinger, Joseph. *Feast of Faith: Approaches to a Theology of the Liturgy*. San Francisco: Ignatius Press, 1986.
◆ Ratzinger, Joseph. *God Is Near Us: The Eucharist, the Heart of Life*. San Francisco: Ignatius Press, 2013.
◆ Ratzinger, Joseph. *Images of Hope: Meditations on Major Feasts*. San Francisco: Ignatius Press, 2006.
◆ Ratzinger, Joseph. *The Spirit of the Liturgy*. San Francisco: Ignatius Press, 2000.
◆ Ratzinger, Joseph. *Theology of the Liturgy: The Sacramental Foundation of Christian Existence*. San Francisco: Ignatius Press, 2014.

CHAPTER 12
The Church in the Public Square

As we have just witnessed, divine worship was one of several subjects that remained a central focus of Joseph Ratzinger throughout his long and distinguished service in the Church. It would be difficult to imagine a topic closer to his heart, but there is another that Benedict arguably considered equally fundamental. This subject is a fitting place to conclude our exploration, for it underpins his entire body of work — namely, what precisely is it that drives Christian belief and guarantees its truth? Reflecting on why he became a theologian so many decades prior, the emeritus pontiff explained that he yearned above all to go to the heart of the matter, which is this: Why do we believe? ("On the Inaugural Volume of My Collected Works," xvi).

As this book nears its conclusion, we too will now ask a question of Benedict. After examining all the challenging subjects that he considered over the course of his ministry, what is it that he thinks would lead someone today to commit to following Jesus Christ in the bosom of the Catholic Church? In reply to this question, the pontiff repeatedly pointed to two realities that he considered privileged manifestations of Catholicism's truth: "I have often affirmed my conviction that the true apology of Christian faith, the most convincing demonstration of its truth against every denial, are the saints, and the beauty that the faith has generated. Today, for faith to grow, we must lead ourselves and the persons we meet to encounter the saints and to enter into contact with the Beautiful" ("The Feeling of Things, the Contemplation of Beauty"). In this chapter, we will delve into this pivotal assertion, pinpointing specific areas where Benedict desired the Church to advance her ministry of evangelization.

In the course of this exploration, we will have an opportunity to observe once again this pontiff's singular effectiveness as an evangelist, which arose from his capacity to get to the essence of things and navigate the narrow path between opposing extremes that push people away from the Church. As we know by now, Benedict was thoroughly persuaded of the biblical revelation that human fulfillment ultimately comes only from knowing the love of Christ crucified. At the same time, we will examine how he followed in the footsteps of the ancient Church by recognizing that the fruitful dissemination of the Gospel requires us to meet people where they are. In the case of those who already follow a religious tradition, this entails showing how the Gospel completes what is good in their pursuit of the divine. Further, it means honoring others' dignity so that our encounter with them is an opportunity to refine and mature our own faith. As for the increasingly large number of those in our society who no longer practice religion, Benedict believes that the same logic applies. The pontiff was convinced that reaching these individuals will require the Church to rediscover her own essence and to demonstrate that, in the cross of Christ Jesus, she has an immeasurably precious gift to offer that the world cannot give.

Beauty That Inspires Conversion

In this book, we have observed that Benedict's theology places particular emphasis on the all-encompassing nature of the Catholic religion. Authentic faith is no mere intellectual affair. In this connection, he often emphasized that the *via pulchritudinis*, or way of beauty, is "a privileged and fascinating path" to the knowledge of the ineffable Triune God (General Audience, November 18, 2009). Why is it that beauty holds such sway over us? The reason, Benedict maintains, is that it speaks a universal language that is uniquely capable of reaching every human being — including those individuals who would not otherwise be open to hearing the Gospel proclaimed directly. Whether it be painting, iconography, architecture, sculpture, music, film, or literature, the pontiff looked to the history of the Church and recognized that her art has always been a vital channel for the communication of the Gospel. As one contemplates these sources of art, the pope maintained, it becomes evident that "some artistic expressions are real highways to God, the supreme Beauty" (General Audience, August 31, 2011).

To grasp Benedict's point, we might consider such wonders as a beautiful sunset, the little hands and feet of a newborn child, an Easter vigil celebrated with devotion, Gregorian chant at a papal Mass at Pentecost, or the smile of Mother Teresa. Benedict recognized a specific feature that unites all these manifestations of beauty. In their respective ways, each is capable of fostering a "pedagogy of desire" in the heart of man. That is to say, they represent avenues by which believers and unbelievers alike can learn to seek that which is above and to recover the taste of authentic joy in our lives.

In a vivid analogy, the pontiff taught that these encounters with God's reflection on earth serve as a spiritual inoculation, "producing antibodies" against the unhealthy caricature of beauty so widespread in society today (General Audience, November 7, 2012). "Too often," the pope noted, "the beauty that is thrust upon us is illusory and deceitful." Benedict noted that this parody of true beauty does not raise our hearts to things above but rather distorts reality and "imprisons [man] within himself and further enslaves him, depriving him of hope and joy" ("The Feeling of Things, the Contemplation of Beauty"). Concocted in no small part by the advertising industry to stir up the lust for power, possession, and pleasure, it involves the use of "images made with supreme skill that are created to tempt the human being irresistibly, to make him want to grab everything and seek the passing satisfaction rather than be open to others" (Meeting with Artists, November 21, 2009).

Inhabiting a world that is dominated by this debased perspective and often hostile to the Church, Benedict held that recourse to the language of authentic beauty is arguably more important than ever. Indeed, in his view, it is indispensable if we wish to compellingly present the Gospel to would-be believers and re-present it to Catholics who find themselves wavering in their faith. Especially in our present-day "culture of images," Ratzinger found that a sacred image "can express much more than what can be said in words, and be an extremely effective and dynamic way of communicating the Gospel message" (Introduction to the Compendium of the Catechism of the Catholic Church, 5).

The "Wound" of Beauty and Its Saving Power

It is commonly said that "beauty lies in the eye of the beholder," and there is certainly some truth to this saying. In some matters (say, whether you like a particular song or movie), there is considerable room for debate among people of good will as to whether the particular object in question should be called beautiful. Yet, confining beauty exclusively to the realm of the subjective leads to serious problems when pushed to its logical conclusion. This can be seen by the fact that there are certain realities that any sane person would recognize as *not* beautiful, and even *repugnant*. For a glaringly obvious example, take the carnage of Auschwitz — not the acts of heroism by the camp's prisoners like St. Maximilian Kolbe, but the brutal acts of aggression perpetrated upon them. If we were to call those atrocities beautiful, then we would have emptied the word "beauty" of all meaning.

So, what is beauty? As readers may have come to expect, Benedict does not provide us with a textbook definition. Instead, drawing on Plato, what he offers is a phenomenological account that seeks to capture the *experience* of beauty from a variety of angles. As this pontiff saw it, the dominant effect of beauty is that it gives us a healthy "shock." It has a jarring effect that "disturbs" us, even to the point of "wounding" the soul. And yet, the net outcome is deeply positive. Encountering beauty draws our soul aloft and out of the rut in which we have entrenched ourselves. It gives us wings, empowering us to soar to transcendent greatness by reawakening in us "a longing for the Ineffable, readiness for sacrifice, the abandonment of self" ("The Feeling of Things, the Contemplation of Beauty"). According to Church Fathers like Dionysius the Areopagite, beauty inspires a yearning for the eternal, beckoning us to union with the divine Beauty of which all created beauty is but a reflection.

One of Benedict's favorite ways to illustrate this dynamic is by looking to traditional church architecture with its power to draw us toward the infinite. Upon crossing the threshold of God's house, he explains, we enter a sacred space and a dimension of time set apart from the ordinary. We witness this embodied, for instance, in the upward thrust of a Gothic cathedral's soaring walls. The pontiff deemed these walls "an invitation to prayer ... intended to express in its architectural lines the soul's longing for God." Regarding sculpture, he elaborated:

> Another merit of Gothic cathedrals is that the whole Christian and civil community participated in their building and decoration in harmonious and complementary ways. The lowly and the powerful, the illiterate and the learned; all participated because in this common house all believers were instructed in the faith. Gothic sculpture in fact has made cathedrals into "stone Bibles," depicting Gospel episodes and illustrating the content of the liturgical year, from the Nativity to the glorification of the Lord. (General Audience, November 18, 2009)

Scene by scene, these masterpieces recounted biblical events, told gospel parables, and brought the ancient saints back to life. Citing the great artist Marc Chagall, Benedict said that the artists who produced these marvels "dipped their brushes in that colored alphabet which is the Bible."

Having said that, the end game of the Church who commissioned these creatives was not just to recount history. The point of it all is the same one that we discussed in the last chapter in the context of pursuing liturgical renewal: holiness. The pontiff did not think that we have to replicate the precise mastery of forefathers, replacing all our churches with Gothic structures and forbidding all music at Mass except for Gregorian chant. The pontiff did not want us to get caught up in what he referred to as an "elitist ghetto," a scenario in which the quest for technical excellence becomes so engrossing that we lose sight of our original love and forget how to relate to ordinary people (*Spirit of the Liturgy*, 147).

In short, Benedict was a firm believer that beauty in our churches and liturgies can continue to impel us toward God and godliness, emboldening Holy Mother Church "to tell the story of salvation and to involve them in this story" (General Audiences, November 18, 2009, and August 31, 2011). This point is crucial, for we have witnessed this pontiff constantly stress that simply knowing the facts of Christianity is far from sufficient. Echoing the thought of his friend Hans Urs von Balthasar, in one classic work of dogmatic theology Ratzinger avowed that a mystery "can be seen only by one who lives it" (*Principles of Catholic Theology*, 51). In another foundational text geared toward disclosing the heart of Catholic doctrine, he explained, "Only by entering does one experience; only by cooperating in the experiment does one ask at all; and only he who asks receives an answer" (*Introduction to Christianity*, 175–76).

Delving into some of Benedict's lesser-known writings can help to illumine the full importance of this last remark. As already mentioned, when he celebrated Mass in Saint Patrick's Cathedral in New York, the pontiff gave a fascinating reflection upon the great house of worship as a parable for faith. Like any Gothic shrine, from the outside its windows appear dark and heavy, even dreary. But, once one enters the church, these same portals suddenly come alive with resplendent radiance passing through their stained glass. The application to Catholicism is evident. As with the stained-glass portals of a Gothic cathedral, so too for the Catholic Church: "It is only from the inside, from the experience of faith and ecclesial life, that we see the Church as she truly is: flooded with grace, resplendent in beauty, adorned by the manifold gifts of the Spirit" (Homily, April 19, 2008).

Through this parable, Benedict communicates poetically a truth he has reiterated in a variety of places and ways throughout his life. The truth of the Catholic Church ultimately can be seen only *from the inside* through a deeply lived experience that requires embarking upon "the experiment of faith":

> A man always sees only as much as he loves. … Without a certain measure of love, one finds nothing. Someone who does not get involved at least for a while in the experiment of faith, in the

experiment of becoming affirmatively involved with the Church, who does not take the risk of looking with the eyes of love, is only exasperating himself. The venture of love is the prerequisite for faith.

Ratzinger then identifies this venture of faith as the antidote to fear and scandal at the "dark areas" of Catholicism that would hold us back from following Christ in his Church:

If it is ventured, then one does not have to hide from the dark areas in the Church. But one discovers that they are not the only thing after all. One discovers that alongside the Church history of scandals there is another Church history that has proved to be fruitful throughout the centuries. ... He finds that the Church has brought forth in history a gleaming path that cannot be ignored. And the beauty that has sprung up in response to her message and is still manifest to us today in incomparable works of art becomes for him a witness to the truth: something that could express itself in that way cannot be mere darkness. The beauty of the great cathedrals, the beauty of the music that has developed within the context of the faith, the dignity of the Church's liturgy, and in general the reality of festive celebration, which one cannot make for oneself but can only receive, the elaboration of the seasons in the liturgical year, in which then and now, time and eternity interpenetrate — all that is in my view no insignificant accident. Beauty is the radiance of truth. ("Why I Am Still in the Church," 152–53)

While this by no means absolves us from the obligation to face up to problems in the Church and to present reasonable arguments in defense of the Catholic Faith, this pontiff makes it clear that we cannot argue people into believing. However, one thing we can certainly do every day is to embrace the fullness of life in Christ, and Benedict points to this as an eminently compelling means by which others will be drawn into the Church. This Christian witness epitomizes what the pope had in mind when pointing to the Church's saints and her beauty as the greatest apology of Christian Faith.

Self-Surrender: The Beauty of a Life Well Lived

Just as merely gazing at an artistic masterpiece is insufficient to convert our hearts to Christ, the same holds true in the other realm that Benedict found pivotal for grasping the truth of Catholicism. That is to say, simply learning about the lives of the saints will only take us so far unless we are also willing to embrace the truths that they upheld. In line with the pontiff's understanding of faith that we explored earlier in this book, Benedict stresses that the guarantors of Catholicism's truth are "the saints, who have undergone the experiment" (*Truth and Tolerance*, 226). As we discussed in Chapter 10, these holy men and women are above all *ordinary people* who by their lives of everyday goodness and unassuming heroism testify to the reality of the beliefs that they profess. In the theology of St. Thomas Aquinas, these individuals draw us to Christ because they have *spiritual beauty*, a well-proportioned life of virtue (*Summa Theologiae*, II–II, q. 145, a. 2).

Still, even this does not fully capture the depth of Benedict's perspective on the saints in relation to knowing the truth of Christianity. To be sure, he emphasizes that the lives of holy people "demonstrate a singular beauty which fascinates and attracts," yet the beauty of Christian existence that Benedict considers "even more effective than art and imagery" ultimately has to be something more intimate — namely, *the life that we ourselves live* (Address, October 25, 2012). That this would be a central theme of Benedict's pontificate was clear already in his first papal homily, in which he memorably shared, "There is nothing more beautiful than to know Him and to speak to others of our friendship with Him" (Homily at the Mass for the Inauguration of his Pontificate, April 24, 2005).

At the conclusion of this same text, Benedict advanced a related point that he returned to later on numerous occasions. Christian evangelists, he insisted, need to share with people the good news that our friendship with Jesus does not hold us back from fulfilling our deepest desires. On the contrary, the pope highlighted that living according to the demands of the Gospel — that is, living in conformity with the love of Jesus Christ — is precisely what opens us to behold the fullness of beauty and experience the abundance of life for which we all yearn.

This perspective connects seamlessly with what we have learned of Benedict's theology in the previous chapters of this book. What characterizes the life of a saint if not the quest to be ever more united to Our Lord in a total gift of self? With this in mind, Benedict revisited the issue of apologetics near the end of his life and accentuated that "the authentic proof of the truth of Christianity" is something that we find in the saints across all times, and it is astonishingly simple: *love* ("Love at the Origin of Missionary Work," in *What Is Christianity?*, 20). As we discovered back in Chapter 7, which dove into the virtue of faith, Benedict stands in a long line of thinkers like St. Gregory the Great. According to these masters of the Catholic tradition, love is a true source of knowledge, and it offers a vantage point into the real that cannot be attained by the intellect alone.

On this matter, Ratzinger never tired of recalling the wisdom of his mentor, Saint Augustine, who exhorted, *Ama, ut videas*, or "Love, so that you may behold!" Ratzinger understood that religion is a discipline whose goodness can only be understood through its exercise. This, he maintains, is similar to the dynamic at play in another pivotal practice:

> Medicine can only be learned in the practice of healing, never merely by means of books and reflection. Similarly, religion can only be understood through religion — an undisputed axiom in more recent philosophy of religion. The fundamental act of religion is prayer, which in the Christian religion acquires a very specific character: it is the act of self-surrender by which we enter the Body of Christ. Thus it is an act of love. ("Seven Theses on Christology and the Hermeneutic of Faith," 189–209)

The Beauty of Christ Crucified

If the best evidence for Christianity lies in the beauty of the Church and her saints, and if the beauty of holiness is something that must be experienced through love, then what, ultimately, is love? As usual, Benedict's answer is as profound as it is uncomplicated. The incarnation of love is beheld in the face of Christ crucified: "The truest beauty is the love of God, who definitively revealed himself to us in the paschal mystery" (*Sacramentum Caritatis*, 35). Christ's total gift of self on the cross is the most beautiful of all human actions, and it challenges the superficial notion of beauty dominant in our culture today. If the classical understanding of beauty lies in a harmony of proportion and form, then the beauty of Our Lord lies in him being the one who is "the fairest of the sons of men" (Ps 45:2), yet who at the same time "had no form or comeliness that we should look at him, / and no beauty that we should desire him" (Is 53:2).

Gazing upon the suffering Christ, Benedict points us to one of life's most important lessons: Beauty is not all sunshine and rainbows. Fyodor Dostoyevsky famously remarked that beauty will save the world, but Benedict reminds us of something easy to forget: Salvific beauty is not any beauty whatsoever, but specifically the redeeming beauty of Christ crucified, which we experience through sharing in his cross. This perspective on beauty therefore embraces pain, disappointment, and even the dark mystery of death. In other words, Jesus on the cross reminds us that authentic beauty, true freedom, and everlasting happiness are only found when we accept suffering as an essential part of God's plan for our sanctification. The reason for this is that the crucible of suffering serves to draw us away from the transitory and detach us from all that is opposed to God.

Paradoxically, then, the perspective of faith tells us that the trials of life contribute to its very glory. Like Olympic athletes relentlessly pursuing perfection, Saint Paul envisioned believers undergoing rigorous training for a race whose goal is the crown of eternal glory (see 1 Cor 9:24–27; 2 Tm 4:7–8). Ratzinger likewise saw the Christian life in this way and confidently affirmed something that can be truly grasped only by those who have had to face down extreme difficulties in life — namely, "The very toughness of the adventure is what makes it beautiful" (*Faith and the Future*, 75).

Love, the Wellspring of the Church's Missionary Commitment

If we were to stop here, one might get the mistaken impression that Christianity is a religion for self-absorbed people interested primarily in their own happiness. As we disciples know well, though, to be a follower of Christ is also to be an *apostle* — one who is "sent" by Our Lord to spread his Gospel to the whole world. This leads us to a final pair of concerns that were dear to Benedict's heart: the rationale behind *why* we ought to evangelize, and then the question of *how* to go about proclaiming Christ in a public arena that is hostile to it.

The Catholic Church has been animated by a missionary impulse from her earliest days. Before his ascension, Jesus commanded his followers, "Go into all the world and preach the gospel to the whole creation" (Mk 16:15). The reason for Our Lord's injunction is straightforward. As the texts of the New Testament unanimously declare, there is ultimately only one road that leads to eternal life, and this Way is the person of Jesus Christ. In our Master's own words, "He who believes and is baptized will be saved; but he who does not believe will be condemned" (Mk 16:16). The foundational motive for evangelization, then, is loving care for people's eternal well-being. It is about getting our brothers and sisters to heaven — and offering them a taste of paradise in their lives even now.

One of the great features of Benedict's approach to evangelization is his emphasis on Christianity's power to fulfill the human person's deepest longings. In keeping with the wisdom of the early Church, he sought to show that embracing Catholicism is not chiefly about compelling people to abandon what they have long known but rather about uncovering its full richness in Jesus Christ. In order to achieve this end, he consistently supported a robust sense of religious freedom, which he described as "an essential element" in society and "not the exclusive patrimony of believers, but of the whole family of the earth's peoples" (January 1, 2011, Message for the World Day of Peace). The fundamental principle guiding this emphasis was aptly expressed by the Second Vatican Council when it explained that a faith imposed upon a person from the outside is not genuine faith seeing as "the act of faith is of its very nature a free act" (*Dignitatis Humanae*, 10).

Returning to this theme in one of his final essays, the emeritus pontiff shared his perspective on what we ought to be emphasizing when proclaiming the Gospel. It is crucial, he explained, to show that "the encounter with [Jesus] is not the intrusion of something foreign that destroys their own culture and their own history" but that meeting Jesus instead represents "an entrance into something greater toward which they are traveling." Like St. Clement of Alexandria, Benedict regarded the world's sacred traditions as "expectant religions." Considering the good within them as a preparation for the Gospel, he believed that non-Christian traditions "are awaiting the encounter with Jesus Christ, the light that comes from him, which alone can lead them completely to their truth" ("Love at the Origin of Missionary Work" in *What Is Christianity?*, 17).

On the basis of this conviction, Benedict always endeavored to nurture the "seeds of the Logos" that the Lord has sown among all peoples. Like Saint Paul who praised the good he found among the Athenians (see Acts 17:16–34), one of the keys to Benedict's success as an evangelist was his capacity to rejoice in the truth wherever it might be found — and to behold in it the providence of God who "desires all men to be saved and to come to the knowledge of the truth" (1 Tm 2:4). Indeed, so strongly was Ratzinger convinced of this reality that he acknowledged the presence of goodness in "pagan saints" outside the visible structure of Catholicism, even as he resolutely professed that all goodness in this world comes from Christ Jesus, the only savior of mankind (Acts 4:12; *Truth and Tolerance*, 226).

In this connection, Cardinal Ratzinger also made the important clarification that this acknowledgment does not thereby mean that everything in other religions is good. In the face of strong and vocal opposition from certain circles, Ratzinger, as prefect of the Congregation for the Doctrine of the Faith, unambiguously affirmed the uniqueness of Christ's Church, which "subsists" (i.e., exists fully) only in the Catholic Church governed by the successor of Saint Peter (*Dominus Iesus*, 16, 22). Reflecting on this near the end of his life, Benedict remarked that it would be naïve and harmful to think that explicit faith in Christ is not of the utmost importance, for religion "is never simply a purely positive or purely negative phenomenon." Seeing as every religion involves an admixture of these dimensions, he prudently observed that an encounter with Christ is necessarily "always simultaneously a purification and a maturation" ("Love at the Origin of Missionary Work" in *What Is Christianity?*, 17).

Remarkably — and this is also one of the traits that made this pontiff's proclamation of the Gospel so compelling — Benedict acknowledged that the need for continual purification is also applicable within the Christian Tradition. Consequently, he actively worked to advance Vatican II's commitment to ecumenism and interreligious dialogue, emphasizing a readiness to learn from those with whom we wished to share the Gospel of Jesus Christ. Indeed, Benedict rejoiced in the truth that an encounter among religions benefits everyone involved: "The encounter is always reciprocal. Christ awaits their history, their wisdom, their vision of things. ... New life springs from the encounter of the expectant religions with Christ ("Love at the Origin of Missionary Work" in *What Is Christianity?*, 17).

Furthermore, the emeritus pontiff supplemented the aforementioned point by underscoring that the Christian Faith must be capable of critiquing its own religious history too. As we learned back in Chapter 2, there is always a need to distinguish the essence of Christianity from its accidentals and to discriminate between legitimate and distorting traditions. On this subject, Benedict says here a final time, "Jesus Christ is the Logos of God, the light that helps us to distinguish between the nature of religion and its distortion" ("Love at the Origin of Missionary Work" in *What Is Christianity?*, 18). In short, for Benedict, the "dialogue of salvation" where we seek to proclaim the Gospel to those of other religious traditions brings the additional benefit of enabling us to rediscover the authentic core of our own faith.

The New Evangelization and the Future of the Church
Historically, the notion of mission has long been closely associated with spreading the good news of Jesus Christ to peoples who had never heard his name. For most Catholics, the notion of missionary work therefore evokes images of the great saints of old, such as St. Isaac Jogues and the North American Martyrs, and the apostles of the East, Saint Thomas who preached in India, and St. Francis Xavier who went as far as Japan. However, Benedict and other popes have placed a heightened emphasis on the urgency of expanding the scope of what we consider mission territory, for this domain now encompasses regions and communities that have repudiated the faith they once knew. In the words of the emeritus pontiff, "Christianity has in many respects grown weary in the countries where its great history has unfolded, and some branches of the large tree that grew from the mustard seed of the Gospel have become dry and fallen to the ground" ("Love at the Origin of Missionary Work," in *What Is Christianity?*, 17). Given the near-total eclipse of faith in the public square within Western civilization,

our recent pontiffs have stressed the need for a "New Evangelization."

We tend to think of this as a more recent phenomenon, given that the fastest-growing denomination in the West is the "nones" who declare no religious affiliation. However, the ever-perceptive Ratzinger recognized the signs of Christianity's societal decline even in his days as a professor. In a 1958 essay, the young priest observed that the Church in the modern era had become "a Church of pagans, who still call themselves Christians, but actually have become pagans," adding that the pace of this downturn was accelerating with the march of time. Reflecting further on this alarming situation, Ratzinger predicted about the Church at the start of the third millennium: "It will become small and will have to start pretty much all over again. It will no longer have use of the structures it built in its years of prosperity. The reduction in the number of faithful will lead to it losing an important part of its social privileges. It will be a more spiritual Church" ("The New Pagans and the Church"). In contrast with previous ages where a Christian culture made it easy to be a believer, Ratzinger foresaw that the Church would soon become more like it was in the beginning: a community of those who have come together not because of social convention but rather through their intentional commitment to follow Jesus Christ.

While this scenario might initially strike us as pessimistic, Ratzinger had confidence that great good would eventually arise from it. The future of the Church, he foretold, will bring forth a new generation of saints, individuals who "are aware of more than mere phrases, people who are modern but have deep roots and live in the fullness of the faith." Amidst all the upheaval — and indeed *precisely because of it* — Ratzinger was optimistic that the Church will "rediscover its own core … its essential being in what has always been its heart: faith in the triune God and in Jesus Christ" (*Faith and the Future*, 93–94).

Unveiling the Countercultural Beauty of Catholicism

If the Church is to reawaken her true nature and attract new disciples in the midst of the modern world, Benedict emphasized that she is going to have to make her presence felt in the public square. In particular, the Church will have to show how she supplies a goodness, truth, and beauty that the world on its own could never hope to provide. In this book, we have showcased a number of gifts that flow from this wellspring: from the beauty of the Christian doctrine of creation, to the Catholic Faith's capacity to elevate our God-given reason, to the incalculable difference that it makes when we have Jesus in our lives, to the fulfillment that comes by living the theological virtues, and finally to the glory that awaits us in eternity and the sacraments that offer us a foretaste of it even now. In all this, Benedict stressed the irreplaceable role of beauty and holiness as the ultimate means by which to know the truth of Christianity, and thereby to find lasting happiness.

However, we must call attention to one further dimension of this enterprise that the Bavarian pontiff considered essential. Granting that evangelization is more impactful when we build on the good of the particular culture we aim to reach, a crucial part of what makes our faith beautiful is that it is also *countercultural.*

According to Benedict, this message has never been timelier than in present-day society, whose antagonism toward Christianity increases with each passing year. Even as Western governments style themselves as forces of tolerance that have broken free from "the foolish, prerational traditions" of faith, in recent times the true nature of the secular enterprise has begun to show itself. Even as the emeritus pontiff noted that this intolerance has not yet turned into full-fledged persecution, he observed that it nevertheless "manifests itself in an increasingly authoritarian way and legislates accordingly" ("Monotheism and Tolerance," in *What Is Christianity?*, 39).

As his theology always does, this pope's analysis of our current societal state ultimately goes back to the issue of truth. In this connection, Benedict observes that tyrannical states are able to seize control over people's lives when truth-based arguments are no longer widely accepted. Pointing to such instances in our contemporary world as "the radical manipulation of man and distortion of the sexes through gender ideology," Benedict further suggests that a major reason for this is that many nowadays regard the very notion of truth with hostility:

> Underlying this concept is the suspicion that the truth is dangerous in itself. For this reason, the basic tendency of modernity moves ever more clearly toward a form of culture that is independent of the truth. Postmodern culture — which makes man his

own creator and disputes the original gift of creation — manifests a will to recreate the world contrary to its truth. ("Monotheism and Tolerance," in *What Is Christianity?*, 41)

If we take our bearings from Scripture, then this should be expected. Like all persecution, the escalating intolerance to faith we are witnessing today arises when the message of the Gospel becomes "inconvenient" for people (see Wis 2:12).

Paradoxically, it is against this backdrop of cultural dissolution that the life-giving distinctiveness of Christianity shines most brilliantly. In a world eager to inform us that the truth is of no consequence and that we ought to liberate ourselves from the shackles of Christian mores, many seekers — especially the young — are discovering the attractiveness of our Faith's enduring traditions. In many ways it would be easier simply to go along with those seeking to overthrow thousands of years of inherited wisdom. The appeal of living the way that we ourselves deem fit, free from obligations on the part of any eternal Authority, is obvious. However, Benedict in his genius recognizes that people yearn to be challenged. In the depths of our hearts, we realize that there must be something more to life than satisfying our impulses and achieving easy goals that we have arbitrarily set for ourselves.

This is where Catholicism enters the picture with its proclamation that the fullness of life is found not by doing our own will, but by boldly following the will of our heavenly Father. Lasting happiness, in other words, arises from conforming our lives to Christ and living according to the demands of his Gospel. As the pontiff approached the end of his life, he emphasized that rising to this occasion will sometimes require that we profess our countercultural convictions in a highly public way. Like the Maccabean martyrs in the face of persecutors who sought to stamp out their Jewish faith, Benedict saw that society today aims "to achieve the extinction of what is essentially Christian." Following in the footsteps of Mattathias, we too must have the audacity to defy unjust laws and proclaim, "We will not obey the king's words by turning aside from our religion to the right hand or to the left" (1 Mc 2:22).

Whatever form our public witness to the Faith might ultimately assume, in the end Benedict underscores that it always "takes its essential form from the Cross of Jesus Christ," who is the definitive "counterbalance to all forms of intolerance" ("Monotheism and Tolerance," in *What Is Christianity?*, 42). This pope here reminds us of Our Lord's teaching that the kingdom of God is not of this world. But what, then, is the alternative? In other words, what is the goal for which people most deeply long, and what is the message that Christianity has to offer society today? In the words of Benedict, it is that the fullness of joy is unachievable without first passing through the crucible of suffering. In short, there is no resurrection without the cross, and therefore, as Benedict articulates, the definitive answer to the riddle of man can be found only in following the way of the crucified and risen Lord, Jesus Christ.

In the autumn of his life, Benedict continued to reflect deeply on evangelization: from its basis, to its goals, to the best ways to put the Church's truths into practice in the mission field. Delving into these writings, it is refreshing to discover that this towering intellect dedicated so much time to pondering the same down-to-earth questions that occupied his mind for decades, in particular the essential place that beauty and love have in the proclamation of the Gospel.

With the publication of the pontiff's remaining writings after his death, it became clear that the retired pontiff also kept up on current events. This only deepened his appreciation for the Gospel of Christ, inspiring him to write on the question of whether the Church's missionary mandate is still essential today. Perhaps more than ever, he concluded that the answer to this question is a resounding "yes." But if salvation is possible outside the visible confines of the Catholic Church, Benedict asked, Why evangelize at all? As the Second Vatican Council and this pope himself taught, one reason is that it often happens that "men, deceived by the Evil One, have become vain in their reasonings and have exchanged the truth of God for a lie, serving the creature rather than the Creator." Moreover, the Church has noted that there are those who, "living and dying in this world without God, are exposed to final despair" (*Lumen Gentium*, 16). As countless souls over the millennia have testified by their own lives, Christ alone saves us from the allure of idolatry and the temptation to despair — both of which Benedict saw as potent forces shaping our culture today like never before.

As for the question of *how* to reach people in a post-Christian era, Benedict repeatedly taught that it is futile to look for cookie-cutter solutions. Catholicism, he always upheld, is not so much a system to be figured out as a quest for the fullness of life. In this volume, we have had ample opportunity to witness Benedict's belief that grasping the truth of Christianity requires that we embark upon the path of becoming like the One whom we seek to follow. That is, the beauty of Catholicism becomes fully evident when we become saints.

Near the end of his earthly pilgrimage, Benedict was asked if there was ever a time in his life when he wondered whether everything the Catholic Church professes about God might turn out to be wrong. The pope frankly granted that this is a reasonable question, but he responded by highlighting that he had been gifted with too many "experiences of faith" for Catholicism to have arisen from nothingness (*Last Testament*, 207). Amidst all the noise in our culture and divisions within the Church today, this point is crucial. There are those who assert that Christianity is indistinguishable from any other religion, with nothing unique or valuable to offer mankind. Others on the opposite extreme insist that their particular intellectual distillation of Catholicism alone gives one access to God. Benedict, however, recognized that these contradictory claims are both missing something crucial. As this pope understood so well, there is ultimately only one sure way to know the fullness of truth and life: by entrusting ourselves to the Church and living her teaching to the full.

READING LIST

◆ Benedict XVI. *What Is Christianity? The Last Writings.* San Francisco: Ignatius Press, 2023.

◆ Ramage, Matthew. *The Experiment of Faith: Pope Benedict XVI on Living the Theological Virtues in a Secular Age.* Washington, DC: The Catholic University of America Press, 2020, chapter 12.

◆ Ramage, Matthew. "The Theological Mind and Method of Pope Benedict XVI as Revealed in His Catechetical Instructions." In

Ressourcement after Vatican II: Essays in Honor of Fr. Joseph Fessio, SJ, 265–90. San Francisco: Ignatius Press, 2019.

♦ Ratzinger, Joseph. *Faith and the Future*. San Francisco: Ignatius Press, 2009.

♦ Ratzinger, Joseph. "The Feeling of Things, the Contemplation of Beauty." Message to the Communion and Liberation Meeting at Rimini. August 24, 2002.

♦ Ratzinger, Joseph. Homily to the College of Cardinals for the Election of the Roman Pontiff. April 18, 2005.

♦ Ratzinger, Joseph. "Seven Theses on Christology and the Hermeneutic of Faith." *Letter and Spirit* 3 (2007): 189–209.

♦ Ratzinger, Joseph. *Truth and Tolerance*. San Francisco: Ignatius Press, 2004.

♦ Ratzinger, Joseph. "Why I Am Still in the Church." In *Fundamental Speeches from Five Decades*, 133–54. San Francisco: Ignatius Press, 2012.

Benedict's Thought as an *Apologia* for the Catholic Faith

Through this book, I hope readers will have come to know Joseph Ratzinger as a shining embodiment of the virtues essential for living the life of Christ in our modern world. On a personal note, having devoted the greater part of two decades to immersing myself in the thought of this extraordinary mind, I have found no finer model for advancing the Faith in our present age. In particular, I never cease to be amazed at the immense fruitfulness of striving to live by Ratzinger's guiding principle of holding fast to what is essential while remaining open to necessary change. As we observed at the outset of this book, no one has put this vision into words better than Ratzinger himself:

> Although the constellations in which I have found myself — and naturally also the periods of life and their different influences — have led to changes and development in the accents of my

> thought, *my basic impulse, precisely during the council, was always to free up the authentic kernel of the faith from encrustations and to give this kernel strength and dynamism. This impulse is the constant of my life.* ... Naturally the office gives an accentuation that isn't present as such when you are a professor. But nonetheless what's important to me is that I have never deviated from this constant, which from my childhood has molded my life, and that I have remained true to it as the basic direction of my life. (*Salt of the Earth*, 79, emphasis added)

As pope, Benedict saw himself as a custodian of the Faith rather than its master. He was a world-class scholar whose insights welled up from his courage to plumb the depth of every topic that he set his mind to exploring. He was blessed with the rare ability to engage in meaningful exchange with anyone, regardless of creed. Furthermore, he was a gentle soul who had the humility to learn from his partners in dialogue. In union with theological giants of the past like St. Thomas Aquinas, he was convinced that "all truth, no matter what its source, is from the Holy Spirit" (Aquinas, *De Veritate*, q. 1, a. 8).

Among students of dogmatic theology, Benedict is esteemed for his comprehensive grasp of the Catholic tradition and proficiency at wedding the best of ancient and modern expertise. Those in the field of biblical studies admire his tireless search for the face of Christ in Scripture and find in his hermeneutical synthesis a sure foundation on which to base their own examination of God's word. Students of the natural sciences are bolstered in their pursuits by Benedict's love for creation and his example of how to unite faith and reason. Believers looking for deeper meaning in life are offered an inspiring path forward through his accessible presentation of the theological virtues. Lovers of the liturgy appreciate the Bavarian pontiff's esteem for the Church's ancient practices combined with a commonsense ability to meet ordinary believers in their present context. Evangelists can find in Benedict's theology a countercultural guide for spreading the Gospel through a bold life dedicated to the pursuit of beauty and holiness.

For these reasons, and others that I have inevitably neglected in this brief volume, a multitude of believers over the past half century have found the thought of this extraordinary individual to be a veritable *apologia* for the Catholic Faith. Indeed, for a significant number of the many students I have had the joy of teaching, it was thanks to engagement with Joseph Ratzinger's example as a believer seeking understanding that they were able to finally find a foothold for their faith. Benedict's writing is for simple and educated believers alike, accessible enough for the beginner but deep enough that it always finds some way to enlighten the specialist. For those just now entering the world of this great pope, a virtue of his work is that there is no bad place to begin exploring. The many interwoven strands of Benedict's reflection tend to make their appearance regardless of the topic at hand at any given moment. But there are perhaps some ideal places to begin this quest, and I have listed some suggestions at the end of each chapter.

For those navigating hurdles in their faith journey — whether they are new to the Faith or lifelong Catholics — Ratzinger's work has arguably proven itself to be life-changing, providing them with faithful, nuanced, and more satisfying answers to their questions. This pontiff's thought is especially valuable for those who have some apprehensiveness about how to profess the Christian Faith amid a multitude of obstacles, yet who are willing to accompany this great thinker as he shows us how to face the toughest questions head-on. His work is formative for those whose yearnings resonate with Ratzinger's desire "to be true to what I have recognized as essential and also to remain open to seeing what should change" (*Salt of the Earth*, 115–16).

I can also attest to the transformative impact of Benedict's wisdom in my own walk of faith. Like many of my readers, my life has presented ample opportunity for trials, including spiritual darkness, ever-present grave illness, and the death of loved ones. I have also studied widely (across the fields of contemporary biblical scholarship, philosophy, classical languages, comparative religion, the empirical sciences, atheist thought, and so on). All the while, I have constantly searched for Catholic thinkers and peers who appreciate the beauty of natural reason and its potential to help us understand our faith better. By the grace of God, I have had the joy of encountering many such individuals along my path. In all this, my companionship with Benedict through his writings — and with friends who share a similar appreciation of them — has strengthened my belief in the truth of the Catholic Faith. Whatever challenge I face in my faith, especially when I doubt whether I will be able to find anyone who has adequately addressed a seemingly insurmountable problem, time and again I have discovered that Ratzinger already answered my question long before I asked it. I just needed to know where to look for this help. I will count this book a success if it has spared some readers the time and effort that I had to invest to reach this point.

Having said that, I do not pretend that this text will provide definitive answers to all the issues that it engages. There is nothing more consistent with Benedict's principles and example than to acknowledge that there is often more than one intelligent, orthodox way to address a given problem. The same insight can be glimpsed in theological giants of the past, like St. Thomas Aquinas. While the Angelic Doctor never held back from condemning error when it was called for, he wisely tempered his judgments with an awareness of this crucial reality: "Some things must be believed by the faithful, while in the case of others there is latitude for debate — and in such matters even the saints at times view things differently" (*In II Sent.*, Lib. 2, d. 12, q. 1, a. 2). Along these lines, Catholic literary giant G. K. Chesterton would write centuries later, "Catholic doctrine and discipline may be walls; but they are the walls of a playground." The point here is that, even as doctrine is indispensable, not everything in Christianity is definitive dogma, and grave harm can be done to souls when we lose sight of that fact.

From this, there follows an eminently practical way each of us can integrate Benedict's wisdom in our lives. In keeping with the overarching theme of this book, perhaps the most timely lesson to be learned is that we should never let debates over secondary matters make us lose sight of what is truly essential — especially our relationships. At the Last Supper, Jesus prayed "that they may all be one," pledging that it will only be through the unity of the faithful "that the world may believe" (Jn 17:20–23). While Benedict could hardly be accused of lacking concern for the truth, everything he lived and taught exemplified the priority of this directive from Our Lord. This great pontiff's ministry of exercising charity in truth and truth in charity stands as a testament to the boundless beauty of the Catholic Faith. In this way, his theology supplies a preeminent model for how we today can embody the Church's timeless imperative to seek unity in essentials, enjoy freedom where possible, and in all things prefer nothing whatsoever to the love of Jesus Christ.

Acknowledgments

I've been a student of Joseph Ratzinger's thought now for over twenty-five years, and I owe a debt of gratitude to numerous teachers and peers who have helped me to enter more deeply into our late pontiff's mind and manner of life. While I can't thank everyone here, I do want to take a moment to express my gratitude for the impact that Ratzinger and my teachers have had on my own biography.

My first deep exposure to Joseph Ratzinger was in fall 2000 when I was an undergraduate at the University of Illinois, where I became deeply involved in the college's outstanding Newman Center. Under the chaplaincy of Msgr. Stuart Swetland and the mentorship of the inimitable Kenneth Howell, I was quickly steeped in the thought of then-Cardinal Ratzinger through classroom study, homilies, and everyday conversation. As the right-hand man of Karol Wojtyła, Ratzinger loomed large in those years of my spiritual and intellectual formation, and I still remember where I was when, as a sophomore sacristan, I finished my first Ratzinger book, *The Spirit of the Liturgy*. Even for those who were not so inclined to reading books and book-length Vatican documents, Ratzinger quickly became a hero for so many of us young people in search of a dynamic orthodoxy that was firm yet full of life.

Shortly thereafter, living in Rome as a seminarian in the early 2000s afforded me an even greater opportunity to get familiar with Ratzinger — and with many misconceptions about him. John Paul II's encyclical *Fides et Ratio* ("Faith and Reason") had not long been out, and I took pleasure in hearing it affectionately referred to as "Fides et Ratzinger."

After becoming debilitated with lupus in Rome, I found myself obliged to shift gears, returning to the United States to work on my M.A. in Theology. We read a lot of Joseph Ratzinger in Franciscan University of Steubenville's graduate program, and I still routinely draw on insights garnered in classes including Scott Hahn's course, Theology and Ministry of the Word, in which I was blessed to read Ratzinger's *God Is Near Us* and *Eschatology* alongside numerous other pivotal texts. Then, in 2006 I arrived for my Ph.D. at Ave Maria University to meet the singularly formative influence of Fr. Joseph Fessio, who is not only a holy priest and responsible for the publication of countless Ratzinger works in English, but was himself a doctoral student of the Bavarian master. Relishing the opportunity to be formed as one of now-Pope Benedict's intellectual grandchildren, our professors assigned Ratzinger books and held impromptu reading groups on Benedict's documents as they came out, such as the 2006 Regensburg Address and the 2007 encyclical *Spe Salvi*.

Father Fessio sought to implement the teachings of Ratzinger in his devout celebration of the liturgy. In an effort to showcase the harmony between the Church of yesteryear and today, he printed booklets entitled *The Mass of Vatican II*, featuring the Latin texts of the *Novus Ordo* liturgy promulgated after the Second Vatican Council to foster active participation in the Mass. Through Father Fessio's liturgies, we discovered the *Novus Ordo* can be every bit as reverent and fruitful as the Church's more ancient rite, referred to as the "extraordinary form of the Church's Liturgy" in Benedict's 2007 *motu proprio*. Inspired by Benedict's commitment to a mutual enrichment between the old and the new, my love for the Mass grew more than ever during this time. I relished the opportunity to lector in English with Latin responses. My future wife sang in the schola, and we had our first date en route to a university-sponsored course on Gregorian chant in Solesmes, France.

Complementing what we experienced every day in Mass, engagement with Benedict's thought in the classrooms of Father Fessio, Fr. Matthew Lamb, Gregory Vall, and my other dear professors cemented in my soul a desire to dedicate my career to putting myself under the tutelage of this pope and bringing his wisdom to bear in the world today. Inspired by our clergy in the chapel and by our teachers in the lecture hall, I wrote my dissertation on how to understand Sacred Scripture with the help of Benedict and Aquinas, who were my two favorite theologians then as they are now.

It is hard to overestimate Benedict's importance in my own intellectual and spiritual journey. I can't say that I'm Catholic today solely because of Benedict, but I can say that my strong confidence in our Faith has much to do with the example of this humble servant of God and incomparable lover of the truth. I came to theology in the first place because I was interested in the biggest questions, and in Benedict I discovered a disciple of Jesus who was willing to face them head-on without downplaying their importance, yet with the unwavering conviction that the Catholic tradition is equal to the challenge.

Taking Benedict as a guide throughout my career, my teaching always tries in some way to apply his wisdom to the most difficult and important issues facing the Church today. This is also reflected in my books for a very simple, autobiographical reason: Time and time again, when facing a challenge in my faith or trying to help someone else in their walk, it is staggering to discover that Benedict had always addressed it years before I did and was ready with a compelling response.

Today, I think about Benedict in much the same way I think about Thomas Aquinas. When I write or teach about Aquinas, there are always great insights to be found. However, what attracts me to his thought is ultimately not so much about the man or his particular insights as it is about the tradition that he has synthesized in an incomparable way. Moreover, not only have I found Ratzinger to be the best modern teacher of the Church's great tradition, but his work enriches that heritage by engaging new discoveries and shining the light of faith on the unique challenges of our age. Relentlessly committed to wedding the best of the ancient with the best of the modern, Joseph Ratzinger better than anyone else fits the bill of the scribe who brings forth treasures old and new from the treasury of God's wisdom (Matthew 13:52). A lover of Christ who kept his gaze fixed firmly on the kingdom of heaven, he showed us how to convincingly live and proclaim the Gospel today. Having been so blessed with the opportunity to immerse myself in this vision for many years now, words cannot express how grateful I am for the opportunity to introduce others to it through this book.

About the Author

D r. Matthew Ramage is a professor of theology at Benedictine College, where he has taught since earning his Ph.D. in systematic theology and biblical studies from Ave Maria University in 2009. A Scholar Associate of the Society of Catholic Scientists and Co-Director of the Center for Integral Ecology at Benedictine, his research concentrates on the theology of Joseph Ratzinger, wedding ancient and modern methods of biblical interpretation, the dialogue between faith and science, and the development of a robustly Catholic approach to care for creation.

Ramage is author, co-author, or translator of over twenty books, including *Dark Passages of the Bible* (CUA Press, 2013), *Jesus, Interpreted* (CUA Press, 2017), *The Experiment of Faith* (CUA Press, 2020), *Christ's Church and World Religions* (Sophia Institute Press, 2020), and *From the Dust of the Earth: Benedict XVI, the Bible, and the Theory of Evolution* (CUA Press, 2022). In addition to his books, Ramage's work has appeared in numerous scholarly journals including *Communio*, *Nova et Vetera*, *Letter and Spirit*, *Scientia et Fides*, and *Scripta Theologica*, as well as popular online venues such as *Homiletic and Pastoral Review*, *Strange Notions*, *Crisis*,

Notre Dame's *Church Life Journal*, and the Word on Fire journal *Evangelization and Culture*.

He has also published lectures through online platforms such as the Thomistic Institute and The Benedictine Dialogues, and released a Faith and Science series through the Center for Media and Culture at Benedictine College. Ramage's monthly column "God's Two Books" is featured at the international outlet *Catholic World Report*.

A widely traveled teacher, Ramage studied in Italy and France and has taught in Greece, India, Ireland, Italy, Israel, and Turkey. He shares a love for linguistics with his wife, Jen, and has competence in Koine Greek, Biblical Hebrew, Latin, Italian, French, Spanish, and German. Wherever he is called upon throughout the United States or abroad, he offers courses at the undergraduate and graduate level, and seminars for lay leaders, teachers, seminarians, and candidates for the permanent diaconate.

When he is not teaching or writing, Ramage enjoys reading, fossil hunting, tending his orchard, road tripping to national parks with his wife and seven children, and aspiring to be a barbeque pitmaster. More on Ramage's writing, teaching, and media appearances can be found on his website www.matthewramage.com.